MW01288695

Rabindranath Tagore

The Plays of Tagore: 8 Philosophical & Allegorical Dramas

e-artnow 2020

*Rabindranath Tagore*

## The Plays of Tagore: 8 Philosophical & Allegorical Dramas

The Post Office, Chitra, The Cycle of Spring, The King of the Dark Chamber, Sanyasi or the Ascetic, Malini, Sacrifice & The King and the Queen, With Author's Autobiography

e-artnow, 2020
Contact: info@e-artnow.org

ISBN 978-80-273-0950-4

# Contents

**THE POST OFFICE**

## DRAMATIS PERSONÆ

- MADHAV
- AMAL, his adopted child
- SUDHA, a little flower girl
- THE DOCTOR
- DAIRYMAN
- WATCHMAN
- GAFFER
- VILLAGE HEADMAN, a bully
- KING'S HERALD
- ROYAL PHYSICIAN

## ACT I

*(Madhav's House)*

MADHAV. What a state I am in! Before he came, nothing mattered; I felt so free. But now that he has come, goodness knows from where, my heart is filled with his dear self, and my home will be no home to me when he leaves. Doctor, do you think he —

PHYSICIAN. If there's life in his fate, then he will live long. But what the medical scriptures say, it seems —

MADHAV. Great heavens, what?

PHYSICIAN. The scriptures have it: "Bile or palsey, cold or gout spring all alike."

MADHAV. Oh, get along, don't fling your scriptures at me; you only make me more anxious; tell me what I can do.

PHYSICIAN (*Taking snuff*) The patient needs the most scrupulous care.

MADHAV. That's true; but tell me how.

PHYSICIAN. I have already mentioned, on no account must he be let out of doors.

MADHAV Poor child, it is very hard to keep him indoors all day long.

PHYSICIAN. What else can you do? The autumn sun and the damp are both very bad for the little fellow-for the scriptures have it:

"In wheezing, swoon or in nervous fret,
In jaundice or leaden eyes —"

MADHAV. Never mind the scriptures, please. Eh, then we must shut the poor thing up. Is there no other method?

PHYSICIAN. None at all: for, "In the wind and in the sun —"

MADHAV. What will your "in this and in that" do for me now? Why don't you let them alone and come straight to the point? What's to be done then? Your system is very, very hard for the poor boy; and he is so quiet too with all his pain and sickness. It tears my heart to see him wince, as he takes your medicine.

PHYSICIAN. effect. That's why the sage Chyabana observes: "In medicine as in good advices, the least palatable ones are the truest." Ah, well! I must be trotting now. (*Exit*)

*(Gaffer enters)*

MADHAV. Well, I'm jiggered, there's Gaffer now.

GAFFER. Why, why, I won't bite you.

MADHAV. No, but you are a devil to send children off their heads.

GAFFER. But you aren't a child, and you've no child in the house; why worry then?

MADHAV. Oh, but I have brought a child into the house.

GAFFER. Indeed, how so?

MADHAV. You remember how my wife was dying to adopt a child?

GAFFER. Yes, but that's an old story; you didn't like the idea.

MADHAV. You know, brother, how hard all this getting money in has been. That somebody else's child would sail in and waste all this money earned with so much trouble-Oh, I hated the idea. But this boy clings to my heart in such a queer sort of way —

GAFFER. So that's the trouble! and your money goes all for him and feels jolly lucky it does go at all.

MADHAV. Formerly, earning was a sort of passion with me; I simply couldn't help working for money. Now, I make money and as I know it is all for this dear boy, earning becomes a joy to me.

GAFFER. Ah, well, and where did you pick him up?

MADHAV. He is the son of a man who was a brother to my wife by village ties. He has had no mother since infancy; and now the other day he lost his father as well.

GAFFER. Poor thing: and so he needs me all the more.

MADHAV. The doctor says all the organs of his little body are at loggerheads with each other, and there isn't much hope for his life. There is only one way to save him and that is to keep him out of this autumn wind and sun. But you are such a terror! What with this game of yours at your age, too, to get children out of doors!

GAFFER. God bless my soul! So I'm already as bad as autumn wind and sun, eh! But, friend, I know something, too, of the game of keeping them indoors. When my day's work is over I am coming in to make friends with this child of yours. (*Exit*)

(*Amal enters*)

AMAL. Uncle, I say, Uncle!

MADHAV. Hullo! Is that you, Amal?

AMAL. Mayn't I be out of the courtyard at all?

MADHAV. No, my dear, no.

AMAL. See, there where Auntie grinds lentils in the quirn, the squirrel is sitting with his tail up and with his wee hands he's picking up the broken grains of lentils and crunching them. Can't I run up there?

MADHAV. No, my darling, no.

AMAL. Wish I were a squirrel! —it would be lovely. Uncle, why won't you let me go about?

MADHAV. Doctor says it's bad for you to be out.

AMAL. How can the doctor know?

MADHAV. What a thing to say! The doctor can't know and he reads such huge books!

AMAL. Does his book-learning tell him everything?

MADHAV. Of course, don't you know!

AMAL (*With a sigh*) Ah, I am so stupid! I don't read books.

MADHAV. Now, think of it; very, very learned people are all like you; they are never out of doors.

AMAL. Aren't they really?

MADHAV. No, how can they? Early and late they toil and moil at their books, and they've eyes for nothing else. Now, my little man, you are going to be learned when you grow up; and then you will stay at home and read such big books, and people will notice you and say, "he's a wonder."

AMAL. No, no, Uncle; I beg of you by your dear feet —I don't want to be learned, I won't.

MADHAV. Dear, dear; it would have been my saving if I could have been learned.

AMAL. No, I would rather go about and see everything that there is.

MADHAV. Listen to that! See! What will you see, what is there so much to see?

AMAL. See that far-away hill from our window —I often long to go beyond those hills and right away.

MADHAV. Oh, you silly! As if there's nothing more to be done but just get up to the top of that hill and away! Eh! You don't talk sense, my boy. Now listen, since that hill stands there upright as a barrier, it means you can't get beyond it. Else, what was the use in heaping up so many large stones to make such a big affair of it, eh!

AMAL. Uncle, do you think it is meant to prevent your crossing over? It seems to me because the earth can't speak it raises its hands into the sky and beckons. And those who live far and sit alone by their windows can see the signal. But I suppose the learned people —

MADHAV. No, they don't have time for that sort of nonsense. They are not crazy like you.

AMAL. Do you know, yesterday I met someone quite as crazy as I am.

MADHAV. Gracious me, really, how so?

AMAL. He had a bamboo staff on his shoulder with a small bundle at the top, and a brass pot in his left hand, and an old pair of shoes on; he was making for those hills straight across that meadow there. I called out to him and asked, "Where are you going?" He answered, "I don't know, anywhere!" I asked again, "Why are you going?" He said, "I'm going out to seek work." Say, Uncle, have you to seek work?

MADHAV. Of course I have to. There's many about looking for jobs.

AMAL. How lovely! I'll go about, like them too, finding things to do.

MADHAV. Suppose you seek and don't find. Then —

AMAL. Wouldn't that be jolly? Then I should go farther! I watched that man slowly walking on with his pair of worn out shoes. And when he got to where the water flows under the fig tree, he stopped and washed his feet in the stream. Then he took out from his bundle some gram-flour, moistened it with water and began to eat. Then he tied up his bundle and shouldered it again; tucked up his cloth above his knees and crossed the stream. I've asked Auntie to let me go up to the stream, and eat my gram-flour just like him.

MADHAV. And what did your Auntie say to that?

AMAL. Auntie said, "Get well and then I'll take you over there." Please, Uncle, when shall I get well?

MADHAV. It won't be long, dear.

AMAL. Really, but then I shall go right away the moment I'm well again.

MADHAV. And where will you go?

AMAL. Oh, I will walk on, crossing so many streams, wading through water. Everybody will be asleep with their doors shut in the heat of the day and I will tramp on and on seeking work far, very far.

MADHAV. I see! I think you had better be getting well first; then —

AMAL. But then you won't want me to be learned, will you, Uncle?

MADHAV. What would you rather be then?

AMAL. I can't think of anything just now; but I'll tell you later on.

MADHAV. Very well. But mind you, you aren't to call out and talk to strangers again.

AMAL. But I love to talk to strangers!

MADHAV. Suppose they had kidnapped you?

AMAL. That would have been splendid! But no one ever takes me away. They all want me to stay in here.

MADHAV. I am off to my work-but, darling, you won't go out, will you?

AMAL. No, I won't. But, Uncle, you'll let me be in this room by the roadside.

(*Exit Madhav*)

DAIRYMAN. Curds, curds, good nice curds.

AMAL. Curdseller, I say, Curdseller.

DAIRYMAN. Why do you call me? Will you buy some curds?

AMAL. How can I buy? I have no money.

DAIRYMAN. What a boy! Why call out then? Ugh! What a waste of time.

AMAL. I would go with you if I could.

DAIRYMAN. With me?

AMAL. Yes, I seem to feel homesick when I hear you call from far down the road.

DAIRYMAN (*Lowering his yoke-pole*) Whatever are you doing here, my child?

AMAL. The doctor says I'm not to be out, so I sit here all day long.

DAIRYMAN. My poor child, whatever has happened to you?

AMAL. I can't tell. You see I am not learned, so I don't know what's the matter with me. Say, Dairyman, where do you come from?

DAIRYMAN. From our village.

AMAL. Your village? Is it very far?

DAIRYMAN. Our village lies on the river Shamli at the foot of the Panch-mura hills.

AMAL. Panch-mura hills! Shamli river! I wonder. I may have seen your village. I can't think when though!

DAIRYMAN. Have you seen it? Been to the foot of those hills?

AMAL. Never. But I seem to remember having seen it. Your village is under some very old big trees, just by the side of the red road-isn't that so?

DAIRYMAN. That's right, child.

AMAL. And on the slope of the hill cattle grazing.

DAIRYMAN. How wonderful! Aren't there cattle grazing in our village! Indeed, there are!

AMAL. And your women with red sarees fill their pitchers from the river and carry them on their heads.

DAIRYMAN. Good, that's right. Women from our dairy village do come and draw their water from the river; but then it isn't everyone who has a red saree to put on. But, my dear child, surely you must have been there for a walk some time.

AMAL. Really, Dairyman, never been there at all. But the first day doctor lets me go out, you are going to take me to your village.

DAIRYMAN. I will, my child, with pleasure.

AMAL. And you'll teach me to cry curds and shoulder the yoke like you and walk the long, long road?

DAIRYMAN. Dear, dear, did you ever? Why should you sell curds? No, you will read big books and be learned.

AMAL. No, I never want to be learned —I'll be like you and take my curds from the village by the red road near the old banyan tree, and I will hawk it from cottage to cottage. Oh, how do you cry—"Curd, curd, good nice curd!" Teach me the tune, will you?

DAIRYMAN. Dear, dear, teach you the tune; what an idea!

AMAL. Please do. I love to hear it. I can't tell you how queer I feel when I hear you cry out from the bend of that road, through the line of those trees! Do you know I feel like that when I hear the shrill cry of kites from almost the end of the sky?

DAIRYMAN. Dear child, will you have some curds? Yes, do.

AMAL. But I have no money.

DAIRYMAN. No, no, no, don't talk of money! You'll make me so happy if you have a little curds from me.

AMAL. Say, have I kept you too long?

DAIRYMAN. Not a bit; it has been no loss to me at all; you have taught me how to be happy selling curds. (*Exit*)

AMAL (*Intoning*) Curds, curds, good nice curds-from the dairy village-from the country of the Panch-mura hills by the Shamli bank. Curds, good curds; in the early morning the women make the cows stand in a row under the trees and milk them, and in the evening they turn the milk into curds. Curds, good curds. Hello, there's the watchman on his rounds. Watchman, I say, come and have a word with me.

WATCHMAN. What's all this row you are making? Aren't you afraid of the likes of me?

AMAL. No, why should I be?

WATCHMAN. Suppose I march you off then?

AMAL. Where will you take me to? Is it very far, right beyond the hills?

WATCHMAN. Suppose I march you straight to the King?

AMAL. To the King! Do, will you? But the doctor won't let me go out. No one can ever take me away. I've got to stay here all day long.

WATCHMAN. Doctor won't let you, poor fellow! So I see! Your face is pale and there are dark rings round your eyes. Your veins stick out from your poor thin hands.

AMAL. Won't you sound the gong, Watchman?

WATCHMAN. Time has not yet come.

AMAL. How curious! Some say time has not yet come, and some say time has gone by! But surely your time will come the moment you strike the gong!

WATCHMAN. That's not possible; I strike up the gong only when it is time.

AMAL. Yes, I love to hear your gong. When it is midday and our meal is over, Uncle goes off to his work and Auntie falls asleep reading her Râmayana, and in the courtyard under the shadow of the wall our doggie sleeps with his nose in his curled up tail; then your gong strikes out, "Dong, dong, dong!" Tell me why does your gong sound?

WATCHMAN. My gong sounds to tell the people, Time waits for none, but goes on forever.

AMAL. Where, to what land?

WATCHMAN. That none knows.

AMAL. Then I suppose no one has ever been there! Oh, I do wish to fly with the time to that land of which no one knows anything.

WATCHMAN. All of us have to get there one day, my child.

AMAL. Have I too?

WATCHMAN. Yes, you too!

AMAL. But doctor won't let me out.

WATCHMAN. One day the doctor himself may take you there by the hand.

AMAL. He won't; you don't know him. He only keeps me in.

WATCHMAN. One greater than he comes and lets us free.

AMAL. When will this great doctor come for me? I can't stick in here any more.

WATCHMAN. Shouldn't talk like that, my child.

AMAL. No. I am here where they have left me —I never move a bit. But when your gong goes off, dong, dong, dong, it goes to my heart. Say, Watchman?

WATCHMAN. Yes, my dear.

AMAL. Say, what's going on there in that big house on the other side, where there is a flag flying high up and the people are always going in and out?

WATCHMAN. Oh, there? That's our new Post Office.

AMAL. Post Office? Whose?

WATCHMAN. Whose? Why, the King's surely!

AMAL. Do letters come from the King to his office here?

WATCHMAN. Of course. One fine day there may be a letter for you in there.

AMAL. A letter for me? But I am only a little boy.

WATCHMAN. The King sends tiny notes to little boys.

AMAL. Oh, how lovely! When shall I have my letter? How do you guess he'll write to me?

WATCHMAN. Otherwise why should he set his Post Office here right in front of your open window, with the golden flag flying?

AMAL. But who will fetch me my King's letter when it comes?

WATCHMAN. The King has many postmen. Don't you see them run about with round gilt badges on their chests?

AMAL. Well, where do they go?

WATCHMAN. Oh, from door to door, all through the country.

AMAL. I'll be the King's postman when I grow up.

WATCHMAN. Ha! ha! Postman, indeed! Rain or shine, rich or poor, from house to house delivering letters-that's very great work!

AMAL. That's what I'd like best. What makes you smile so? Oh, yes, your work is great too. When it is silent everywhere in the heat of the noonday, your gong sounds, Dong, dong, dong, — and sometimes when I wake up at night all of a sudden and find our lamp blown out, I can hear through the darkness your gong slowly sounding, Dong, dong, dong!

WATCHMAN. There's the village headman! I must be off. If he catches me gossiping with you there'll be a great to do.

AMAL. The headman? Whereabouts is he?

WATCHMAN. Right down the road there; see that huge palm-leaf umbrella hopping along? That's him!

AMAL. I suppose the King's made him our headman here?

WATCHMAN. Made him? Oh, no! A fussy busy-body! He knows so many ways of making himself unpleasant that everybody is afraid of him. It's just a game for the likes of him, making trouble for everybody. I must be off now! Mustn't keep work waiting, you know! I'll drop in again to-morrow morning and tell you all the news of the town. (*Exit*)

AMAL. It would be splendid to have a letter from the King every day. I'll read them at the window. But, oh! I can't read writing. Who'll read them out to me, I wonder! Auntie reads her Râmayana; she may know the King's writing. If no one will, then I must keep them carefully and read them when I'm grown up. But if the postman can't find me? Headman, Mr. Headman, may I have a word with you?

HEADMAN. Who is yelling after me on the highway? Oh, you wretched monkey!

AMAL. You're the headman. Everybody minds you.

HEADMAN (*Looking pleased*) Yes, oh yes, they do! They must!

AMAL. Do the King's postmen listen to you?

HEADMAN. They've got to. By Jove, I'd like to see —

AMAL. Will you tell the postman it's Amal who sits by the window here?

HEADMAN. What's the good of that?

AMAL. In case there's a letter for me.

HEADMAN. A letter for you! Whoever's going to write to you?

AMAL. If the King does.

HEADMAN. Ha! ha! What an uncommon little fellow you are! Ha! ha! the King indeed, aren't you his bosom friend, eh! You haven't met for a long while and the King is pining, I am sure. Wait till to-morrow and you'll have your letter.

AMAL. Say, Headman, why do you speak to me in that tone of voice? Are you cross?

HEADMAN. Upon my word! Cross, indeed! You write to the King! Madhav is devilish swell nowadays. He'd made a little pile; and so kings and padishahs are everyday talk with his people. Let me find him once and I'll make him dance. Oh, you snipper-snapper! I'll get the King's letter sent to your house-indeed I will!

AMAL. No, no, please don't trouble yourself about it.

HEADMAN. And why not, pray! I'll tell the King about you and he won't be very long. One of his footmen will come along presently for news of you. Madhav's impudence staggers me. If the King hears of this, that'll take some of his nonsense out of him. (*Exit*)

AMAL. Who are you walking there? How your anklets tinkle! Do stop a while, dear, won't you?

(A Girl enters)

GIRL. I haven't a moment to spare; it is already late!

AMAL. I see, you don't wish to stop; I don't care to stay on here either.

GIRL. You make me think of some late star of the morning! Whatever's the matter with you?

AMAL. I don't know; the doctor won't let me out.

GIRL. Ah me! Don't then! Should listen to the doctor. People'll be cross with you if you're naughty. I know, always looking out and watching must make you feel tired. Let me close the window a bit for you.

AMAL. No, don't, only this one's open! All the others are shut. But will you tell me who you are? Don't seem to know you.

GIRL. I am Sudha.

AMAL. What Sudha?

SUDHA. Don't you know? Daughter of the flower-seller here.

AMAL. What do *you* do?

SUDHA. I gather flowers in my basket.

AMAL. Oh, flower gathering! That is why your feet seem so glad and your anklets jingle so merrily as you walk. Wish I could be out too. Then I would pick some flowers for you from the very topmost branches right out of sight.

SUDHA. Would you really? Do you know more about flowers than I?

AMAL. Yes, I *do*, quite as much. I know all about Champa of the fairy tale and his seven brothers. If only they let me, I'll go right into the dense forest where you can't find your way. And where the honey-sipping hummingbird rocks himself on the end of the thinnest branch, I will flower out as a champa. Would you be my sister Parul?

SUDHA. You are silly! How can I be sister Parul when I am Sudha and my mother is Sasi, the flower-seller? I have to weave so many garlands a day. It would be jolly if I could lounge here like you!

AMAL. What would you do then, all the day long?

SUDHA. I could have great times with my doll Benay the bride, and Meni the pussycat and-but I say it is getting late and I mustn't stop, or I won't find a single flower.

AMAL. Oh, wait a little longer; I do like it so!

SUDHA. Ah, well-now don't you be naughty. Be good and sit still and on my way back home with the flowers I'll come and talk with you.

AMAL. And you'll let me have a flower then?

SUDHA. No, how can I? It has to be paid for.

AMAL. I'll pay when I grow up-before I leave to look for work out on the other side of that stream there.

SUDHA. Very well, then.

AMAL. And you'll come back when you have your flowers?

SUDHA. I will.

AMAL. You will, really?

SUDHA. Yes, I will.

AMAL. You won't forget me? I am Amal, remember that.

SUDHA. I won't forget you, you'll see. (*Exit*)

(*A Troop of Boys enter*)

AMAL. Say, brothers, where are you all off to? Stop here a little.

BOYS. We're off to play.

AMAL. What will you play at, brothers?

BOYS. We'll play at being ploughmen.

FIRST BOY (*Showing a stick*) This is our ploughshare.

SECOND BOY. We two are the pair of oxen.

AMAL. And you're going to play the whole day?

BOYS. Yes, all day long.

AMAL. And you'll come back home in the evening by the road along the river bank?

BOYS. Yes.

AMAL. Do you pass our house on your way home?

BOYS. You come out to play with us, yes do.

AMAL. Doctor won't let me out.

BOYS. Doctor! Suppose the likes of you mind the doctor. Let's be off; it is getting late.

AMAL. Don't. Why not play on the road near this window? I could watch you then.

THIRD BOY. What can we play at here?

AMAL. With all these toys of mine lying about. Here you are, have them. I can't play alone. They are getting dirty and are of no use to me.

BOYS. How jolly! What fine toys! Look, here's a ship. There's old mother Jatai; say, chaps, ain't he a gorgeous sepoy? And you'll let us have them all? You don't really mind?

AMAL. No, not a bit; have them by all means.

BOYS. You don't want them back?

AMAL. Oh, no, I shan't want them.

BOYS. Say, won't you get a scolding for this?

AMAL. No one will scold me. But will you play with them in front of our door for a while every morning? I'll get you new ones when these are old.

BOYS. Oh, yes, we will. Say, chaps, put these sepoys into a line. We'll play at war; where can we get a musket? Oh, look here, this bit of reed will do nicely. Say, but you're off to sleep already.

AMAL. I'm afraid I'm sleepy. I don't know, I feel like it at times. I have been sitting a long while and I'm tired; my back aches.

BOYS It's only early noon now. How is it you're sleepy? Listen! The gong's sounding the first watch.

AMAL. Yes, dong, dong, dong, it tolls me to sleep.

BOYS We had better go then. We'll come in again to-morrow morning.

AMAL. I want to ask you something before you go. You are always out-do you know of the King's postmen?

BOYS Yes, quite well.

AMAL. Who are they? Tell me their names.

BOYS One's Badal, another's Sarat. There's so many of them.

AMAL. Do you think they will know me if there's a letter for me?

BOYS Surely, if your name's on the letter they will find you out.

AMAL. When you call in to-morrow morning, will you bring one of them along so that he'll know me?

BOYS Yes, if you like.
CURTAIN

## ACT II

*(Amal in Bed)*

AMAL. Can't I go near the window to-day, Uncle? Would the doctor mind that too?

MADHAV. Yes, darling, you see you've made yourself worse squatting there day after day.

AMAL. Oh, no, I don't know if it's made me more ill, but I always feel well when I'm there.

MADHAV. No, you don't; you squat there and make friends with the whole lot of people round here, old and young, as if they are holding a fair right under my eaves-flesh and blood won't stand that strain. Just see-your face is quite pale.

AMAL. Uncle, I fear my fakir'll pass and not see me by the window.

MADHAV. Your fakir, whoever's that?

AMAL. He comes and chats to me of the many lands where he's been. I love to hear him.

MADHAV. How's that? I don't know of any fakirs.

AMAL. This is about the time he comes in. I beg of you, by your dear feet, ask him in for a moment to talk to me here.

*(Gaffer Enters in a Fakir's Guise)*

AMAL. There you are. Come here, Fakir, by my bedside.

MADHAV. Upon my word, but this is —

GAFFER *(Winking hard)* I am the fakir.

MADHAV. It beats my reckoning what you're not.

AMAL. Where have you been this time, Fakir?

FAKIR To the Isle of Parrots. I am just back.

MADHAV. The Parrots' Isle!

FAKIR. Is it so very astonishing? Am I like you, man? A journey doesn't cost a thing. I tramp just where I like.

AMAL *(Clapping)* How jolly for you! Remember your promise to take me with you as your follower when I'm well.

FAKIR. Of course, and I'll teach you such secrets too of travelling that nothing in sea or forest or mountain can bar your way.

MADHAV. What's all this rigmarole?

GAFFER. Amal, my dear, I bow to nothing in sea or mountain; but if the doctor joins in with this uncle of yours, then I with all my magic must own myself beaten.

AMAL. No. Uncle shan't tell the doctor. And I promise to lie quiet; but the day I am well, off I go with the Fakir and nothing in sea or mountain or torrent shall stand in my way.

MADHAV. Fie, dear child, don't keep on harping upon going! It makes me so sad to hear you talk so.

AMAL. Tell me, Fakir, what the Parrots' Isle is like.

GAFFER. It's a land of wonders; it's a haunt of birds. There's no man; and they neither speak nor walk, they simply sing and they fly.

AMAL. How glorious! And it's by some sea?

GAFFER. Of course. It's on the sea.

AMAL. And green hills are there?

GAFFER. Indeed, they live among the green hills; and in the time of the sunset when there is a red glow on the hillside, all the birds with their green wings flock back to their nests.

AMAL. And there are waterfalls!

GAFFER. Dear me, of course; you don't have a hill without its waterfalls. Oh, it's like molten diamonds; and, my dear, what dances they have! Don't they make the pebbles sing as they rush over them to the sea. No devil of a doctor can stop them for a moment. The birds looked upon me as nothing but a man, quite a trifling creature without wings-and they would have nothing to do with me. Were it not so I would build a small cabin for myself among their crowd of nests and pass my days counting the sea waves.

AMAL. How I wish I were a bird! Then —

GAFFER. But that would have been a bit of a job; I hear you've fixed up with the dairyman to be a hawker of curds when you grow up; I'm afraid such business won't flourish among birds; you might land yourself into serious loss.

MADHAV. Really this is too much. Between you two I shall turn crazy. Now, I'm off.

AMAL. Has the dairyman been, Uncle?

MADHAV. And why shouldn't he? He won't bother his head running errands for your pet fakir, in and out among the nests in his Parrots' Isle. But he has left a jar of curd for you saying that he is rather busy with his niece's wedding in the village, and he has got to order a band at Kamlipara.

AMAL. But he is going to marry me to his little niece.

GAFFER. Dear me, we are in a fix now.

AMAL. He said she would find me a lovely little bride with a pair of pearl drops in her ears and dressed in a lovely red *sâree;* and in the morning she would milk with her own hands the black cow and feed me with warm milk with foam on it from a brand new earthen cruse; and in the evenings she would carry the lamp round the cow-house, and then come and sit by me to tell me tales of Champa and his six brothers.

GAFFER. How delicious! The prospect tempts even me, a hermit! But never mind, dear, about this wedding. Let it be. I tell you when you wed there'll be no lack of nieces in his household.

MADHAV. Shut up! This is more than I can stand. (*Exit*)

AMAL. Fakir, now that Uncle's off, just tell me, has the King sent me a letter to the Post Office?

GAFFER. I gather that his letter has already started; but it's still on the way.

AMAL. On the way? Where is it? Is it on that road winding through the trees which you can follow to the end of the forest when the sky is quite clear after rain?

GAFFER. That's so. You know all about it already.

AMAL. I do, everything.

GAFFER. So I see, but how?

AMAL. I can't say; but it's quite clear to me. I fancy I've seen it often in days long gone by. How long ago I can't tell. Do you know when? I can see it all: there, the King's postman coming down the hillside alone, a lantern in his left hand and on his back a bag of letters climbing down for ever so long, for days and nights, and where at the foot of the mountain the waterfall becomes a stream he takes to the footpath on the bank and walks on through the rye; then comes the sugarcane field and he disappears into the narrow lane cutting through the tall stems of sugarcanes; then he reaches the open meadow where the cricket chirps and where there is not a single man to be seen, only the snipe wagging their tails and poking at the mud with their bills. I can feel him coming nearer and nearer and my heart becomes glad.

GAFFER. My eyes aren't young; but you make me see all the same.

AMAL. Say, Fakir, do you know the King who has this Post Office?

GAFFER. I do; I go to him for my alms every day.

AMAL. Good! When I get well, I must have my alms too from him, mayn't I?

GAFFER. You won't need to ask, my dear, he'll give it to you of his own accord.

AMAL. No, I would go to his gate and cry, "Victory to thee, O King!" and dancing to the tabor's sound, ask for alms. Won't it be nice?

GAFFER. It would be splendid, and if you're with me, I shall have my full share. But what'll you ask?

AMAL. I shall say, "Make me your postman, that I may go about lantern in hand, delivering your letters from door to door. Don't let me stay at home all day!"

GAFFER. What is there to be sad for, my child, even were you to stay at home?

AMAL. It isn't sad. When they shut me in here first I felt the day was so long. Since the King's Post Office I like it more and more being indoors, and as I think I shall get a letter one day, I feel quite happy and then I don't mind being quiet and alone. I wonder if I shall make out what'll be in the King's letter?

GAFFER. Even if you didn't wouldn't it be enough if it just bore your name?

(*Madhav enters*)

MADHAV. Have you any idea of the trouble you've got me into, between you two?

GAFFER. What's the matter?

MADHAV. I hear you've let it get rumored about that the King has planted his office here to send messages to both of you.

GAFFER. Well, what about it?

MADHAV. Our headman Panchanan has had it told to the King anonymously.

GAFFER. Aren't we aware that everything reaches the King's ears?

MADHAV. Then why don't you look out? Why take the King's name in vain? You'll bring me to ruin if you do.

AMAL. Say, Fakir, will the King be cross?

GAFFER. Cross, nonsense! And with a child like you and a fakir such as I am. Let's see if the King be angry, and then won't I give him a piece of my mind.

AMAL. Say, Fakir, I've been feeling a sort of darkness coming over my eyes since the morning. Everything seems like a dream. I long to be quiet. I don't feel like talking at all. Won't the King's letter come? Suppose this room melts away all on a sudden, suppose —

GAFFER (*Fanning Amal*) The letter's sure to come to-day, my boy.

(*Doctor enters*)

DOCTOR And how do you feel to-day?

AMAL. Feel awfully well to-day, Doctor. All pain seems to have left me.

DOCTOR (*Aside to Madhav*) Don't quite like the look of that smile. Bad sign that, his feeling well! Chakradhan has observed —

MADHAV. For goodness sake, Doctor, leave Chakradhan alone. Tell me what's going to happen?

DOCTOR. Can't hold him in much longer, I fear! I warned you before-This looks like a fresh exposure.

MADHAV. No, I've used the utmost care, never let him out of doors; and the windows have been shut almost all the time.

DOCTOR. There's a peculiar quality in the air to-day. As I came in I found a fearful draught through your front door. That's most hurtful. Better lock it at once. Would it matter if this kept your visitors off for two or three days? If someone happens to call unexpectedly-there's the back door. You had better shut this window as well, it's letting in the sunset rays only to keep the patient awake.

MADHAV. Amal has shut his eyes. I expect he is sleeping. His face tells me-Oh, Doctor, I bring in a child who is a stranger and love him as my own, and now I suppose I must lose him!

DOCTOR. What's that? There's your headman sailing in! —What a bother! I must be going, brother. You had better stir about and see to the doors being properly fastened. I will send on a strong dose directly I get home. Try it on him-it may save him at last, if he can be saved at all. (*Exeunt Madhav and Doctor.*)

(*The Headman enters*)

HEADMAN. Hello, urchin!

GAFFER (*Rising hastily*) 'Sh, be quiet.

AMAL. No, Fakir, did you think I was asleep? I wasn't. I can hear everything; yes, and voices far away. I feel that mother and father are sitting by my pillow and speaking to me.

(*Madhav enters*)

HEADMAN. I say, Madhav, I hear you hobnob with bigwigs nowadays.

MADHAV. Spare me your jests, Headman, we are but common people.

HEADMAN. But your child here is expecting a letter from the King.

MADHAV. Don't you take any notice of him, a mere foolish boy!

HEADMAN. Indeed, why not! It'll beat the King hard to find a better family! Don't you see why the King plants his new Post Office right before your win- dow? Why there's a letter for you from the King, urchin.

AMAL (*Starting up*) Indeed, really!

HEADMAN. How can it be false? You're the King's chum. Here's your letter (*showing a blank slip of paper*). Ha, ha, ha! This is the letter.

AMAL. Please don't mock me. Say, Fakir, is it so?

GAFFER. Yes, my dear. I as Fakir tell you it is his letter.

AMAL. How is it I can't see? It all looks so blank to me. What is there in the letter, Mr. Headman?

HEADMAN. The King says, "I am calling on you shortly; you had better arrange puffed rice offerings for me. —Palace fare is quite tasteless to me now." Ha! ha! ha!

MADHAV (*With folded palms*) I beseech you, headman, don't you joke about these things —

GAFFER. Cutting jokes indeed, dare he!

MADHAV. Are you out of your mind too, Gaffer?

GAFFER. Out of my mind, well then I am; I can read plainly that the King writes he will come himself to see Amal, with the state physician.

AMAL. Fakir, Fakir, 'sh, his trumpet! Can't you hear?

HEADMAN. Ha! ha! ha! I fear he won't until he's a bit more off his head.

AMAL. Mr. Headman, I thought you were cross with me and didn't love me. I never could think you would fetch me the King's letter. Let me wipe the dust off your feet.

HEADMAN. This little child does have an instinct of reverence. Though a little silly, he has a good heart.

AMAL. It's hard on the fourth watch now, I suppose-Hark the gong, "Dong, dong, ding," "Dong, dong, ding." Is the evening star up? How is it I can't see —

GAFFER. Oh, the windows are all shut, I'll open them.

(*A knocking outside*)

MADHAV. What's that? —Who is it-what a bother!

VOICE (*From outside*) Open the door.

MADHAV Say, Headman-Hope they're not robbers.

HEADMAN Who's there? —It's Panchanan, the headman, calls-Aren't you afraid of the like of me? Fancy! The noise has ceased! Panchanan's voice carries far. —Yes, show me the biggest robbers!

MADHAV (*Peering out of the window*) I should think the noise has ceased. They've smashed the door.

*(The King's Herald enters)*

HERALD. Our Sovereign King comes to-night!

HEADMAN. My God!

AMAL. At what hour of the night, Herald?

HERALD. On the second watch.

AMAL. When from the city gates my friend the watchman will strike his gong, "ding dong ding, ding dong ding" —then?

HERALD. Yes, then. The King sends his greatest physician to attend on his young friend.

*(State Physician enters)*

STATE PHYSICIAN. What's this? How close it is here! Open wide all the doors and windows. *(Feeling Amal's body)* How do you feel, my child?

AMAL. I feel very well, Doctor, very well. All pain is gone. How fresh and open! I can see all the stars now twinkling from the other side of the dark.

PHYSICIAN. Will you feel well enough to leave your bed with the King when he comes in the middle watches of the night?

AMAL. Of course, I'm dying to be about for ever so long. I'll ask the King to find me the polar star. —I must have seen it often, but I don't know exactly which it is.

PHYSICIAN. He will tell you everything. *(To Madhav)* Will you go about and arrange flowers through the room for the King's visit? *(Indicating the Headman)* We can't have that person in here.

AMAL. No, let him be, Doctor. He is a friend. It was he who brought me the King's letter.

PHYSICIAN. Very well, my child. He may remain if he is a friend of yours.

MADHAV *(Whispering into Amal's ear)* My child, the King loves you. He is coming himself. Beg for a gift from him. You know our humble circumstances.

AMAL. Don't you worry, Uncle. —I've made up my mind about it.

MADHAV. What is it, my child?

AMAL. I shall ask him to make me one of his postmen that I may wander far and wide, delivering his message from door to door.

MADHAV *(Slapping his forehead)* Alas, is that all?

AMAL. What'll be our offerings to the King, Uncle, when he comes?

HERALD. He has commanded puffed rice.

AMAL. Puffed rice! Say, Headman, you're right. You said so. You knew all we didn't.

HEADMAN. If you send word to my house then I could manage for the King's advent really nice —

PHYSICIAN. No need at all. Now be quiet all of you. Sleep is coming over him. I'll sit by his pillow; he's dropping into slumber. Blow out the oil-lamp. Only let the star-light stream in. Hush, he slumbers.

MADHAV (*Addressing Gaffer*) What are you standing there for like a statue, folding your palms. —I am nervous. —Say, are they good omens? Why are they darkening the room? How will star-light help?

GAFFER. Silence, unbeliever.

(*Sudha enters*)

SUDHA. Amal!

PHYSICIAN. He's asleep.

SUDHA. I have some flowers for him. Mayn't I give them into his own hand?

PHYSICIAN. Yes, you may.

SUDHA. When will he be awake?

PHYSICIAN. Directly the King comes and calls him.

SUDHA. Will you whisper a word for me in his ear?

PHYSICIAN. What shall I say?

SUDHA. Tell him Sudha has not forgotten him.
CURTAIN

**CHITRA**

## PREFACE

This lyrical drama was written about twenty-five years ago. It is based on the following story from the Mahabharata.

In the course of his wanderings, in fulfilment of a vow of penance, Arjuna came to Manipur. There he saw Chitrangada, the beautiful daughter of Chitravahana, the king of the country. Smitten with her charms, he asked the king for the hand of his daughter in marriage. Chitravahana asked him who he was, and learning that he was Arjuna the Pandara, told him that Prabhanjana, one of his ancestors in the kingly line of Manipur, had long been childless. In order to obtain an heir, he performed severe penances. Pleased with these austerities, the god Shiva gave him this boon, that he and his successors should each have one child. It so happened that the promised child had invariably been a son. He, Chitravahana, was the first to have only a daughter Chitrangada to perpetuate the race. He had, therefore, always treated her as a son and had made her his heir.

Continuing, the king said:

"The one son that will be born to her must be the perpetuator of my race. That son will be the price that I shall demand for this marriage. You can take her, if you like, on this condition."

Arjuna promised and took Chitrangada to wife, and lived in her father's capital for three years. When a son was born to them, he embraced her with affection, and taking leave of her and her father, set out again on his travels.

## THE CHARACTERS

GODS:
MADANA (Eros).
VASANTA (Lycoris).


MORTALS:
CHITRA, daughter of the King of Manipur.
ARJUNA, a prince of the house of the Kurus. He is of the Kshatriya or "warrior caste," and during the action is living as a Hermit retired in the forest.

VILLAGERS from an outlying district of Manipur.


NOTE. —The dramatic poem "Chitra" has been performed in India without scenery-the actors being surrounded by the audience. Proposals for its production here having been made to him, he went through this translation and provided stage directions, but wished these omitted if it were printed as a book.

## SCENE I

CHITRA. Art thou the god with the five darts, the Lord of Love?

MADANA. I am he who was the first born in the heart of the Creator. I bind in bonds of pain and bliss the lives of men and women!

CHITRA. I know, I know what that pain is and those bonds. —And who art thou, my lord?

VASANTA. I am his friend-Vasanta-the King of the Seasons. Death and decrepitude would wear the world to the bone but that I follow them and constantly attack them. I am Eternal Youth.

CHITRA. I bow to thee, Lord Vasanta.

MADANA. But what stern vow is thine, fair stranger? Why dost thou wither thy fresh youth with penance and mortification? Such a sacrifice is not fit for the worship of love. Who art thou and what is thy prayer?

CHITRA. I am Chitra, the daughter of the kingly house of Manipur. With godlike grace Lord Shiva promised to my royal grandsire an unbroken line of male descent. Nevertheless, the divine word proved powerless to change the spark of life in my mother's womb —so invincible was my nature, woman though I be.

MADANA. I know, that is why thy father brings thee up as his son. He has taught thee the use of the bow and all the duties of a king.

CHITRA. Yes, that is why I am dressed in man's attire and have left the seclusion of a woman's chamber. I know no feminine wiles for winning hearts. My hands are strong to bend the bow, but I have never learnt Cupid's archery, the play of eyes.

MADANA. That requires no schooling, fair one. The eye does its work untaught, and he knows how well, who is struck in the heart.

CHITRA. One day in search of game I roved alone to the forest on the bank of the Purna river. Tying my horse to a tree trunk I entered a dense thicket on the track of a deer. I found a narrow sinuous path meandering through the dusk of the entangled boughs, the foliage vibrated with the chirping of crickets, when of a sudden I came upon a man lying on a bed of dried leaves, across my path. I asked him haughtily to move aside, but he heeded not. Then with the sharp end of my bow I pricked him in contempt. Instantly he leapt up with straight, tall limbs, like a sudden tongue of fire from a heap of ashes. An amused smile flickered round the corners of his mouth, perhaps at the sight of my boyish countenance. Then for the first time in my life I felt myself a woman, and knew that a man was before me.

MADANA. At the auspicious hour I teach the man and the woman this supreme lesson to know themselves. What happened after that?

CHITRA. With fear and wonder I asked him "Who are you?" "I am Arjuna," he said, "of the great Kuru clan." I stood petrified like a statue, and forgot to do him obeisance. Was this indeed Arjuna, the one great idol of my dreams! Yes, I had long ago heard how he had vowed a twelve-years' celibacy. Many a day my young ambition had spurred me on to break my lance with him, to challenge him in disguise to single combat, and prove my skill in arms against him. Ah, foolish heart, whither fled thy presumption? Could I but exchange my youth with all its aspirations for the clod of earth under his feet, I should deem it a most precious grace. I know not in what whirlpool of thought I was lost, when suddenly I saw him vanish through the trees. O foolish woman, neither didst thou greet him, nor speak a word, nor beg forgiveness, but stoodest like a barbarian boor while he contemptuously walked away! . . . Next morning I laid aside my man's clothing. I donned bracelets, anklets, waist-chain, and a gown of purple red silk. The unaccustomed dress clung about my shrinking shame; but I hastened on my quest, and found Arjuna in the forest temple of Shiva.

MADANA. Tell me the story to the end. I am the heart-born god, and I understand the mystery of these impulses.

CHITRA. Only vaguely can I remember what things I said, and what answer I got. Do not ask me to tell you all. Shame fell on me like a thunderbolt, yet could not break me to pieces, so utterly hard, so like a man am I. His last words as I walked home pricked my ears like red hot needles. "I have taken the vow of celibacy. I am not fit to be thy husband!" Oh, the vow of a man! Surely thou knowest, thou god of love, that unnumbered saints and sages have surrendered the merits of their life-long penance at the feet of a woman. I broke my bow in two and burnt my arrows in the fire. I hated my strong, lithe arm, scored by drawing the bowstring. O Love, god Love, thou hast laid low in the dust the vain pride of my manlike strength; and all my man's training lies crushed under thy feet. Now teach me thy lessons; give me the power of the weak and the weapon of the unarmed hand.

MADANA. I will be thy friend. I will bring the world-conquering Arjuna a captive before thee, to accept his rebellion's sentence at thy hand.

CHITRA. Had I but the time needed, I could win his heart by slow degrees, and ask no help of the gods. I would stand by his side as a comrade, drive the fierce horses of his war-chariot, attend him in the pleasures of the chase, keep guard at night at the entrance of his tent, and help him in all the great duties of a Kshatriya, rescuing the weak, and meting out justice where it is due. Surely at last the day would have come for him to look at me and wonder, "What boy is this? Has one of my slaves in a former life followed me like my good deeds into this?" I am not the woman who nourishes her despair in lonely silence, feeding it with nightly tears and covering it with the daily patient smile, a widow from her birth. The flower of my desire shall never drop into the dust before it has ripened to fruit. But it is the labour of a life time to make one's true self known and honoured. Therefore I have come to thy door, thou world-vanquishing Love, and thou, Vasanta, youthful Lord of the Seasons, take from my young body this primal injustice, an unattractive plainness. For a single day make me superbly beautiful, even as beautiful as was the sudden blooming of love in my heart. Give me but one brief day of perfect beauty, and I will answer for the days that follow.

MADANA. Lady, I grant thy prayer.

VASANTA. Not for the short span of a day, but for one whole year the charm of spring blossoms shall nestle round thy limbs.

## SCENE II

ARJUNA. Was I dreaming or was what I saw by the lake truly there? Sitting on the mossy turf, I mused over bygone years in the sloping shadows of the evening, when slowly there came out from the folding darkness of foliage an apparition of beauty in the perfect form of a woman, and stood on a white slab of stone at the water's brink. It seemed that the heart of the earth must heave in joy under her bare white feet. Methought the vague veilings of her body should melt in ecstasy into air as the golden mist of dawn melts from off the snowy peak of the eastern hill. She bowed herself above the shining mirror of the lake and saw the reflection of her face. She started up in awe and stood still; then smiled, and with a careless sweep of her left arm unloosed her hair and let it trail on the earth at her feet. She bared her bosom and looked at her arms, so flawlessly modelled, and instinct with an exquisite caress. Bending her head she saw the sweet blossoming of her youth and the tender bloom and blush of her skin. She beamed with a glad surprise. So, if the white lotus bud on opening her eyes in the morning were to arch her neck and see her shadow in the water, would she wonder at herself the livelong day. But a moment after the smile passed from her face and a shade of sadness crept into her eyes. She bound up her tresses, drew her veil over her arms, and sighing slowly, walked away like a beauteous evening fading into the night. To me the supreme fulfilment of desire seemed to have been revealed in a flash and then to have vanished. . . . But who is it that pushes the door?
Enter Chitra, dressed as a woman..

Ah! it is she. Quiet, my heart! . . . Fear me not, lady! I am. a Kshatriya.

CHITRA. Honoured sir, you are my guest. I live in this temple. I know not in what way I can show you hospitality.

ARJUNA. Fair lady, the very sight of you is indeed the highest hospitality. If you will not take it amiss I would ask you a question.

CHITRA. You have permission.

ARJUNA. What stern vow keeps you immured in this solitary temple, depriving all mortals of a vision of so much loveliness?

CHITRA. I harbour a secret desire in my heart, for the fulfilment of which I offer daily prayers to Lord Shiva.

ARJUNA. Alas, what can you desire, you who are the desire of the whole world! From the easternmost hill on whose summit the morning sun first prints his fiery foot to the end of the sunset land have I travelled. I have seen whatever is most precious, beautiful and great on the earth. My knowledge shall be yours, only say for what or for whom you seek.

CHITRA. He whom I seek is known to all. Arjuna Indeed! Who may this favourite of the gods be, whose fame has captured your heart? Chitra Sprung from the highest of all royal houses, the greatest of all heroes is he.

ARJUNA. Lady, offer not such wealth of beauty as is yours on the altar of false reputation. Spurious fame spreads from tongue to tongue like the fog of the early dawn before the sun rises. Tell me who in the highest of kingly lines is the supreme hero?

CHITRA. Hermit, you are jealous of other men's fame. Do you not know that all over the world the royal house of the Kurus is the most famous?

ARJUNA. The house of the Kurus!

CHITRA. And have you never heard of the greatest name of that far-famed house?

ARJUNA. From your own lips let me hear it.

CHITRA. Arjuna, the conqueror of the world. I have culled from the mouths of the multitude that imperishable name and hidden it with care in my maiden heart. Hermit, why do you look perturbed? Has that name only a deceitful glitter? Say so, and I will not hesitate to break this casket of my heart and throw the false gem to the dust.

ARJUNA. Be his name and fame, his bravery and prowess false or true, for. mercy's sake do not banish him from your heart-for he kneels at your feet even now.

CHITRA. You, Arjuna!

ARJUNA. Yes, I am he, the love-hungered guest at your door.

CHITRA. Then it is not true that Arjuna has taken a vow of chastity for twelve long years?

ARJUNA. But you have dissolved my vow even as the moon dissolves the night's vow of obscurity.

CHITRA. Oh, shame upon you! What have you seen in me that makes you false to yourself? Whom do you seek in these dark eyes, in these milk-white arms, if you are ready to pay for her the price of your probity? Not my true self, I know. Surely this cannot be love, this is not man's highest homage to woman! Alas, that this frail disguise, the body, should make one blind to the light of the deathless spirit! Yes, now indeed, I know, Arjuna, the fame of your heroic manhood is false.

ARJUNA. Ah, I feel how vain is fame, the pride of prowess! Everything seems to me a dream. You alone are perfect; you are the wealth of the world, the end of all poverty, the goal of all efforts, the one woman! Others there are who can be but slowly known. While to see you for a moment is to see perfect completeness once and for ever.

CHITRA. Alas, it is not I, not I, Arjuna! It is the deceit of a god. Go, go, my hero, go. Woo not falsehood, offer not your great heart to an illusion. Go.

## SCENE III

CHITRA. No, impossible. To face that fervent gaze that almost grasps you like clutching hands of the hungry spirit within; to feel his heart struggling to break its bounds urging its passionate cry through the entire body-and then to send him away like a beggar-no, impossible.

Enter MADANA and VASANTA.. Ah, god of love, what fearful flame is this with which

thou hast enveloped me! I burn, and I burn whatever I touch.

MADANA. I desire to know what happened last night.

CHITRA. At evening I lay down on a grassy bed strewn with the petals of spring flowers, and recollected the wonderful praise of my beauty I had heard from Arjuna; —drinking drop by drop the honey that I had stored during the long day. The history of my past life like that of my former existences was forgotten. I felt like a flower, which has but a few fleeting hours to listen to all the humming flatteries and whispered murmurs of the woodlands and then must lower its eyes from the Sky, bend its head and at a breath give itself up to the dust without a cry, thus ending the short story of a perfect moment that has neither past nor future.

VASANTA. A limitless life of glory can bloom and spend itself in a morning.

MADANA. Like an endless meaning in the narrow span of a song.

CHITRA. The southern breeze caressed me to sleep. From the flowering Malati bower overhead silent kisses dropped over my body. On my hair, my breast, my feet, each flower chose a bed to die on. I slept. And, suddenly in the depth of my sleep, I felt as if some intense eager look, like tapering fingers of flame, touched my slumbering body. I started up and saw the Hermit standing before me. The moon had moved to the west, peering through the leaves to espy this wonder of divine art wrought in a fragile human frame. The air was heavy with perfume; the silence of the night was vocal with the chirping of crickets; the reflections of the trees hung motionless in the lake; and with his staff in his hand he stood, tall and straight and still, like a forest tree. It seemed to me that I had, on opening my eyes, died to all realities of life and undergone a dream birth into a shadow land. Shame slipped to my feet like loosened clothes. I heard his call —"Beloved, my most beloved!" And all my forgotten lives united as one and responded to it. I said, "Take me, take all I am!" And I stretched out my arms to him. The moon set behind the trees. One curtain of darkness covered all. Heaven and earth, time and space, pleasure and pain, death and life merged together in an unbearable ecstasy. . . . With the first gleam of light, the first twitter of birds, I rose up and sat leaning on my left arm. He lay asleep with a vague smile about his lips like the crescent moon in the morning. The rosy red glow of the dawn fell upon his noble forehead. I sighed and stood up. I drew together the leafy lianas to screen the streaming sun from his face. I looked about me and saw the same old earth. I remembered what I used to be, and ran and ran like a deer afraid of her own shadow, through the forest path strewn with shephali flowers. I found a lonely nook, and sitting down covered my face with both hands, and tried to weep and cry. But no tears came to my eyes.

MADANA. Alas, thou daughter of mortals! I stole from the divine Storehouse the fragrant wine of heaven, filled with it one earthly night to the brim, and placed it in thy hand to drink — yet still I hear this cry of anguish!

CHITRA (BITTERLY). Who drank it? The rarest completion of life's desire, the first union of love was proffered to me, but was wrested from my grasp? This borrowed beauty, this falsehood that enwraps me, will slip from me taking with it the only monument of

40

that sweet union, as the petals fall from an overblown flower; and the woman ashamed of her naked poverty will sit weeping day and night. Lord Love, this cursed appearance companions me like a demon robbing me of all the prizes of love-all the kisses for which my heart is athirst.

MADANA. Alas, how vain thy single night had been! The barque of joy came in sight, but the waves would not let it touch the shore.

CHITRA. Heaven came so close to my hand that I forgot for a moment that it had not reached me. But when I woke in the morning from my dream I found that my body had become my own rival. It is my hateful task to deck her every day, to send her to my beloved and see her caressed by him. O god, take back thy boon!

MADANA. But if I take it from you how can you stand before your lover? To snatch away the cup from his lips when he has scarcely drained his first draught of pleasure, would not that be cruel? With what resentful anger he must regard thee then?

CHITRA. That would be better far than this. I will reveal my true self to him, a nobler thing than this disguise. If he rejects it, if he spurns me and breaks my heart, I will bear even that in silence.

VASANTA. Listen to my advice. When with the advent of autumn the flowering season is over then comes the triumph of fruitage. A time will come of itself when the heat-cloyed bloom of the body will droop and Arjuna will gladly accept the abiding fruitful truth in thee. O child, go back to thy mad festival.

## SCENE IV

CHITRA. Why do you watch me like that, my warrior?

ARJUNA. I watch how you weave that garland. Skill and grace, the twin brother and sister, are dancing playfully on your finger tips. I am watching and thinking.

CHITRA. What are you thinking, sir?

ARJUNA. I am thinking that you, with this same lightness of touch and sweetness, are weaving my days of exile into an immortal wreath, to crown me when I return home.

CHITRA. Home! But this love is not for a home!

ARJUNA. Not for a home?

CHITRA. No. Never talk of that. Take to your home what is abiding and strong. Leave the little wild flower where it was born; leave it beautifully to die at the day's end among all fading blossoms and decaying leaves. Do not take it to your palace hall to fling it on the stony floor which knows no pity for things that fade and are forgotten.

ARJUNA. Is ours that kind of love?

CHITRA. Yes, no other! Why regret it? That which was meant for idle days should never outlive them. Joy turns into pain when the door by which it should depart is shut against it. Take it and keep it as long as it lasts. Let not the satiety of your evening claim more than the desire of your morning could earn. . . . The day is done. Put this garland on. I am tired. Take me in your arms, my love. Let all vain bickerings of discontent die away at the sweet meeting of our lips.

ARJUNA. Hush! Listen, my beloved, the sound of prayer bells from the distant village temple steals upon the evening air across the silent trees!

## SCENE V

VASANTA. I cannot keep pace with thee, my friend! I am tired. It is a hard task to keep alive the fire thou hast kindled. Sleep overtakes me, the fan drops from my hand, and cold ashes cover the glow of the fire. I start up again from my slumber and with all my might rescue the weary flame. But this can go on no longer.

MADANA. I know, thou art as fickle as a child. Ever restless is thy play in heaven and on earth. Things that thou for days buildest up with endless detail thou dost shatter in a moment without regret. But this work of ours is nearly finished. Pleasure-winged days fly fast, and the year, almost at its end, swoons in rapturous bliss.

## SCENE VI

ARJUNA. I woke in the morning and found that my dreams had distilled a gem. I have no casket to inclose it, no king's crown whereon to fix it, no chain from which to hang it, and yet have not the heart to throw it away. My Kshatriya's right arm, idly occupied in holding it, forgets its duties.
Enter CHITRA..

CHITRA. Tell me your thoughts, sir!

ARJUNA. My mind is busy with thoughts of hunting today. See, how the rain pours in torrents and fiercely beats upon the hillside. The dark shadow of the clouds hangs heavily over the forest, and the swollen stream, like reckless youth, overleaps all barriers with mocking laughter. On such rainy days we five brothers would go to the Chitraka forest to chase wild beasts. Those were glad times. Our hearts danced to the drumbeat of rumbling clouds. The woods resounded with the screams of peacocks. Timid deer could not hear our approaching steps for the patter of rain and the noise of waterfalls; the leopards would leave their tracks on the wet earth, betraying their lairs. Our sport over, we dared each other to swim across turbulent streams on our way back home. The restless spirit is on me. I long to go hunting.

CHITRA. First run down the quarry you are now following. Are you quite certain that the enchanted deer you pursue must needs be caught? No, not yet. Like a dream the wild creature eludes you when it seems most nearly yours. Look how the wind is chased by the mad rain that discharges a thousand arrows after it. Yet it goes free and unconquered. Our sport is like that, my love! You give chase to the fleet-footed spirit of beauty, aiming at her every dart you have in your hands. Yet this magic deer runs ever free and untouched.

ARJUNA. My love, have you no home where kind hearts are waiting for your return? A home which you once made sweet with your gentle service and whose light went out when you left it for this wilderness?

CHITRA. Why these questions? Are the hours of unthinking pleasure over? Do you not know that I am no more than what you see before you? For me there is no vista beyond. The dew that hangs on the tip of a Kinsuka petal has neither name nor destination. It offers no answer to any question. She whom you love is like that perfect bead of dew.

ARJUNA. Has she no tie with the world? Can she be merely like a fragment of heaven dropped on the earth through the carelessness of a wanton god?

CHITRA. Yes.

ARJUNA. Ah, that is why I always seem about to lose you. My heart is unsatisfied, my mind knows no peace. Come closer to me, unattainable one! Surrender yourself to the bonds of name and home and parentage. Let my heart feel you on all sides and live with you in the peaceful security of love.

CHITRA. Why this vain effort to catch and keep the tints of the clouds, the dance of the waves, the smell of the flowers?

ARJUNA. Mistress mine, do not hope to pacify love with airy nothings. Give me something to clasp, something that can last longer than pleasure, that can endure even through suffering.

CHITRA. Hero mine, the year is not yet full, and you are tired already! Now I know that it is Heaven's blessing that has made the flower's term of life short. Could this body of mine have drooped and died with the flowers of last spring it surely would have died with honour. Yet, its days are numbered, my love. Spare it not, press it dry of honey, for fear your beggar's heart come back to it again and again with unsated desire, like a thirsty bee when summer blossoms lie dead in the dust.

## SCENE VII

MADANA. Tonight is thy last night.

VASANTA. The loveliness of your body will return tomorrow to the inexhaustible stores of the spring. The ruddy tint of thy lips freed from the memory of Arjuna's kisses, will bud anew as a pair of fresh asoka leaves, and the soft, white glow of thy skin will be born again in a hundred fragrant jasmine flowers.

CHITRA. O gods, grant me this my prayer! Tonight, in its last hour let my beauty flash its brightest, like the final flicker of a dying flame.

MADANA. Thou shalt have thy wish.

# SCENE VIII

VILLAGERS. Who will protect us now?

ARJUNA. Why, by what danger are you threatened?

VILLAGERS. The robbers are pouring from the northern hills like a mountain flood to devastate our village.

ARJUNA. Have you in this kingdom no warden?

VILLAGERS. Princess Chitra was the terror of all evil doers. While she was in this happy land we feared natural deaths, but had no other fears. Now she has gone on a pilgrimage, and none knows where to find her.

ARJUNA. Is the warden of this country a woman?

VILLAGERS. Yes, she is our father and mother in one.. (Exeunt.
Enter CHITRA..

CHITRA. Why are you sitting all alone?

ARJUNA. I am trying to imagine what kind of woman Princess Chitra may be. I hear so many stories of her from all sorts of men.

CHITRA. Ah, but she is not beautiful. She has no such lovely eyes as mine, dark as death. She can pierce any target she will, but not our hero's heart.

ARJUNA. They say that in valour she is a man, and a woman in tenderness.

CHITRA. That, indeed, is her greatest misfortune. When a woman is merely a woman; when she winds herself round and round men's hearts with her smiles and sobs and services and caressing endearments; then she is happy. Of what use to her are learning and great achievements? Could you have seen her only yesterday in the court of the Lord Shiva's temple by the forest path, you would have passed by without deigning to look at her. But have you grown so weary of woman's beauty that you seek in her for a man's strength? With green leaves wet from the spray of the foaming waterfall, I have made our noonday bed in a cavern dark as night. There the cool of the soft green mosses thick on the black and dripping stone, kisses your eyes to sleep. Let me guide you thither.

ARJUNA. Not today, beloved.

CHITRA. Why not today?

47

ARJUNA. I have heard that a horde of robbers has neared the plains. Needs must I go and prepare my weapons to protect the frightened villagers.

CHITRA. You need have no fear for them. Before she started on her pilgrimage, Princess Chitra had set strong guards at all the frontier passes.

ARJUNA. Yet permit me for a short while to set about a Kshatriya's work. With new glory will I ennoble this idle arm, and make of it a pillow more worthy of your head.

CHITRA. What if I refuse to let you go, if I keep you entwined in my arms? Would you rudely snatch yourself free and leave me? Go then! But you must know that the liana, once broken in two, never joins again. Go, if your thirst is quenched. But, if not, then remember that the goddess of pleasure is fickle, and waits for no man. Sit for a while, my lord! Tell me what uneasy thoughts tease you. Who occupied your mind today? Is it Chitra?

ARJUNA. Yes, it is Chitra. I wonder in fulfilment of what vow she has gone on her pilgrimage. Of what could she stand in need?

CHITRA. Her needs? Why, what has she ever had, the unfortunate creature? Her very qualities are as prison walls, shutting her woman's heart in a bare cell. She is obscured, she is unfulfilled. Her womanly love must content itself dressed in rags; beauty is denied her. She is like the spirit of a cheerless morning, sitting upon the stony mountain peak, all her light blotted out by dark clouds. Do not ask me of her life. It will never sound sweet to man's ear.

ARJUNA. I am eager to learn all about her. I am like a traveller come to a strange city at midnight. Domes and towers and garden-trees look vague and shadowy, and the dull moan of the sea comes fitfully through the silence of sleep. Wistfully he waits for the morning to reveal to him all the strange wonders. Oh, tell me her story.

CHITRA. What more is there to tell?

ARJUNA. I seem to see her, in my mind's eye, riding on a white horse, proudly holding the reins in her left hand, and in her right a bow, and like the Goddess of Victory dispensing glad hope all round her. Like a watchful lioness she protects the litter at her dugs with a fierce love. Woman's arms, though adorned with naught but unfettered strength, are beautiful! My heart is restless, fair one, like a serpent reviving from his long winter's sleep. Come, let us both race on swift horses side by side, like twin orbs of light sweeping through space. Out from this slumbrous prison of green gloom, this dank, dense cover of perfumed intoxication, choking breath.

CHITRA. Arjuna, tell me true, if, now at once, by some magic I could shake myself free from this voluptuous softness, this timid bloom of beauty shrinking from the rude and healthy touch of the world, and fling it from my body like borrowed clothes, would you be able to bear it? If I stand up straight and strong with the strength of a daring heart spurning the wiles and arts of twining weakness, if I hold my head high like a tall young mountain fir, no longer trailing in the dust like a liana, shall I then appeal to man's eye?

No, no, you could not endure it. It is better that I should keep spread about me all the dainty playthings of fugitive youth, and wait for you in patience. When it pleases you to return, I will smilingly pour out for you the wine of pleasure in the cup of this beauteous body. When you are tired and satiated with this wine, you can go to work or play; and when I grow old I will accept humbly and gratefully whatever corner is left for me. Would it please your heroic soul if the playmate of the night aspired to be the helpmeet of the day, if the left arm learnt to share the burden of the proud right arm?

ARJUNA. I never seem to know you aright. You seem to me like a goddess hidden within a golden image. I cannot touch you, I cannot pay you my dues in return for your priceless gifts. Thus my love is incomplete. Sometimes in the enigmatic depth of your sad look, in your playful words mocking at their own meaning, I gain glimpses of a being trying to rend asunder the languorous grace of her body, to emerge in a chaste fire of pain through a vaporous veil of smiles. Illusion is the first appearance of Truth. She advances towards her lover in disguise. But a time comes when she throws off her ornaments and veils and stands clothed in naked dignity. I grope for that ultimate you, that bare simplicity of truth. Why these tears, my love? Why cover your face with your hands? Have I pained you, my darling? Forget what I said. I will be content with the present. Let each separate moment of beauty come to me like a bird of mystery from its unseen nest in the dark bearing a message of music. Let me for ever sit with my hope on the brink of its realization, and thus end my days.

## SCENE IX

CHITRA AND ARJUNA. Chitra (cloaked) My lord, has the cup been drained to the last drop? Is this, indeed, the end? No, when all is done something still remains, and that is my last sacrifice at your feet. I brought from the garden of heaven flowers of incomparable beauty with which to worship you, god of my heart. If the rites are over, if the flowers have faded, let me throw them out of the temple [unveiling in her original male attire]. Now, look at your worshipper with gracious eyes. I am not beautifully perfect as the flowers with which I worshipped. I have many flaws and blemishes. I am a traveller in the great world-path, my garments are dirty, and my feet are bleeding with thorns. Where should I achieve flower-beauty, the unsullied loveliness of a moment's life? The gift that I proudly bring you is the heart of a woman. Here have all pains and joys gathered, the hopes and fears and shames of a daughter of the dust; here love springs up struggling toward immortal life. Herein lies an imperfection which yet is noble and grand. If the flower-service is finished, my master, accept this as your servant for the days to come! I am Chitra, the king's daughter. Perhaps you will remember the day when a woman came to you in the temple of Shiva, her body loaded with ornaments and finery. That shameless woman came to court you as though she were a man. You rejected her; you did well. My lord, I am that woman. She was my disguise. Then by the boon of gods I obtained for a year the most radiant form that a mortal ever wore, and wearied my hero's heart with the burden of that deceit. Most surely I am not that woman. I am Chitra. No goddess to be worshipped, nor yet the object of common pity to be brushed aside like a moth with indifference. If you deign to keep me by your side in the path of danger and daring, if you allow me to share the great duties of your life, then you will know my true self. If your babe, whom I am nourishing in my womb be born a son, I shall myself teach him to be a second Arjuna, and send him to you when the time comes, and then at last you will truly know me. Today I can only offer you Chitra, the daughter of a king.

ARJUNA. Beloved, my life is full.

# THE CYCLE OF SPRING

I DEDICATE THIS BOOK
TO MY BOYS OF THE SHANTINIKETAN
WHO HAVE FREED
THE FOUNTAIN OF YOUTH
HIDDEN IN THE HEART OF THIS OLD POET
AND TO DINENDRANATH
WHO IS
THE GUIDE OF THESE BOYS IN THEIR FESTIVALS
AND TREASURE-HOUSE OF ALL MY SONGS

# INTRODUCTION

## CHARACTERS OF THE PRELUDE

King, Vizier, General (Bijoy Varma)

  Chinese Ambassador, Pundit (Sruti-bhushan)

  Poet (Kabi-shekhar), Guards, Courtiers, Herald

    The stage is on two levels: the higher, at the back, for the Song-preludes alone, concealed by a purple curtain; the lower only being discovered when the drop goes up. Diagonally across the extreme left of the lower stage, is arranged the king's court, with various platforms, for the various dignitaries ascending to the canopied throne. The body of the stage is left free for the "Play" when that develops.

*(Enter some* Courtiers.)

  (The names of the speakers are not given in the margin, as they can easily be guessed.)

Hush! Hush!

What is the matter?

The King is in great distress.

How dreadful!

Who is that over there, playing on his flute?

Why? What's the matter?

The King is greatly disturbed.

How dreadful!

What are those wild children doing, making so much noise?

They are the Mandal family.

Then tell the Mandal family to keep their children quiet.

Where can that Vizier have gone to?

Here I am. What's the matter?

Haven't you heard the news?

No, what?

The King is greatly troubled in his mind.

Well, I've got some very important news about the frontier war.

War we may have, but not the news.

Then the Chinese Ambassador is waiting to see His Majesty.

Let him wait. Anyhow he can't see the King.

Can't see the King? —Ah, here is the King at last. Look at him coming this way, with a mirror in his hand. "Long live the King. Long live the King."

If it please Your Majesty, it is time to go to the Court.

Time to go? Yes, time to go, but not to the Court.

What does Your Majesty mean?

Haven't you heard? The bell has just been rung to dismiss the Court.

When? What bell? We haven't heard any bell.

How could you hear? They have rung it in my ears alone.

Oh, Sire. No one can have had the impertinence to do that.

Vizier! They are ringing it now.

Pardon me, Sire, if I am very stupid; but I cannot understand.

Look at this, Vizier, look at this.

Your Majesty's hair — —

Can't you see there's a bell-ringer there?

Oh, Your Majesty. Are you playing a joke?

The joke is not mine, but His, who has got the whole world by the ear, and is having His jest. Last night, when the Queen was putting a garland of jasmines round my neck, she cried out with alarm, "King, what is this? Here are two grey hairs behind your ear."

Oh, please, Sire, don't worry so much about a little thing like that. Why! The royal physician — —

Vizier! The founder of our dynasty had his royal physician, too. But what could he do? Death has left his card of invitation behind my ear. The Queen wanted, then and there, to pluck out the grey hairs. But I said, "Queen, what's the use? You may remove Death's invitation, but can you remove Death, the Inviter?" So, for the present — —

Yes, Sire, for the present, let us attend to business.

Business, Vizier! I have no time for business. Send for the Pundit. Send for Sruti-bhushan.

But, Sire, the General — —

The General? —No, no, not the General. Send for the Pundit.

But, the news from the frontier — —

Vizier, the news has come to me from the last great frontier of all, the frontier of Death. Send for the Pundit.

But if Your Majesty will give me one moment, the Ambassador from the great Emperor of China — —

Vizier, a greater Emperor has sent his embassy to me. Call Sruti-bhushan.

Very well, Sire. But your father-in-law — —

It is not my father-in-law whom I want now. Send for the Pundit.

But, if it please you to hear me this once. The poet, Kabi-shekhar, is waiting with his new book called the *Garden of Poesy*.

Let your poet disport himself, jumping about on the topmost branches of his Garden of Poesy, but send for the Pundit.

Very well, Sire. I will send for him at once.

Tell him to bring his book of devotions with him, called the *Ocean of Renunciation*.

Yes, Sire.

But, Vizier. Who are those outside making all that noise? Go out and stop them at once. I must have peace.

If it please Your Majesty, there is a famine in Nagapatam and the headmen of the villages are praying to be allowed to see your face.

My time is short, Vizier. I must have peace.

They say their time is shorter. They are at death's door. They, too, want peace, —peace from the burning of hunger.

Vizier! The burning of hunger is quenched at last on the funeral pyre.

Then these wretched people — —

Wretched! —Listen to the advice of a wretched King to his wretched subjects. It is futile to be impatient, and try to break through the net of the inexorable Fisherman. Sooner or later, Death the Fisherman will have his haul.

Well then?

Let me have the Pundit, and his *Book of Renunciation*.

And in this scarcity — —

Vizier! The real scarcity is of time, and not of food. We are all suffering from starvation of time. None of us has enough of it, neither the King, nor his people.

Then — —

Then know, that our petitions for more time will all go to the last fire of doom. So why strain our voice in prayer? —Ah, here is Sruti-bhushan at last. My reverence to you.

Pundit, do tell the King that the Goddess of Fortune deserts him who gives way to melancholy.

Sruti-bhushan, what is my Vizier whispering to you?

He tells me, King, to instruct you in the ways of fortune.

What instruction can you give?

There is a verse in my book of devotions which runs as follows:

> Fortune, as fickle as lotus-flower,
> Closes her favours when comes the hour.
> Oh, foolish man, how can you trust her,
> Who comes of a sudden, and goes in a fluster?

Ah, Pundit. One breath of your teaching blows out the false flame of ambition. Our teacher has said:

> "Teeth fall out, hair grows grey;
> Yet man clings to hope that plays him false."

Well, King, now that you have introduced the subject of hope, let me give you another verse from the *Ocean of Renunciation*. It runs as follows:

> That fetters are binding, all are aware;
> But fetters of hope are strange, I declare.
> Hope's captive is tossed in the whirlpool's wake,
> And only grows still when the fetters break.

Ah, Pundit. Your words are priceless. Vizier, give him a hundred gold sequins at once. What's that noise outside?

It is the famine-stricken people.

Tell them to hold their peace.

Let Sruti-bhushan, with his book of devotions, go and try to bring them peace; and, in the meanwhile, Your Majesty might discuss war matters ——

No, no. Let the war matters come later. I can't let Sruti-bhushan go yet.

King, you said something to me, a moment ago, about a gift of gold. Now mere gold, by itself, does not confer any permanent benefit. It is said in my book of devotions, called the *Ocean of Renunciation*:

> He who gives gold, gives only pain;
> When the gold is spent grief comes again.
> When a lakh, or crore, of gold is spent,
> Grief only remains in the empty tent.

Ah, Pundit. How exquisite. So you don't want any gold, my Master?

No, King, I don't want gold, but something more permanent, which would make your merit permanent also. I should be quite content, if you gave me the living of Kanchanpur. For it is said in the *Renunciation* ——

No, Pundit, I quite understand. You needn't quote scripture to support your claim. I understand quite well-Vizier!

Yes, Your Majesty.

See that the rich province of Kanchanpur is settled on the Pundit. —What's the matter now outside there? What are they crying for?

If it please Your Majesty, it is the people.

Why do they cry so repeatedly?

Their cry is repeated, I admit, but the reason remains most monotonously the same. They are starving.

But, King, I must tell you before I forget it. It is the one desire of my wife to make her whole body jingle, from head to foot, in praise of your munificence; but, alas, the sound is too feeble for want of proper ornaments.

I understand you, Pundit. Vizier! Order ornaments from the Court Jeweller for Sruti-bhushan's wife immediately.

And, King, while he is about it, would you tell the Vizier, that we are both of us distracted in our devotions by house-repairs. Let him ask the royal masons to put up a thoroughly well-built house, where we can practise our devotions in peace.

Very well, Pundit. —Vizier!

Yes, Your Majesty.

Give the order at once.

Sire, your treasury is empty. Funds are wanting.

Pooh! That's an old story. I hear that every year. It is your business to increase the funds, and mine to increase the wants. What do you say, Sruti-bhushan?

King, I cannot blame the Vizier. He is looking after your treasures in this world. We are looking after your treasures in the next. So where he sees want, we see wealth. Now, if you would only let me dive deep once more into the *Ocean of Renunciation* you will find it written as follows:

> That King's coffers are well stored,
> Where wealth alone on worth is poured.

Pundit, your company is most valuable.

Your Majesty, Sruti-bhushan knows its value to a farthing. Come, Sruti-bhushan, make haste. Let us collect all the wealth you need for your Treasury of Devotion. For wealth has the ugly habit of diminishing fast. If we are not quick about it, little will remain to enable us to observe our renunciation with all splendour.

Yes, Vizier, let us go at once. (*To the King.*) When he is making such a fuss about a tiny matter like this, it is best to pacify him first and then return to you afterwards.

Pundit, I am afraid that, some day, you will leave my royal protection altogether, and retire to the forest.

King, so long as I find contentment in a King's palace, it is as good as a hermitage for my peace of mind. I must now leave you, King. Vizier, let us go.

(*The Vizier and Pundit go out.*

Oh, dear me! Whatever shall I do? Here's the Poet coming. I am afraid he'll make me break all my good resolutions. —Oh, my grey hairs, cover my ears, so that the Poet's allurements may not enter.

Why, King, what's the matter? I hear you want to send away your Poet.

What have I to do with poets, when poetry brings me this parting message?

What parting message?

Look at this behind my ear. Don't you see it?

See what? Grey hairs? Why, King, don't you worry about that.

Poet, Nature is trying to rub out the green of youth, and to paint everything white.

No, no, King. You haven't understood the artist. On that white ground, Nature will paint new colours.

I don't see any sign of colours yet.

They are all within. In the heart of the white dwell all the colours of the rainbow.

Oh, Poet, do be quiet. You disturb me when you talk like that.

King, if this youth fades, let it fade. Another Queen of Youth is coming. And she is putting a garland of pure white jasmines round your head, in order to be your bride. The wedding festival is being made ready, behind the scene.

Oh, dear, Poet. You will undo everything. Do go away. Ho there, Guard. Go at once and call Sruti-bhushan.

What will you do with him, King, when he comes?

I will compose my mind, and practise my renunciation.

Ah, King, when I heard that news, I came at once. For I can be your companion in this practice of renunciation.

You?

Yes, I, King. We Poets exist for this very purpose. We set men free from their desires.

I don't understand you. You talk in riddles.

What? You don't understand me? And yet you have been reading my poems all this while! — There is renunciation in our words, renunciation in the metre, renunciation in our music. That is why fortune always forsakes us; and we, in turn always forsake fortune. We go about, all day long, initiating the youths in the sacred cult of fortune-forsaking.

What does it say to us?

It says:

"Ah, brothers, don't cling to your goods and chattels,
And sit ever in the corner of your room.
Come out, come out into the open world.
Come out into the highways of life.
Come out, ye youthful Renouncers."

But, Poet, do you really mean to say that the highway of the open world is the pathway of renunciation?

Why not, King? In the open world all is change, all is life, all is movement. And he who ever moves and journeys with this life-movement, dancing and playing on his flute as he goes, he is the true Renouncer. He is the true disciple of the minstrel Poet.

But how then can I get peace? I must have peace.

Oh, King, we haven't the least desire for peace. We are the Renouncers.

But ought we not to get that treasure, which is said to be never-changing?

No, we don't covet any never-changing treasures. We are the Renouncers.

What do you mean? Oh, dear, Poet, you will undo everything, if you talk like that. You are destroying my peace of mind. Call Sruti-bhushan. Let some one call the Pundit.

What I mean, King, is this. We are the true Renouncers, because change is our very secret. We lose, in order to find. We have no faith in the never-changing.

What do you mean?

Haven't you noticed the detachment of the rushing river, as it runs splashing from its mountain cave? It gives itself away so swiftly, and only thus it finds itself. What is never-changing, for the river, is the desert sand, where it loses its course.

Ah, but listen, Poet-listen to those cries there outside. That is your world. How do you deal with that?

King, they are your starving people.

My people, Poet? Why do you call them that? They are the world's people, not mine. Have I created their miseries? What can your youthful Poet Renouncers do to relieve sufferings like theirs? Tell me that.

King, it is we alone who can truly bear those sufferings, because we are like the river that flows on in gladness, thus lightening our burden, and the burden of the world. But the hard, metalled road is fixed and never-changing. And so it makes the burden more burdensome. The heavy loads groan and creak along it, and cut deep gashes in its breast. We Poets call to every one to carry all their joys and sorrows lightly, in a rhythmic measure. Our call is the Renouncers' call.

Ah, Poet, now I don't care a straw for Sruti-bhushan. Let the Pundit go hang. But, do you know what my trouble is now? Though I can't, for the life of me, understand your words, the music haunts me. Now, it's just the other way round with the Pundit. His words are clear enough, and they obey the rules of syntax quite correctly. But the tune! —No, it's no use telling you any further.

King, our words don't speak, they sing.

Well, Poet, what do you want to do now?

King, I'm going to have a race through those cries, which are rising outside your gate.

What do you mean? Famine relief is for men of business. Poets oughtn't to have anything to do with things like that.

King, business men always make their business so out of tune. That is why we Poets hasten to tune it.

Now come, my dear Poet, do speak in plainer language.

King, they work, because they must. We work, because we are in love with life. That is why they condemn us as unpractical, and we condemn them as lifeless.

But who is right, Poet? Who wins? You, or they?

We, King, we. We always win.

But, Poet, your proof— —

King, the greatest things in the world disdain proof. But if you could for a time wipe out all the poets and all their poetry from the world, then you would soon discover, by their very absence, where the men of action got their energy from, and who really supplied the life-sap to their harvest-field. It is not those who have plunged deep down into the Pundit's *Ocean of Renunciation*, nor those who are always clinging to their possessions; it is not those who have become adepts in turning out quantities of work, nor those who are ever telling the dry beads of duty, —it is not these who win at last. But it is those who love, because they live. These truly win, for they truly surrender. They accept pain with all their strength and with all their strength they remove pain. It is they who create, because they know the secret of true joy, which is the secret of detachment.

Well then, Poet, if that be so, what do you ask me to do now?

I ask you, King, to rise up and move. That cry outside yonder is the cry of life to life. And if the life within you is not stirred, in response to that call without, then there is cause for anxiety indeed, —not because duty has been neglected, but because you are dying.

But, Poet, surely we must die, sooner or later?

No, King, that's a lie. When we feel for certain that we are alive, then we know for certain that we shall go on living. Those who have never put life to the test, in all possible ways, these keep on crying out:

> Life is fleeting, Life is waning,
> Life is like a dew-drop on a lotus leaf.

But, isn't life inconstant?

Only because its movement is unceasing. The moment you stop this movement, that moment you begin to play the drama of Death.

Poet, are you speaking the truth? Shall we really go on living?

Yes, we shall really go on living.

Then, Poet, if we are going to go on living, we must make our life worth its eternity. Is not that so?

Yes, indeed.

Ho, Guard.

Yes, Your Royal Highness.

Call the Vizier at once.

Yes, Your Royal Highness.

(*Vizier enters.*)

What is Your Majesty's pleasure?

Vizier! Why on earth have you kept me waiting so long?

I was very busy, Your Majesty.

Busy? What were you busy about?

I was dismissing the General.

Why should you dismiss the General? We have got to discuss war matters with him.

And arrangements had to be made for the state-departure of the Chinese Ambassador.

What do you mean by his state-departure?

If it please Your Majesty, you did not grant him an interview. So he — —

Vizier! You surprise me. Is this the way you manage state affairs? What has happened to you? Have you lost your senses?

Then, again. Sire, I was trying to find a way to pull down the Poet's house. At first, no one would undertake it. Then, at last, all the Pundits of the Royal School of Grammar and Logic came up with their proper tools and set to work.

Vizier! Are you mad this morning? Pull down the Poet's house? Why, you might as well kill all the birds in the garden and make them up into a pie.

If it please Your Majesty, you need not be annoyed. We shan't have to pull down the house after all; for the moment Sruti-bhushan heard it was to be demolished, he decided to take possession of it himself.

What, Vizier! That's worse still. Why! The Goddess of Music would break her harp in pieces against my head, if she even heard of such a thing. No, that can't be.

Then, Your Majesty, there was another thing to be got through. We had to deliver over the province of Kanchanpur to the Pundit.

No, Vizier! What a mess you are making. That must go to our Poet.

To me, King? No. My poetry never accepts reward.

Well, well. Let the Pundit have it.

And, last of all, Sire. I have issued orders to the soldiers to disperse the crowd of famine-stricken people.

Vizier, you are doing nothing but blunder. The best way to disperse the famished people is with food, not force.

(Guard enters.)

May it please Your Royal Highness.

What's the matter, Guard?

May it please Your Royal Highness, here is Sruti-bhushan, the Pundit, coming back with his *Book of Devotions*.

Oh, stop him, Vizier, stop him. He will undo everything. Don't let him come upon me unawares like this. In a moment of weakness, I may suddenly find myself out of my depths in the *Ocean of Renunciation*. Poet! Don't give me time for that. Do something. Do anything. Have you got anything ready to hand? Any play toward? Any poem? Any masque? Any — —

Yes, King. I have got the very thing. But whether it is a drama, or a poem, or a play, or a masque, I cannot say.

Shall I be able to understand the sense of what you have written?

No, King, what a poet writes is not meant to have any sense.

What then?

To have the tune itself.

What do you mean? Is there no philosophy in it?

No, none at all, thank goodness.

What does it say, then?

King, it says "I exist." Don't you know the meaning of the first cry of the new-born child? The child, when it is born, hears at once the cries of the earth and water and sky, which surround him, —and they all cry to him, "We exist," and his tiny little heart responds, and cries out in its turn, "I exist." My poetry is like the cry of that new-born child. It is a response to the cry of the Universe.

Is it nothing more than that, Poet?

No, nothing more. There is life in my song, which cries, "In joy and in sorrow, in work and in rest, in life and in death, in victory and in defeat, in this world and in the next, all hail to the 'I exist.'"

Well, Poet, I can assure you, if your play hasn't got any philosophy in it, it won't pass muster in these days.

That's true, King. The newer people, of this modern age, are more eager to amass than to realize. They are, in their generation, wiser than the children of light.

Whom shall we ask, then, for an audience? Shall we ask the young students of our royal school?

No, King, they cut up poetry with their logic. They are like the young-horned deer trying their new horns on the flower-beds.

Whom should I ask, then?

Ask those whose hair is turning grey.

What do you mean, Poet?

The youth of these middle-aged people is a youth of detachment. They have just crossed the waters of pleasure, and are in sight of the land of pure gladness. They don't want to eat fruit, but to produce it.

I, at least, have now reached that age of discretion, and ought to be able to appreciate your songs. Shall I ask the General?

Yes, ask him.

And the Chinese Ambassador?

Yes, ask him too.

I hear my father-in-law has come.

Well, ask him too, but I have my doubts about his youthful sons.

But don't forget his daughter.

Don't worry about her. She won't let herself be forgotten.

And Sruti-bhushan? Shall I ask him?

No, King, no. Decidedly, no. I have no grudge against him. Why should I inflict this on him?

Very well, Poet. Off with you. Make your stage preparations.

No, King. We are going to act this play without any special preparations. Truth looks tawdry when she is overdressed.

But, Poet, there must be some canvas for a background.

No. Our only background is the mind. On that we shall summon up a picture with the magic wand of music.

Are there any songs in the play?

Yes, King. The door of each act will be opened by the key of song.

What is the subject of the songs?

The Disrobing of Winter.

But, Poet, we haven't read about that in any Mythology.

In the world-myth this song comes round in its turn. In the play of the seasons, each year, the mask of the Old Man, Winter, is pulled off, and the form of Spring is revealed in all its beauty. Thus we see that the old is ever new.

Well, Poet, so much for the songs: but what about the remainder?

Oh, that is all about life.

Life? What is life?

This is how it runs: A band of young companions has run off in pursuit of one Old Man. They have taken a vow to catch him. They enter into a cave; they take hold of him, and then — —

Then, what? What did they see?

Ah. That will be told in its own good time.

But, I haven't understood one thing. Your drama and your songs, —have they different subjects, or the same?

The same, King. The play of Spring in nature is the counterpart of the play of Youth in our lives. It is simply from the lyrical drama of the World Poet that I have stolen this plot.

Who, then, are the chief characters?

One is called the Leader.

Who is he, Poet?

He is the guiding impulse in our life. Another is Chandra.

Who is he?

He who makes life dear to us.

And who else?

Then there is Dada, to whom duty is the essence of life, not joy.

Is there any one else?

Yes, the blind Minstrel.

Blind?

Because he does not see with his eyes, therefore he sees with his whole body and mind and soul.

Who else is there, in your play, among the chief actors?

You are there, King.

I?

Yes, you, King. For if you stayed out of it, instead of coming into it, then the King would begin to abuse the Poet and send for Sruti-bhushan again. And then there would be no hope of salvation for him. For the World Poet himself would be defeated. And the South Wind of Spring would have to retire, without receiving its homage.

## ACT I

The Heralds of Spring are abroad. There are songs in the rustling bamboo leaves, in birds' nests, and in blossoming branches.

## SONG-PRELUDE

The purple secondary curtain[1] goes up, disclosing the elevated rear stage with a skyey background of dark blue, on which appear the horn of the crescent moon and the silver points of stars. Trees in the foreground, with two rope swings entwined with garlands of flowers. Flowers everywhere in profusion. On the extreme left the mouth of a dark cavern dimly seen. Boys representing the "Bamboo" disclosed, swinging.

## SONG OF THE BAMBOO

O South Wind, the Wanderer, come and rock me,
Rouse me into the rapture of new leaves.
I am the wayside bamboo tree, waiting for your breath
To tingle life into my branches.

O South Wind, the Wanderer, my dwelling is in the end of the lane.
I know your wayfaring, and the language of your footsteps.
Your least touch thrills me out of my slumber,
Your whisper gleans my secrets.

*(Enter a troop of girls, dancing, representing birds.)*

## SONG OF THE BIRD

The sky pours its light into our hearts,
We fill the sky with songs in answer.
We pelt the air with our notes
When the air stirs our wings with its madness.
O Flame of the Forest,
All your flower-torches are ablaze;
You have kissed our songs red with the passion of your youth.
In the spring breeze the mango-blossoms launch their messages to the unknown
And the new leaves dream aloud all day.
O Sirish, you have cast your perfume-net round our hearts,
Drawing them out in songs.

*(Disclosed among the branches of trees, suddenly lighted up, boys representing champak blossoms.)*

## SONG OF THE BLOSSOMING CHAMPAK

My shadow dances in your waves, everflowing river,
I, the blossoming champak, stand unmoved on the bank, with my flower-vigils.
My movement dwells in the stillness of my depth,
In the delicious birth of new leaves,
In flood of flowers,
In unseen urge of new life towards the light.
Its stirring thrills the sky, and the silence of the dawn is moved.


### MORNING

( *The rear stage is now darkened. On the main stage, bright, enter a band of youths whose number may be anything between three and thirty. They sing.*)

The fire of April leaps from forest to forest,
Flashing up in leaves and flowers from all nooks and corners.
The sky is thriftless with colours,
The air delirious with songs.
The wind-tost branches of the woodland
Spread their unrest in our blood.
The air is filled with bewilderment of mirth;
And the breeze rushes from flower to flower, asking their names.

(In the following dialogue only the names of the principal characters are given. Wherever the name is not given the speaker is one or other of the Youths.)

April pulls hard, brother, April pulls very hard.

How do you know that?

If he didn't, he would never have pulled Dada outside his den.

Well, I declare. Here is Dada, our cargo-boat of moral-maxims, towed against the current of his own pen and ink.

#### Chandra

But you mustn't give April all the credit for that. For I, Chandra, have hidden the yellow leaves of his manuscript book among the young buds of the *pial* forest, and Dada is out looking for it.

The manuscript book banished! What a good riddance!

We ought to strip off Dada's grey philosopher's cloak also.

#### Chandra

Yes, the very dust of the earth is tingling with youth, and yet there's not a single touch of Spring in the whole of Dada's body.

#### Dada

Oh, do stop this fooling. What a nuisance you are making of yourselves! We aren't children any longer.

#### Chandra

Dada, the age of this earth is scarcely less than yours; and yet it is not ashamed to look fresh.

Dada, you are always struggling with those quatrains of yours, full of advice that is as old as death, while the earth and the water are ever striving to be new.

Dada, how in the world can you go on writing verses like that, sitting in your den?

#### Dada

Well, you see, I don't cultivate poetry, as an amateur gardener cultivates flowers. *My* poems have substance and weight in them.

Yes, they are like the turnips, which cling to the ground.

Dada

Well, then, listen to me ———

How awful! Here's Dada going to run amuck with his quatrains.

Oh dear, oh dear! The quatrains are let loose. There's no holding them in.

To all passers-by I give notice that Dada's quatrains have gone mad, and are running amuck.

Chandra

Dada! Don't take any notice of their fun. Go on with your reading. If no one else can survive it, I think I can. I am not a coward like these fellows.

Come on, then, Dada. We won't be cowards. We will keep our ground, and not yield an inch, but only listen.

We will receive the spear-thrusts of the quatrains on our breast, not on our back.

But for pity's sake, Dada, give us only one-not more.

Dada

Very well. Now listen:

> If bamboos were made only into flutes,
> They would droop and die with very shame,
> They hold their heads high in the sky,
> Because they are variously useful.

Please, gentlemen, don't laugh. Have patience while I explain. The meaning is ———

The meaning?

What? Must the infantry charge of meaning follow the cannonading of your quatrains, to complete the rout?

Dada

Just one word to make you understand. It means, that if the bamboos were no better than those noisy instruments ———

No, Dada, we must not understand.

I defy you to make us understand.

Dada, if you use force to make us understand we shall use force to force ourselves not to understand.

Dada

The gist of the quatrain is this, that if we do no good to the world, then ———

Then the world will be very greatly relieved.

Dada

There is another verse that makes it clearer:

> There are numerous stars in the midnight sky,
> Which hang in the air for no purpose;
> If they would only come down to earth,
> For the street lighting they might be useful.

I see we must make clearer our meaning. Catch him. Let's raise him up, shoulder high, and take him back to his den.

Dada

Why are you so excited to-day? Have you any particular business to do?

Yes, we have very urgent business, —very urgent indeed.

Dada

What is your business about?

We are out to seek a play for our Spring festival.

Dada

Play! Day and night, play!

(*They sing.*)

We are free, my friends, from the fear of work,
For we know that work is play, — the play of life.
It is Play, to fight and toss, between life and death;
It is Play that flashes in the laughter of light in the infinite heart;
It roars in the wind, and surges in the sea.

Oh, here comes our Leader. Brothers-our Leader, our Leader.

Leader

Hallo! What a noise you make!
Was it that which made you come out of doors?

Leader

Yes.
Well, we did it for that very purpose.

Leader

You don't want me to remain indoors?
Why remain indoors? This outer world has been made with a lavish expenditure of sun and moon and stars. Let us enjoy it, and then we can save God's face for indulging in such extravagance.

Leader

What were you discussing?
This:

*(They sing.)*

Play blooms in flower and ripens in fruit
In the sunshine of eternal youth.
Play bursts up in the blood-red fire, and licks into ashes the decaying and the dead.

Our Dada's objection was about this play.

Dada

Shall I tell you the reason why?
Yes, Dada, you may tell us, but we shan't promise to listen.

Dada

Here it is:

Time is the capital of work,
And Play is its defalcation.
Play rifles the house, and then wastes its spoil,
Therefore the wise call it worse than useless.

Chandra

But surely, Dada, you are talking nonsense. Time itself is Play. Its only object is Pas-time.

Dada

Then what is Work?

Chandra

Work is the dust raised by the passing of Time.

Dada

Leader, you must give us your answers.

Leader

No. I never give answers. I lead on from one question to another. That is my leadership.

Dada

Everything else has its limits, but your childishness is absolutely unbounded.
Do you know the reason? It is because we are really nothing but children. And everything else has its limitations except the child.

Dada

Won't you ever attain Age?

No, we shall never attain Age.

We shall die old, but never attain Age.

Chandra

When we meet Age, we shall shave his head, and put him on a donkey, and send him across the river.

Oh, you can save yourself the trouble of shaving his head for Age is bald.

(*They sing.*)

Our hair shall never turn grey,
Never.
There is no blank in this world for us, no break in our road,
It may be an illusion that we follow,
But it shall never play us false,
Never.


(*The Leader sings.*)

Our hair shall never turn grey,
Never.
We will never doubt the world and shut our eyes to ponder.
Never.
We will not grope in the maze of our mind.
We flow with the flood of things, from the mountain to the sea,
We will never be lost in the desert sand,
Never.


We can tell, by his looks, that Dada will some day go to that Old Man, to receive his lessons.

Leader

Which Old Man?

The Old Man of the line of Adam.

He dwells in a cave, and never thinks of dying.

Leader

Where did you learn about him?

Oh, every one talks about him, And it is in the books also.

Leader

What does he look like?

Some say he is white, like the skull of a dead man. And some say he is dark, like the socket of a skeleton's eye.

But haven't you heard any news of him, Leader?

Leader

I don't believe in him at all.

Well, that goes entirely against current opinion. That Old Man is more existent than anything else. He lives within the ribs of creation.

According to our Pundit, it is we who have no existence. You can't be certain whether we are, or are not.

Chandra

We? Oh, we are too brand new altogether. We haven't yet got our credentials to prove that we exist.

Leader

Have you really gone and opened communication with the Pundits?

Why? What harm is there in that, Leader?

Leader

You will become pale, like the white mist in autumn. Even the least colour of blood will disappear from your mind. I have a suggestion.

What, Leader? What?

Leader

You were looking out for a play?

Yes, yes, we got quite frantic about it.

We thought it over so vigorously, that people had to run to the King's court to lodge a complaint.

Leader

Well, I can suggest a play which will be new.

What? —What? —Tell us.

Leader

Go and capture the Old Man.

That is new, no doubt, but we very much doubt if it's a play.

Leader

I am sure you won't be able to do it.

Not do it? We shall.

Leader

No, never.

Well then, suppose we do capture him, what will you give us?

Leader

I shall accept you as my preceptor.

Preceptor! You want to make us grey, and cold, and old, before our time.

Leader

Then, what do you want me to do?

If we capture him, then we shall take away your leadership.

Leader

That will be a great relief to me. You have made all my bones out of joint already. Very well, then it's all settled?

Yes, settled. We shall bring him to you by the next full moon of Spring.

But what are we going to do with him?

Leader

You shall let him join in your Spring Festival.

Oh no, that will be outrageous. Then the mango flowers will run to seed at once.

And all the cuckoos will become owls.

And the bees will go about reciting Sanskrit verses, making the air hum with m's and n's.

Leader

And your skull will be so top-heavy with prudence, that it will be difficult for you to keep on your feet.

How awful!

Leader

And you will have rheumatics in all your joints.

How awful!

Leader

And you will become your own elder brothers, pulling your own ears to set yourselves right.

How awful!

Leader

And — —

No more "ands." We are ready to surrender.

We will abandon our game of capturing the Old Man.

67

We will put it off till the cold weather. In this Springtime, your company will be enough for us.

Leader

Ah, I see! You have already got the chill of the Old Man in your bones.

Why? What are the symptoms?

Leader

You have no enthusiasm. You back out at the very start. Why don't you make a trial?

Very well. Agreed. Come on.

Let us go after the Old Man. We will pluck him out, like a grey hair, wherever we find him.

Leader

But the Old Man is an adept in the business of plucking out. His best weapon is the hoe.

You needn't try to frighten us like that. When we are out for adventure, we must leave behind all fears, all quatrains, all Pundits, and all Scriptures.

(*They sing.*)

We are out on our way
And we fear not the Robber, the Old Man.
Our path is straight, it is broad,
Our burden is light, for our pocket is bare,
Who can rob us of our folly?
For us there is no rest, nor ease, nor praise, nor success,
We dance in the measure of fortune's rise and fall,
We play our game, or win or lose,
And we fear not the Robber.

## ACT II

## SONG-PRELUDE

*(Spring's Heralds try to rob Winter of his outfit of age.)*
Rear stage lighted up, disclosing Old Winter teased by the boys and girls representing
Spring's Heralds.

## SONG OF THE HERALDS OF SPRING

We seek our playmates,
Waking them up from all corners before it is morning.
We call them in bird songs,
Beckon them in nodding branches.
We spread our spell for them in the splendour of clouds.


We laugh at solemn Death
Till he joins in our laughter.
We tear open Time's purse,
Taking back his plunder from him.
You shall lose your heart to us, O Winter.
It will gleam in the trembling leaves
And break into flowers.

## SONG OF WINTER

Leave me, let me go.
I sail for the bleak North, for the peace of the frozen shore.
Your laughter is untimely, my friends.
You turn my farewell tunes into the welcome song of the Newcomer,
And all things draw me back again into the dancing ring of their hearts.

## SONG OF THE HERALDS OF SPRING

Life's spies are we, lurking in ambush everywhere.
We wait to rob you of your last savings of withered hours to scatter them in the way-
ward winds.
We shall bind you in flower chains where Spring keeps his captives,
For we know you carry your jewels of youth hidden in your grey rags.

*(NOON)*

( *The rear stage is darkened. The band of Youths enters on the main stage. No actual change in the scenery is necessary-this being left to the imagination of the audience.*)

Ferryman! Ferryman! Open your door.

Ferryman

What do you want?
We want the Old Man.

Ferryman

Which old man?
Not which old man. We want *the* Old Man.

Ferryman

Who is he?
The true and original Old Man.

Ferryman

Oh! I understand. What do you want him for?
For our Spring Festival.

Ferryman

For your Spring Festival? Are you become mad?
Not a sudden becoming. We have been like this from the beginning.
And we shall go on like this to the end.

(*They sing.*)

The Piper pipes in the centre, hidden from sight.
And we become frantic, we dance.
The March wind, seized with frenzy,
Runs and reels, and sways with noisy branches.
The sun and stars are drawn in the whirl of rapture.

Now, Ferryman, give us news of the Old Man.
You ply your boat from one landing stage to another. Surely you know where —— 

Ferryman

My business is limited only to the path. But whose path it is, and what it means, I have no occasion to enquire. For my goal is the landing-stage, not the house.

Very well. Let us go, let us try all the ways.

(They sing.)

The Piper pipes in the centre, hidden from sight.
Ah, the turbulent tune, to whose time the oceans dance,
And dance our heaving hearts.
Fling away all burdens and cares, brother,
Do not be doubtful of your path,
For the path wakes up of itself
Under the dancing steps of freedom.

Ferryman

There comes the Watchman. Ask him. I know about the way; but he knows about the way-farers.

Watchman

Who are you?
We are just what you see. That's our only description.

Watchman

But what do you want?
We want the Old Man.

Watchman

Which old man?

That eternal Old Man.

Watchman

How absurd! While you are seeking him, he is after you.

Why?

Watchman

He is fond of warming his cold blood with the wine of hot youth.

We'll give him a warm enough reception. All we want is to see him. Have you seen him?

Watchman

My watch is at night. I see my people, but don't know their features. But, look here, every one knows that he is the great kidnapper; and you want to kidnap him! It's midsummer madness.

The secret is out. It doesn't take long to discover that we are mad.

Watchman

I am the Watchman. The people I see passing along the road are all very much alike. Therefore, when I see anything queer, it always strikes me.

Just listen to him. All the respectable people of our neighbourhood say just the same thing—that we are queer.

Yes, we're queer. There's no mistake about that.

Watchman

But all this is utter childishness.

Do you hear that? It's exactly what our Dada says.

We have been going on with our childishness through unremembered ages.

And now we have become confirmed children.

And we have a leader, who is a perfect veteran in childhood. He rushes along so recklessly, that he drops off his age at every step he runs.

Watchman

And who are you?

We are butterflies, freed from the cocoon of Age.

Watchman

(*Aside.*) Mad. Raving mad.

Ferryman

Then what will you all do now?

Chandra

We shall go — —

Watchman

Where?

Chandra

That we haven't decided.

Watchman

You have decided to go, but not where to go?

Chandra

Yes, that will be settled as we go along.

Watchman

What does that mean?

Chandra

It means this song.

(*They sing.*)

We move and move without rest,
We move while the wanderers' stars shine in the sky and fade.
We play the tune of the road

While our limbs scatter away the laughter of movement,
And our many-coloured mantle of youth flutters about in the air.


Watchman

Is it your custom to answer questions by songs?

Chandra

Yes, otherwise the answer becomes too unintelligible.

Watchman

Then you think your songs intelligible?

Chandra

Yes, quite, because they contain music.

(*They sing.*)

We move and move without rest.
World, the Rover, loves his comrades of the road.
His call comes across the sky.
The seasons lead the way, strewing the path with flowers.


Watchman

No ordinary being ever breaks out singing, like this, in the middle of talking.

Chandra

Again we are found out. We are no ordinary beings.

Watchman

Have you got no work to do?

Chandra

No, we are on a holiday.

Watchman

Why?

Chandra

Lest our time should all be wasted.

Watchman

I don't quite understand you.

Chandra

Then we shall be obliged to sing again.

Watchman

No, no. There's no need to do that. I don't hope to understand you any better, even if you do sing.

Chandra

Everybody has given up the hope of understanding us.

Watchman

But how can things get on with you, if you behave like this?

Chandra

Oh, there's no need for things to get on with us, so long as we ourselves get on.

Watchman

Mad! Quite mad! Raving mad!

Chandra

Why, here comes our Dada.
Dada, what made you lag behind?

Chandra

Don't you know? We are free as the wind, because we have no substance in us. But Dada is like the rain-cloud of August. He must stop, every now and then, to unburden himself.

Dada

Who are you?

**Ferryman**

I am the Ferryman.

**Dada**

And who are you?

**Watchman**

I am the Watchman.

**Dada**

I am delighted to see you. I want to read you something that I have written. It contains nothing frivolous, but only the most important lessons.

**Ferryman**

Very good. Let us have it then.

**Watchman**

Our master used to tell us that there are plenty of men to say good things, but very few to listen. That requires strength of mind. Now, go on, Sir, go on.

**Dada**

I saw, in the street, one of the King's officers dragging along a merchant. The King had made up a false charge, in order to get his money. This gave me an inspiration. You must know that I never write a single line which is not inspired by some actual fact. You can put my verses to the test in the open streets and markets — —

**Ferryman**

Please, Sir, do let us hear what you have written.

**Dada**

The sugar-cane filling itself with juice
Is chewed and sucked dry by all beggars.
O foolish men, take your lesson from this;
Those trees are saved, which are fruitful.

You will understand that the sugar-cane gets into trouble, simply because it tries to keep its juice. But nobody is so foolish as to kill the tree that freely gives fruit.

**Watchman**

What splendid writing, Ferryman!

**Ferryman**

Yes, Watchman, it contains great lessons for us.

**Watchman**

It gives me food for thought. If only I had here our neighbour, the Scribe! I should like to take this down. Do send round to tell the people of the place to assemble.

**Chandra**

But, Ferryman, you promised to come out with us. Yet, if once Dada begins to quote his quatrains, there will be — —

**Ferryman**

Go along with you. None of your madness here. We are fortunate now in having met our master. Let us improve the occasion with good words. We are all of us getting old. Who knows when we shall die?

All the more reason why you should cultivate our company.

**Chandra**

You can always find another Dada. But when once we are dead, God will never repeat the blunder of another absurdity like us again.

(*Enter Oilman.*)

**Oilman**

Ho! Watchman.

Watchman

Who is there? Is that the Oilman?

Oilman

The child I was bringing up was kidnapped last night.

Watchman

By whom?

Oilman

By the Old Man.

Youths

(*Together.*) Old Man? You don't mean it. Old Man?

Oilman

Yes, Sirs, the Old Man; what makes you so glad?

Oh, that's a bad habit of ours. We become glad for no reason whatever.

Watchman

(*Aside.*) Mad! Raving mad! Have you seen the Old Man?

Oilman

I think I saw him in the distance last night.

First Youth

What did he look like?

Oilman

Black. More black than our brother here, the Watchman. Black as night, with two eyes on his breast shining like two glow-worms.

That won't suit us. That would be awkward for our Spring Festival.

Chandra

We shall have to change our date from the full moon to the dark moon. For the dark moon has no end of eyes on her breast.

Watchman

But I warn you, my friends, you are not doing wisely.

No, we are not.

We are found out again. We never do anything wisely. It is contrary to our habit.

Watchman

Do you take this to be a joke? I warn you, my friends, it is dangerous.

Dangerous? That's the best joke of all.

(*They sing.*)

We are neither too good nor wise,
That is all the merit we have.
Our calumny spreads from land to land,
And danger dogs our steps.
We take great care to forget what is taught us,
We say things different from the book,
Bringing upon us trouble,
And rebuke from the learned.

Watchman

Ah, Sir, you spoke about some Leader. Where is he? He could have kept you in order, if he were with you.

He never stays with us, lest he should have to keep us in order.

He simply launches us on our way, and then slips off.

Watchman

That's a poor idea of leadership.

Chandra

74

He is never concerned about his leadership. That is why we recognize him as our Leader.

Watchman

Then he has got a very easy task.

Chandra

It is no easy task to lead men. But it is easy enough to drive them.

(*They sing.*)

> We are not too good nor wise,
> That is all the merit we have.
> In a luckless moment we were born,
> When the star of wisdom was the dimmest.
> We can hope for no profit from our adventures,
> We move on, because we must.

Dada, come on. Let us go.

Watchman

No, no, Sir. Don't you get yourself into mischief in their company.

Ferryman

You read your verses, Sir, to us. Our neighbours will be here soon. They will be greatly profited.

Dada

No. I'm not going to move a step from here.

Then let us move. The men in the street can't bear us.

That's because we rattle them too much.

You hear the hum of human bees, they smell the honey of Dada's quatrains.

Youths

(*Together.*) They come! They come!

(*Enter Village folk.*)

Villager

Is it true that there is going to be a reading?

Who are you? Are *you* going to read?

No. We commit all kinds of atrocities, but not that. This one merit will bring us salvation.

Villager

What do they say? They seem to be talking in riddles.

Chandra

We only say things which we perfectly understand ourselves, and they are riddles to you. Dada repeats to you things which you understand perfectly and these sound to you the very essence of wisdom.

(*Boy enters.*)

Boy

I couldn't catch him.

Whom?

Boy

The Old Man, whom you are seeking.

Have you seen him?

Boy

Yes, I thought I saw him going by in a car.

Where? In what direction?

Boy

I couldn't make out exactly. The dust raised by his wheels is still whirling in the air.

Then let us go.

He has filled the sky with dead leaves.

(*They go out.*

                              Watchman
They are mad! Quite mad! Raving mad!

## ACT III

## SONG-PRELUDE

(*Winter is being unmasked-his hidden youth about to be disclosed.*)
The rear stage lighted up, disclosing Winter and the Heralds of Spring.

## SONG OF THE HERALDS OF SPRING

How grave he looks, how laughably old,
How solemnly quiet among death preparations!
Come, friends, help him to find himself before he reaches home.
Change his pilgrim's robe into the dress of the singing youth,
Snatch away his bag of dead things
And confound his calculations.

(*Another group sings.*)

The time comes when the world shall know that you're not banished in your own shadows;
Your heart shall burst in torrents
Out of the clasp of the ice;
And your North wind turn its face
Against the haunts of the flitting phantoms.
There sounds the magician's drum,
And the sun waits with laughter in his glance,
To see your grey turn into green.

(*Evening*)
(*The rear stage is darkened; the light on the main stage dimmed to the greyness of dark.*)
Band of Youths

They all cry, "There, there," and when we look for it, we find nothing but dust and dry leaves.

I thought I had a glimpse of the flag on his car through the cloud.

It is difficult to follow his track. Now it seems East: now it seems West.

And so we are tired, chasing shadows all day long. And the day has been lost.

I tell you the truth. Fear comes more and more into my mind, as the day passes.

We have made a mistake. The morning light whispered in our ears, "Bravo, march on." And now, the evening light is mocking us for that.

I am afraid we have been deceived. I am beginning to feel greater respect for Dada's quatrains than before. We shall all be soon sitting down on the ground composing quatrains.

And then the whole neighbourhood will come, swarming round us. And they will get such immense benefit from our wisdom that they will never leave us.

And we shall settle down like a great big boulder, cold and immovable.

And they will cling to us, as we sit there, like a thick fog.

What would our Leader think of us, I wonder, if he could hear us now?

I am sure it is our Leader, who has led us astray. He makes us toil for nothing, while he himself remains idle.

Let us go back and fight with him. We will tell him that we won't move a step further, but sit with our legs tucked under us. These legs are wretched vagabonds. They are always trudging the road.

We will keep our hands fast behind our backs.

There is no mischief in the back; all the trouble is in the front.

Of all our limbs, the back is the most truthful. It says to us, "Lie down."

When we are young, that braggart breast is a great swell; but, in the end, we can only rely on our back.

The little stream that flows past our village comes to my mind. That morning we thought that it said to us, "Forward! Forward!" But what it really said was, "False! False!" The world is all false.

Our Pundit used to tell us that.

We shall go straight to the Pundit, when we get back.

We shall never stir one step outside the limit of the Pundit's Scriptures.

What a mistake we made. We thought that moving itself was something heroic.

But really not to move, that is heroic, because it is defying the whole moving world.

Brave rebels that we are, we shall *not* move. We shall have the audacity to sit still, and never move an inch.

"Life and youth are fleeting," the Scripture says. Let life and youth go to the dogs, we shall not move.

"Our minds and wealth are fleeting," adds the Scripture. "Give them up and sit still," say we.

Let us go back to the point from which we started.

But that would be to move.

What then?

There sit down, where we have come to.

And let us imagine that there we had been before we ever came there.

Yes, yes, that will keep our minds still. If we know that we have come from somewhere else, then the mind longs for that somewhere else.

That land of somewhere else is a very dangerous place.

There the ground moves, and also the roads. But as for us — —

(*They sing.*)

> We cling to our seats and never stir,
> We allow our flowers to fade in peace, and avoid the trouble of bearing fruit.
> Let the starlights blazon their eternal folly,
> We quench our flames.
> Let the forest rustle and the ocean roar,
> We sit mute.
> Let the call of the flood-tide come from the sea,
> We remain still.

Do you hear that laughter?

Yes, yes, it is laughter.

What a relief! We have never heard that sound for an age.

We had been choking, for want of the breath of laughter.

This laughter comes to us like the April rain.

Whose is it?

Cannot you guess? It is our Chandra.

What a marvellous gift of laughter he has! It is like a waterfall. It dashes all the black stones out of the path.

It is like sunlight. It cuts the mist to pieces with its sword.

Now all danger of quatrain fever is over. Let us get up.

From this moment there will be nothing but work for us. As the Scripture says, "Everything in this world is fleeting, and he only lives who does his duty and achieves fame."

Why are you quoting that? Are you still suffering from the quatrain fever?

What do you mean by fame? Does the river take any heed of its foam? Fame is that foam on life's stream.

*(Enter Chandra with a blind Minstrel.)*

Well, Chandra, what makes you so glad?

Chandra

I have got the track of the Old Man.

From whom?

Chandra

From this old Minstrel.

He seems to be blind.

Chandra

Yes, that is why he has not got to seek the road.

What do you say? Shall you be able to lead us right?

Minstrel

Yes.

But how?

Minstrel

Because I can hear the footsteps.

We also have ears, but —— ——

Minstrel

I hear with my whole being.

Chandra

They all started up with fear, when I asked about the Old Man. Only this Minstrel seemed to have no fear. I suppose because he cannot see, he is not afraid.

Minstrel

Do you know why I have no fear? When the sun of my life set, and I became blind, the dark night revealed all its lights, and, from that day forward, I have been no more afraid of the dark.

Then let us go. The evening star is up.

Minstrel

Let me sing, and walk on as I sing, and you follow me. I cannot find my way, if I do not sing.

What do you mean?

Minstrel

My songs precede, I follow.

*(He sings.)*

Gently, my friend, gently walk to your silent chamber.
I know not the way, I have not the light,
Dark is my life and my world.
I have only the sound of your steps to guide me in this wilderness.


Gently, my friend, gently walk along the dark shore.
Let the hint of the way come in whisper,
Through the night, in the April breeze.
I have only the scent of your garland to guide me in this wilderness.

## ACT IV

### SONG-PRELUDE

(*There enter a troupe of young things, and they introduce themselves in a song as follows:*)

### THE SONG OF RETURNING YOUTH

Again and again we say "Good-bye,"
To come back again and again.
Oh, who are you?
I am the flower vakul.
And who are you?
I am the flower parul.
And who are these?
We are mango blossoms landed on the shore of light.
We laugh and take leave when the time beckons us.
We rush into the arms of the ever-returning.
But who are you?
I am the flower shimul.
And who are you?
I am the kamini bunch,
And who are these?
We are the jostling crowd of new leaves.

(*Winter is revealed as Spring and answers to the questions put by the chorus of young things.*)

### THE SONG OF BURDENS DROPPED

Do you own defeat at the hand of youth?
Yes.
Have you met at last the ageless Old, who ever grows new?
Yes.
Have you come out of the walls that crumble and bury those whom they shelter?
Yes.

(*Another group sings.*)

Do you own defeat at the hands of life?
Yes.
Have you passed through death to stand at last face to face with the Deathless?
Yes.
Have you dealt the blow to the demon dust, that swallows your city Immortal?
Yes.

(*Spring's flowers surround him and sing.*)

## THE SONG OF FRESH BEAUTY

We waited by the wayside counting moments till you appeared in the April morning.
You come as a soldier-boy winning life at death's gate, —
Oh, the wonder of it.
We listen amazed at the music of your young voice.
Your mantle is blown in the wind like the fragrance of the Spring.
The white spray of malati flowers in your hair shines like star-clusters.
A fire burns through the veil of your smile, —
Oh, the wonder of it.
And who knows where your arrows are hidden which smite death?

*(Night)*
( *The rear stage is darkened, and the light on the main stage dimmed to the heavy purple blackness of mourning.*)
*(Enter the Band of Youths.)*

Chandra has gone away again, leaving us behind.
It is difficult to keep him still.
We get our rest by sitting down, but he gets his by walking on.
He has gone across the river with the blind minstrel, in whose depth of blindness Chandra is seeking the invisible light.
That is why our Leader calls him the Diver.
Our life becomes utterly empty, when Chandra is away.
Do you feel as though something was in the air?
The sky seems to be looking into our face, like a friend bidding farewell.
This little stream of water is trickling through the *casuarina* grove. It seems like the tears of midnight.
We have never gazed upon the earth before with such intentness.
When we run forward at full speed, our eyes keep gazing in front of us, and we see nothing on either side of us.
If things did not move on and vanish, we should see no beauty anywhere.
If youth had only the heat of movement, it would get parched and withered. But there is ever the hidden tear, which keeps it fresh.
The cry of the world is not only "I have," but also "I give." In the first dawning light of creation, "I have" was wedded to "I give." If this bond of union were to snap, then everything would go to ruin.
I don't know where that blind Minstrel has landed us at last.
It seems as though these stars in the sky above us are the gazing of countless eyes we met in all forgotten ages. It seems as if, through the flowers, there came the whisper of those we have forgotten, saying Remember us.
Our hearts will break if we do not sing.
*(They sing.)*

Did you leave behind you your love, my heart, and miss peace through all your days?
And is the path you followed lost and forgotten, making your return hopeless?
I go roaming listening to brooks' babble, to the rustle of leaves.
And it seems to me that I shall find the way, that reaches the land of lost love beyond the evening stars.

What a strange tune is this, that comes out of the music of Spring.
It seems like the tune of yellow leaves.
Spring has stored up its tears in secret for us all this while.

It was afraid we should not understand it, because we were so youthful.

It wanted to beguile us with smiles.

But we shall sleep our hearts tonight in the sadness of the other shore.

Ah, the dear earth! The beautiful earth! She wants all that we have-the touch of our hands, the song of our hearts.

She wants to draw out from us all that is within, hidden even from ourselves.

This is her sorrow, that she finds out some things only to know that she has not found all. She loses before she attains.

Ah, the dear earth! We shall never deceive you.

(They sing.)

I shall crown you with my garland, before I take leave.

You ever spoke to me in all my joys and sorrows.

And now, at the end of the day, my own heart will break in speech.

Words came to me, but not the tune, and the song that I never sang to you remains hidden behind my tears.


Brother, did you notice that some one seemed to have passed by?

The only thing you feel is this passing by.

I felt the touch of the mantle of some wayfarer.

We came out to capture somebody, but now we feel the longing to be captured ourselves.

Ah, here comes the Minstrel. Where have you brought us? The breath of the wayfaring world touches us here, —the breath of the starry sky.

We came seeking a new form of play. But now we have forgotten what play it was.

We wanted to catch the Old Man.

And everybody said that he was terrifying, a bodiless head, a gaping mouth, a dragon eager to swallow the moon of the youth of the world. But now we are no longer afraid. The flowers go, the leaves go, the waves in the river go, and we shall also follow them. Ah, blind Minstrel, strike your lute and sing to us. Who knows what is the hour of the night?

(The Minstrel sings.)

Let me give my all to him, before I am asked, whom the world offers its all.

When I came to him for my gifts, I was not afraid;

And I will not fear, when I come to him, to give up what I have.

The morning accepts his gold with songs, the evening pays him back the debt of gold and is glad.

The joy of the blooming flower comes to fruit with shedding of its leaves.

Hasten, my heart, and spend yourself in love, before the day is done.


Minstrel, why is Chandra still absent?

Minstrel

Don't you know that he has gone?

Gone? —Where?

Minstrel

He said, I shall go and conquer him.

Whom?

Minstrel

The One who is feared by all. He said, "Why else am I young?"

Ah, that was fine. —Dada goes to read his quatrains to the village people, and Chandra has disappeared, —for what purpose nobody knows.

Minstrel

He said, "Men have always been fighting for a cause. It is the shock of that, which ruffles the breeze of this Spring."

The shock?

Minstrel

Yes, the message that man's fight is not yet over.

Is this the message of Spring?

Minstrel

Yes. Those, who have been made immortal by death, have sent their message in these fresh leaves of Spring. It said, "We never doubted the way. We never counted the cost: we rushed out: we blossomed. If we had sat down to debate, then where would be the Spring?"

Has that made Chandra mad?

Minstrel

He said —— —

(*The Minstrel sings.*)

The Spring flowers have woven my wreath of victory,
The South wind breathes its breath of fire in my blood.
The voice of the house-corner wails in vain from behind.
Death stands before me, offering its crown.
The tempest of youth sweeps the skyharp with its fingers;
My heart dances in its wild rhythm.
Gathering and storing are not for me,
I spend and scatter.
And prudence and comfort bid me adieu in despair.

But where has he gone to?

Minstrel

He said, "I cannot keep waiting by the wayside any longer. I must go and meet him, and conquer him."

But which way did he take?

Minstrel

He has entered the cave.

How is that? It is so fearfully dark. Did he, without making any enquiries —— —

Minstrel

Yes, he went in to make enquiries himself.

When will he come back?

I don't believe he will ever come back.

But if Chandra leaves us, then life is not worth living.

What shall we say to our Leader?

The Leader also will leave us.

Didn't he leave any message for us before he disappeared?

Minstrel

He said, "Wait for me. I shall return."

Return? How are we to know it?

Minstrel

He said, "I will conquer, and then come back again."

Then we shall wait for him all night.

But, Minstrel, where have we got to wait for him?

Minstrel

Before that cave, from whence the stream of water comes flowing out.

Which way did he go to get there?

The darkness there is like a dark sword.

Minstrel

He followed the sound of the night-bird's wings.

Why did you not go with him?

He left me behind to give you hope.

When did he go?

In the first hour of the watch.

Now the third hour has passed, I think. The air is chilly.

I dreamt that three women, with their hair hanging loose — —

Oh, leave off your dream-women. I am sick of your dreams.

Everything appears darkly ominous. I didn't notice before the hooting of the owl. But now — —

Do you hear that dog whining on the far bank of the river?

It seems as though a witch were riding upon him and lashing him.

Surely, if it had been possible, Chandra would have come back by now.

How I wish this night were over.

Do you hear the woman's cry?

Oh, the women, the women. They are ever crying and weeping. But they cannot turn those back, who must go forward.

It is getting unbearable to sit still like this. Men imagine all sorts of things when they sit still. Let us go also. As soon as we are started on our way fear will leave us.

But who will show us the way?

There is the blind Minstrel.

What do you say, Minstrel? Can you show us the way?

Yes.

But we can hardly believe you. How can you find out the path by simply singing?

If Chandra never comes back, you shall.

We never knew that we loved Chandra so intensely. We made light of him all these days.

When we are in the playing mood, we become so intent on the play, that we neglect the playmate.

But, if he once comes back, we shall never neglect him any more.

I am afraid that we have often given him pain.

Yet his love rose above all that. We never knew how beautiful he was, when we could see him every day.

*(They sing.)*

When there was light in my world
You stood outside my eyes.
Now that there is none,
You come into my heart.
When there were dolls for me, I played;
You smiled and watched from the door.
Now that the dolls have crumbled to dust,
You come and sit by me.
And I have only my heart for my music,
When my lute-strings have broken.


That Minstrel sits so still and silent. I don't like it.

He looks ominous, —like the lowering autumn cloud.

Let us dismiss him.

No, no. It gives us heart, when he sits there.

Don't you see that there is no sign of fear in his face?

It seems as if some messages were striking his forehead. His body appears to espy some one in the distance. There seem to be eyes on the tips of his fingers.

Simply by watching him, we can see that some one is coming through the dark.

Look. He is standing up. He is turning towards the East, and making his obeisance.

Yet there is nothing to be seen, not even a streak of light.

Why not ask him what it is that he sees?

No, don't disturb him.

Do you know, it seems to me that the morning has dawned in him.

As if the ferry-boat of light had reached the shore of his forehead.

His mind is still, like the morning sky.

The storm of birds' songs will burst out presently.

He is striking his lute. His heart is singing.

Hush. He is singing.

(The Minstrel sings.)

Victory to thee, victory for ever,
O brave heart.
Victory to life, to joy, to love,
To eternal light.
The night shall wane, the darkness shall vanish,
Have faith, brave heart.
Wake up from sleep, from languor of despair,
Receive the light of new dawn with a song.


(A ray of light hovers before the cavern.)

Ah! There he is. Chandra! Chandra!

Hush. Don't make any noise. I cannot see him distinctly.

Ah! It cannot be any other than Chandra.

Oh, what joy!

Chandra! Come!

Chandra! How could you leave us for so long?

Have you been able to capture the Old Man?

Chandra

Yes, I have.

But we don't see him.

Chandra

He is coming.

But what did you see in the cave? Tell us.

Chandra

No, I cannot tell you.

Why?

Chandra

If my mind were a voice, then I could tell you.

But could you see him, whom you captured? Was he the Old Man of the World?

The Old Man who would like to drink up the sea of youth in his insatiable thirst.

Was it the One who is like the dark night, whose eyes are fixed on his breast, whose feet are turned the wrong way round, who walks backwards?

Was it the One who wears the garland of skulls, and lives in the burning-ground of the dead?

Chandra

I do not know, I cannot say. But he is coming. You shall see him.

Minstrel

Yes, I see him.

*(The light strengthens and gradually throughout the scene grows to a culminating brilliance at the close.)*

Where?

Minstrel

Here.

He is coming out of the cave. —Some one is coming out of the cave.

How wonderful.

Chandra

Why, it is you!

Our Leader!

Our Leader!

Our Leader!

Where is the Old Man?

Leader

He is nowhere.

Nowhere?

Leader

Yes, nowhere.

Then what is he?

Leader

He is a dream.

Then you are the real?

Leader

Yes.

And we are the real?

Leader

Yes.

Those who saw you from behind imagined you in all kinds of shapes.

We didn't recognize you through the dust.

You seemed old.

And then you came out of the cave, —and now you look like a boy.

It seems just as if we had seen you for the first time.

Chandra

You are first every time. You are first over and over again.

Leader

Chandra! You must own your defeat. You couldn't catch the Old Man.

Chandra

Let our festival begin. The sun is up.

Minstrel, if you keep so still, you will swoon away. Sing something.

*(The Minstrel sings.)*

I lose thee, to find thee back again and again,
My beloved.
Thou leavest me, that I may receive thee all the more, when thou returnest.
Thou canst vanish behind the moment's screen
Only because thou art mine for evermore,
My beloved.
When I go in search of thee, my heart trembles, spreading ripples across my love.
Thou smilest through thy disguise of utter absence, and my tears sweeten thy smile.

Do you hear the hum?

Yes.

They are not bees, but the people of the place.

Then Dada must be near at hand with his quatrains.

Dada

Is this the Leader?

Yes, Dada.

Dada

Oh, I am so glad you have come. I must read my collection of quatrains.

No. No. Not the whole collection, but only one.

Dada

Very well. One will do.

The sun is at the gate of the East, his drum of victory sounding in the sky.
The Night says I am blessed, my death is bliss.
He receives his alms of gold, filling his wallet, —and departs.

That is to say — —

No. We don't want your that is to say.

Dada

It means — —

Whatever it means, we are determined not to know it.

Dada

What makes you so desperate?

It is our festival day.

Dada

Ah! Is that so? Then let me go to all the neighbours — —

No, you mustn't go there.

Dada

But is there any need for me here?

Yes.

Then my quatrains — —

Chandra

We shall colour your quatrains with such a thick brush, that no one will know whether they have any meaning at all.

And then you will be without any means.

The neighbourhood will desert you.

The Watchman will take you to be a fool.

And the Pundit will take you to be a blockhead.

And your own people will consider you to be useless.

And the outside people will consider you queer.

Chandra

But we shall crown you, Dada, with a crown of new leaves.

We shall put a garland of jasmine round your neck.

And there will be no one else except ourselves who will know your true worth.


## THE SONG OF THE FESTIVAL OF SPRING

*(In which all the persons of the drama, not excepting Sruti-bhushan, unite on the main stage in the dance of Spring.)*

Come and rejoice, for April is awake.
Fling yourselves into the flood of being, bursting the bondage of the past.
April is awake.
Life's shoreless sea is heaving in the sun before you.
All the losses are lost, and death is drowned in its waves.
Plunge into the deep without fear, with the gladness of April in your heart.

## Footnote

# THE KING OF THE DARK CHAMBER

(A street. A few wayfarers, and a CITY GUARD)

FIRST MAN. Ho, Sir!

CITY GUARD. What do you want?

SECOND MAN. Which way should we go? We are strangers here.
Please tell us which street we should take.

CITY GUARD. Where do you want to go?

THIRD MAN. To where those big festivities are going to be held, you know. Which way do we go?

CITY GUARD. One street is quite as good as another here. Any street will lead you there. Go straight ahead, and you cannot miss the place. (Exit.)

FIRST MAN. Just hear what the fool says: "Any street will lead you there!" Where, then, would be the sense of having so many streets?

SECOND MAN. You needn't be so awfully put out at that, my man. A country is free to arrange its affairs in its own way. As for roads in our country-well, they are as good as non-existent; narrow and crooked lanes, a labyrinth of ruts and tracks. Our King does not believe in open thoroughfares; he thinks that streets are just so many openings for his subjects to fly away from his kingdom. It is quite the contrary here; nobody stands in your way, nobody objects to your going elsewhere if you like to; and yet the people are far from deserting this kingdom. With such streets our country would certainly have been depopulated in no time.

FIRST MAN. My dear Janardan, I have always noticed that this is a great fault in your character.

JANARDAN. What is?

FIRST MAN. That you are always having a fling at your country.
How can you think that open highways may be good for a country?
Look here, Kaundilya; here is a man who actually believes that
open highways are the salvation of a country.

KAUNDILYA. There is no need, Bhavadatta, of my pointing out afresh that Janardan is blessed with an intelligence which is remarkably crooked, which is sure to land him in danger some day. If the King comes to hear of our worthy friend, he will make it a pretty hard job for him to find any one to do him his funeral rites when he is dead.

BHAVADATTA. One can't help feeling that life becomes a burden in this country; one misses the joys of privacy in these streets — this jostling and brushing shoulders with strange people day and night makes one long for a bath. And nobody can tell exactly what kind of people you are meeting with in these public roads — ugh!

KAUNDILYA. And it is Janardan who persuaded us to come to this precious country! We never had any second person like him in our family. You knew my father, of course; he was a great man, a pious man if ever there was one. He spent his whole life within a circle of a radius of 49 cubits drawn with a rigid adherence to the injunctions of the scriptures, and never for a single day did he cross this circle. After his death a serious difficulty arose-how cremate him within the limits of the 49 cubits and yet outside the house? At length the priests decided that though we could not go beyond the scriptural number, the only way out of the difficulty was to reverse the figure and make it 94 cubits; only thus could we cremate him outside the house without violating the sacred books. My word, that was strict observance! Ours is indeed no common country.

BHAVADATTA. And yet, though Janardan comes from the very same soil, he thinks it wise to declare that open highways are best for a country.
(Enter GRANDFATHER with a band of boys)

GRANDFATHER. Boys, we will have to vie with the wild breeze of the south to-day —and we are not going to be beaten. We will sing till we have flooded all streets with our mirth and song.

## SONG.

The southern gate is unbarred. Come, my spring, come!
Thou wilt swing at the swing of my heart, come, my spring, come!
Come in the lisping leaves, in the youthful surrender of flowers;
Come in the flute songs and the wistful sighs of the woodlands!
Let your unfastened robe wildly flap in the drunken wind!
Come, my spring, come!

(Exeunt.)
(Enter a band of CITIZENS)

FIRST CITIZEN. After all, one cannot help wishing that the King had allowed himself to be seen at least this one day. What a great pity, to live in his kingdom and yet not to have seen him for a single day!

SECOND CITIZEN. If you only knew the real meaning of all this mystery! I could tell you if you would keep a secret.

FIRST CITIZEN. My dear fellow, we both live in the same quarter of the town, but have you ever known me letting out any man s secret? Of course, that matter of your brother's finding a hidden fortune while digging for a well-well, you know well enough why I had to give it out. You know all the facts.

SECOND CITIZEN. Of course I know. And it is because I know that I ask, could you keep a secret if I tell you? It may mean ruination to us all, you know, if you once let it out.

THIRD CITIZEN. You are a nice man, after all, Virupaksha! Why are you so anxious to bring down a disaster which as yet only may happen? Who will be responsible for keeping your secret all his life?

VIRUPAKSHA. It is only because the topic came up-well, then, I shall not say anything. I am not the man to say things for nothing. You had yourself brought up the question that the King never showed himself; and I only remarked that it was not for nothing that the King shut himself up from the public gaze.

FIRST CITIZEN. Pray do tell us why, Virupaksha.

VIRUPAKSHA. Of course I don't mind telling you-for we are all good friends, aren't we? There can be no harm. (With a low voice.) The King-is-hideous to look at, so he has made up his mind never to show himself to his subjects.

FIRST CITIZEN. Ha! that's it! It must be so. We have always wondered...why, the mere sight of a King in all countries makes one's soul quake like an aspen leaf with fear; but why should our King never have been seen by any mortal soul? Even if he at least came out and consigned us all to the gibbet, we might be sure that our King was no hoax. After all, there is much in Virupaksha's explanation that sounds plausible enough.

THIRD CITIZEN. Not a bit—I don't believe in a syllable of it.

VIRUPAKSHA. What, Vishu, do you mean to say that I am a liar?

VISHU. I don't exactly mean that-but I cannot accept your theory. Excuse me, I cannot help if I seem a bit rude or churlish.

VIRUPAKSHA. Small wonder that you can't believe my words-you who think yourself sage enough to reject the opinions of your parents and superiors. How long do you think you could have stayed in this country if the King did not remain in hiding? You are no better than a flagrant heretic.

VISHU. My dear pillar of orthodoxy! Do you think any other King would have hesitated to cut off your tongue and make it food for dogs? And you have the face to say that our King is horrid to look at!

VIRUPAKSHA. Look here, Vishu. will you curb your tongue?

VISHU. It would be superfluous to point out whose tongue needs the curbing.

FIRST CITIZEN. Hush, my dear friends-this looks rather bad.... It seems as if they are resolved to put me in danger as well. I am not going to be a party to all this.(Exit.)

(Enter a number of men, dragging in GRANDFATHER, in boisterous exuberance)

SECOND CITIZEN. Grandpa, something strikes me to-day...

GRANDFATHER. What is it?

SECOND CITIZEN. This year every country has sent its people to our festival, but every one asks, "Everything is nice and beautiful-but where is your King?" and we do not know what to answer. That is the one big gap which cannot but make itself felt to every one in our country.

GRANDFATHER. "Gap," do you say! Why, the whole country is all filled and crammed and packed with the King: and you call him a "gap"! Why,he has made every one of us a crowned King!


## SONG.

We are all Kings in the kingdom of our King.
Were it not so, how could we hope in our heart to meet him!
We do what we like, yet we do what he likes;
We are not bound with the chain of fear at the feet of a slave-owning King.
Were it not so, how could we hope in our heart to meet him!
Our King honours each one of us, thus honours his own very self.
No littleness can keep us shut up in its walls of untruth for aye.
Were it not so, how could we have hope in our heart to meet

him!
We struggle and dig our own path, thus reach his path at the
end.
We can never get lost in the abyss of dark night.
Were it not so, how could we hope in our heart to meet him!

THIRD CITIZEN. But, really, I cannot stand the absurd things people say about our King simply because he is not seen in public.

FIRST CITIZEN. Just fancy! Any one libelling me can be punished, while nobody can stop the mouth of any rascal who chooses to slander the King.

GRANDFATHER. The slander cannot touch the King. With a mere breath you can blow out the flame which a lamp inherits from the sun, but if all the world blow upon the sun itself its effulgence remains undimmed and unimpaired as before.

(Enter VISHVAVASU and VIRUPAKSHA)

VISHU. Here's Grandfather! Look here, this man is going about telling everybody that our King does not come out because he is ugly.

GRANDFATHER. But why does that make you angry, Vishu? His King must be ugly, because how else could Virupaksha possess such features in his kingdom? He fashions his King after the image of himself he sees in the mirror.

VIRUPAKSHA. Grandfather, I shall mention no names, but nobody would think of dis-believing the person who gave me the news.

GRANDFATHER. Who could be a higher authority than yourself!

VIRUPAKSHA. But I could give you proofs...

FIRST CITIZEN. The impudence of this fellow knows no bounds! Not content with spreading a ghastly rumour with an unabashed face, he offers to measure his lies with inso-lence!

SECOND CITIZEN. Why not make him measure his length on the ground?

GRANDFATHER. Why so much heat, my friends? The poor fellow is going to have his own festive day by singing the ugliness of his King. Go along, Virupaksha, you will find plenty of people ready to believe you: may you be happy in their company.(Exeunt.)

(Re-enter the party of FOREIGNERS)

BHAVADATTA. It strikes me, Kaundilya, that these people haven't got a King at all. They have somehow managed to keep the rumour afloat.

KAUNDILYA. You are right, I think. We all know that the supreme thing that strikes one's eye in any country is the King, who of course loses no opportunity of exhibiting himself.

JANARDAN. But look at the nice order and regularity prevailing all over the place-how do you explain it without a King?

BHAVADATTA. So this is the wisdom you have arrived at by living so long under a ruler! Where would be the necessity of having a King if order and harmony existed already?

JANARDAN. All these people have assembled to rejoice at this festival. Do you think they could come together like this in a country of anarchy?

BHAVADATTA. My dear Janardan, you are evading the real issue, as usual. There can be no question about the order and regularity, and the festive rejoicing too is plain enough: there is no difficulty so far. But where is the King? Have you seen him? Just tell us that.

JANARDAN. What I want to say is this: you know from your experience that there can be chaos and anarchy even if a King be present: but what do we see here?

KAUNDILYA. You are always coming back to your quibbling. Why can you not give a straight answer to Bhavadatta's question-Have you, or have you not, seen the King? Yes or no? (Exeunt.)

(Enter a band of MEN, singing)

## SONG.

My beloved is ever in my heart
That is why I see him everywhere,
He is in the pupils of my eyes
That is why I see him everywhere.
I went far away to hear his own words,
But, ah, it was vain!
When I came back I heard them
In my own songs.
Who are you who seek him like a beggar
from door to door!
Come to my heart and see his face in the
tears of my eyes!

(Enter HERALDS and ADVANCE GUARDS of the KING)

FIRST HERALD. Stand off! Get away from the street, all of you!

FIRST CITIZEN. Eh, man, who do you think you are? You weren't of course born with such lofty strides, my friend? —Why should we stand off, my dear sir? Why should we budge? Are we street dogs, or what?

SECOND HERALD. Our King is coming this way.

SECOND CITIZEN. King? Which King?

FIRST HERALD. Our King, the King of this country.

FIRST CITIZEN. What, is the fellow mad? Whoever heard of our King coming out heralded by these vociferous gentry?

SECOND HERALD. The King will no longer deny himself to his subjects. He is coming to command the festivities himself.

SECOND CITIZEN. Brother, is that so?

SECOND HERALD. Look, his banner is flying over there.

SECOND CITIZEN. Ah, yes, that is a flag indeed.

SECOND HERALD. Do you see the red *Kimshuk* flower painted on it?

SECOND CITIZEN. Yes, yes, it is the *Kimshuk* indeed! —what a bright scarlet flower!

FIRST HERALD. Well! do you believe us now?

SECOND CITIZEN. I never said I didn't. That fellow Kumbha started all this fuss. Did I say a word?

FIRST HERALD. Perhaps, though a pot-bellied man, he is quite empty inside; an empty vessel sounds most, you know.

SECOND HERALD. Who is he? Is he any kinsman of yours?

SECOND CITIZEN. Not at all. He is just a cousin of our village chief's father-in-law, and he does not even live in the same part of our village with us.

SECOND HERALD. Just so: he quite looks the seventh cousin of somebody's father-in-law, and his understanding appears also to bear the stamp of uncle-in-lawhood.

KUMBHA. Alas, my friends, many a bitter sorrow has given my poor mind a twist before it has become like this. It is only the other day that a King came and paraded the streets, with as many titles in front of him as the drums that made the town hideous by their din,... What did I not do to serve and please him! I rained presents on him, I hung about him like a beggar-and in the end I found the strain on my resources too hard to bear. But what was the end of all that pomp and majesty? When people sought grants and presents from him, he could not somehow discover an auspicious day in the Calendar: though all days were red-letter days when we had to pay our taxes!

SECOND HERALD. Do you mean to insinuate that our King is a bogus King like the one you have described?

FIRST HERALD. Mr. Uncle-in-law, I believe the time has come for you to say good-bye to Aunty-in-law.

KUMBHA. Please, sirs, do not take any offence. I am a poor creature-my sincerest apologies, sirs: I will do anything to be excused. I am quite willing to move away as far as you like.

SECOND HERALD. All right, come here and form a line. The King will come just now-we shall go and prepare the way for him. (They go out.)

SECOND CITIZEN. My dear Kumbha, your tongue will be your death one day.

KUMBHA. Friend Madhav, it isn't my tongue, it is fate. When the bogus King appeared I never said a word, though that did not prevent my striking at my own feet with all the self-confidence of innocence. And now, when perhaps the real King has come, I simply must blurt out treason. It is fate, my dear friend!

MADHAV. My faith is, to go on obeying the King-it does not matter whether he is a real one or a pretender. What do we know of Kings that we should judge them! It is like throwing stones in the dark-you are almost sure of hitting your mark. I go on obeying and acknowledging-if it is a real King, well and good: if not, what harm is there?

KUMBHA. I should not have minded if the stones were nothing better than stones. But they are often precious things: here, as elsewhere, extravagance lands us in poverty, my friend.

MADHAV. Look! There comes the King! Ah, a King indeed! What a figure, what a face! Whoever saw such beauty-lily-white, creamy-soft! What now, Kumbha? What do you think now?

KUMBHA. He looks all right-yes, he may be the real King for all I know.

MADHAV. He looks as if he were moulded and carved for kingship, a figure too exquisite and delicate for the common light of day.

(Enter the "KING")

(Transcriber's note: The author indicates the trumped up King as "KING" in this play, enclosing the word King in double quotes to help us distinguish the imposter from the real one.)

MADHAV. Prosperity and victory attend thee, O King! We have been standing here to have a sight of thee since the early morning. Forget us not, your Majesty, in your favours.

KUMBHA. The mystery deepens. I will go and call Grandfather.(Goes out.)

(Enter another band of MEN)

FIRST MAN. The King, the King! Come along, quick, the King is passing this way.

SECOND MAN. Do not forget me, O King! I am Vivajadatta, the grandson of Udayadatta of Kushalivastu. I came here at the first report of thy coming —I did not stop to hear what people were saying: all the loyalty in me went out towards thee, O Monarch, and brought me here.

THIRD MAN. Rubbish! I came here earlier than you-before the cockcrow. Where were you then? O King, I am Bhadrasena, of Vikramasthali. Deign to keep thy servant in thy memory!

"KING". I am much pleased with your loyalty and devotion.

VIVAJADATTA. Your Majesty, many are the grievances and complaints we have to make to thee: to whom could we turn our prayers so long, when we could not approach thy august presence?

"KING". Your grievances will all be redressed. (Exit.)

FIRST MAN. It won't do to lag behind, boys-the King will lose sight of us if we get mixed up with the mob.

SECOND MAN. See there-look what that fool Narottam is doing! He has elbowed his way through all of us and is now sedulously fanning the King with a palm leaf!

MADHAV. Indeed! Well, well, the sheer audacity of the man takes one's breath away.

SECOND MAN. We shall have to pitch the fellow out of that place-is he fit to stand beside the King?

MADHAV. Do you imagine the King will not see through him? His loyalty is obviously a little too showy and profuse.

FIRST MAN. Nonsense! Kings can't scent hypocrites as we do —I should not be surprised if the King be taken in by that fool's strenuous fanning.

(Enter KUMBHA with GRANDFATHER)

KUMBHA. I tell you-he has just passed by this street.

GRANDFATHER. Is that a very infallible test of Kingship?

KUMBHA. Oh no, he did not pass unobserved: not one or two men but hundreds and thousands on both sides of the street have seen him with their own eyes.

GRANDFATHER. That is exactly what makes the whole affair suspicious. When ever has our King set out to dazzle the eyes of the people by pomp and pageantry? He is not the King to make such a thundering row over his progress through the country.

KUMBHA. But he may just have chosen to do so on this important occasion: you cannot really tell.

GRANDFATHER. Oh yes, you can! My King cherishes no weathercock fancy, no fantastic vein.

KUMBHA. But, Grandfather, I wish I could only describe him! So soft, so delicate and exquisite like a waxen doll! As I looked on him, I yearned to shelter him from the sun, to protect him with my whole body.

GRANDFATHER. Fool, O precious ass that you are! *My* King a waxen doll, and you to protect him!

KUMBHA. But seriously, Grandpa, he is a superb god, a miracle of beauty: I do not find a single other figure in this vast assembly that can stand beside his peerless loveliness.

GRANDFATHER. If my King chose to make himself shown, your eyes would not have noticed him. He would not stand out like that amongst others-he is one of the people, he mingles with the common populace.

KUMBHA. But did I not tell you I saw his banner?

GRANDFATHER. What did you see displayed on his banner?

KUMBHA. It had a red *Kimshuk* flower painted on it-the bright and glittering scarlet dazzled my eyes.

GRANDFATHER. *My* King has a thunderbolt within a lotus painted on his flag.

KUMBHA. But every one is saying, the King is out in this festival: *every one.*

GRANDFATHER. Why, so he is, of course: but he has no heralds, no army, no retinue, no music bands or lights to accompany him.

KUMBHA. So none could recognise him in his incognito, it seems.

GRANDFATHER. Perhaps there are a few that can.

KUMBHA. And those that can recognise him-does the King grant them whatever they ask for?

GRANDFATHER. But they never ask for anything. No beggar will ever know the King. The greater beggar appears like the King to the eyes of the lesser beggar. O fool, the man that has come out to-day attired in crimson and gold to beg from you-it is him whom you are trumpeting as your King!...Ah, there comes my mad friend! Oh come, my brothers! we cannot spend the day in idle wrangling and prating-let us now have some mad frolic, some wild enjoyment!

(Enter the MAD FRIEND, who sings)

Do you smile, my friends? Do you laugh, my brothers? I roam
in search of the golden stag! Ah yes, the fleet-foot vision
that ever eludes me!

Oh, he flits and glimpses like a flash and then is gone, the untamed rover of the wilds! Approach him and he is afar in a trice, leaving a cloud of haze and dust before thy eyes!

Yet I roam in search of the golden stag, though I may never catch him in these wilds! Oh, I roam and wander through woods and fields and nameless lands like a restless vagabond, never caring to turn my back.

You all come and buy in the marketplace and go back to your homes laden with goods and provisions: but me the wild winds of unscalable heights have touched and kissed-Oh, I know not when or where!

I have parted with my all to get what never has become mine! And yet think my moanings and my tears are for the things I thus have lost!

With a laugh and a song in my heart I have left all sorrow and grief far behind me: Oh, I roam and wander through woods and fields and nameless lands-never caring to turn my vagabond's back!

## II

(A DarkChamber. QUEEN SUDARSHANA. Her Maid of Honour,
SURANGAMA)

SUDARSHANA. Light, light! Where is light? Will the lamp never be lighted in this chamber?

SURANGAMA. My Queen, all your other rooms are lighted-will you never long to escape from the light into a dark room like this?

SUDARSHANA. But why should this room be kept dark?

SURANGAMA. Because otherwise you would know neither light nor darkness.

SUDARSHANA. Living in this dark room you have grown to speak darkly and strangely — I cannot understand you, Surangama. But tell me, in what part of the palace is this chamber situated? I cannot make out either the entrance or the way out of this room.

SURANGAMA. This room is placed deep down, in the very heart of the earth. The King has built this room specially for your sake.

SUDARSHANA. Why, he has no dearth of rooms-why need he have made this chamber of darkness specially for me?

SURANGAMA. You can meet others in the lighted rooms: but only in this dark room can you meet your lord.

SUDARSHANA. No, no —I cannot live without light —I am restless in this stifling dark. Surangama, if you can bring a light into this room, I shall give you this necklace of mine.

SURANGAMA. It is not in my power, O Queen. How can I bring light to a place which he would have kept always dark!

SUDARSHANA. Strange devotion! And yet, is it not true that the
King punished your father?

SURANGAMA. Yes, that is true. My father used to gamble. All the young men of the country used to gather at my father's house-and they used to drink and gamble.

SUDARSHANA. And when the King sent away your father in exile, did it not make you feel bitterly oppressed?

SURANGAMA. Oh, it made me quite furious. I was on the road to ruin and destruction: when that path was closed for me, I seemed left without any support, without any succour or shelter. I raged and raved like a wild beast in a cage-how I wanted to tear every one to pieces in my powerless anger!

SUDARSHANA. But how did you get this devotion towards that same
King?

SURANGAMA . How can I tell? Perhaps I could rely and depend on him because he was so hard, so pitiless!

SUDARSHANA. When did this change of feeling take place?

SURANGAMA. I could not tell you —I do not know that myself. A day came when all the rebel in me knew itself beaten, and then my whole nature bowed down in humble resignation on the dust of the earth. And then I saw...I saw that he was as matchless in beauty as in terror. Oh. I was saved, I was rescued.

SUDARSHANA. Tell me, Surangama, I implore you, won't you tell me what is the King like to look at? I have not seen him yet for a single day. He comes to me in darkness, and leaves me in this dark room again. How many people have I not asked-but they all return vague and dark answers-it seems to me that they all keep back something.

SURANGAMA. To tell you the truth, Queen, I could not say well what he is like. No-he is not what men call handsome.

SUDARSHANA. You don't say so? Not handsome!

SURANGAMA. No, my Queen, he is not handsome. To call him beautiful would be to say far too little about him.

SUDARSHANA. All your words are like that-dark, strange, and vague. I cannot under-stand what you mean.

SURANGAMA. No, I will not call him handsome. And it is because he is not beautiful that he is so wonderful, so superb, so miraculous!

SUDARSHANA. I do not quite understand you-though I like to hear you talk about him. But I must see him at any cost. I do not even remember the day when I was married to him. I have heard mother say that a wise man came before my marriage and said, "He who will wed your daughter is without a second on this earth." How often have I asked her to describe his appearance to me, but she only answers vaguely, and says she cannot say-she saw him through a veil, faintly and obscurely. But if he is the best among men, how can I sit still without seeing him?

SURANGAMA. Do you not feel a faint breeze blowing?

SUDARSHANA. A breeze? Where?

SURANGAMA. Do you not smell a soft perfume?

SUDARSHANA. No, I don't.

SURANGAMA. The large door has opened...he is coming; my King is coming in.

SUDARSHANA. How can you perceive when he comes?

SURANGAMA. I cannot say: I seem to hear his footsteps in my own heart. Being his servant of this dark chamber, I have developed a sense —I can know and feel without seeing.

SUDARSHANA. Would that I had this sense too, Surangama!

SURANGAMA. You will have it, O Queen...this sense will awaken in you one day. Your longing to have a sight of him makes you restless, and therefore all your mind is strained and warped in that direction. When you are past this state of feverish restlessness, everything will become quite easy.

SUDARSHANA. How is it that it is easy to you, who are a servant, and so difficult to me, the Queen?

SURANGAMA. It is because I am a mere servant that no difficulty baulks me. On the first day, when he left this room to my care, saying, "Surangama, you will always keep this chamber ready for me: this is all your task," then I did not say, even in thought, "Oh, give me the work of those who keep the other rooms lighted." No, but as soon as I bent all my mind to my task, a power woke and grew within me, and mastered every part of me unopposed.... Oh, there he comes!...he is standing outside, before the door. Lord! O King!

SONG outside.

> Open your door. I am waiting.
> The ferry of the light from the dawn to the dark is done for
> the day,
> The evening star is up.
> Have you gathered your flowers, braided your hair,
> And donned your white robe for the night?
> The cattle have come to their folds and birds to their nests.
> The cross paths that run to all quarters have merged into one
> in the dark.
> Open your door. I am waiting.

SURANGAMA. O King, who can keep thy own doors shut against thee? They are not locked or bolted-they will swing wide open if you only touch them with thy fingers. Wilt thou not even touch them? Wilt thou not enter unless I go and open the doors?

## SONG.

> At a breath you can remove my veils, my lord!
> If I fall asleep on the dust and hear not your call, would you
> wait till I wake?
> Would not the thunder of your chariot wheel make the earth
> tremble?
> Would you not burst open the door and enter your own house
> unbidden?

> Then do you go, O Queen, and open the door for him: he will not enter otherwise.

SUDARSHANA. I do not see anything distinctly in the dark —I do not know where the doors are. You know everything here-go and open the doors for me.

> (SURANGAMA opens the door, bows to the KING, and goes out. The
> KING will remain invisible throughout this play.)

SUDARSHANA. Why do you not allow me to see you in the light?

KING. So you want to see me in the midst of a thousand things in broad daylight! Why should I not be the only thing you can feel in this darkness?

SUDARSHANA. But I must see you —I am longing to have a sight of you.

KING. You will not be able to bear the sight of me-it will only give you pain, poignant and overpowering.

SUDARSHANA. How can you say that I shall be unable to bear your sight? Oh, I can feel even in this dark how lovely and wonderful you are: why should I be afraid of you in the light? But tell me, can you see me in the dark?

KING. Yes, I can.

SUDARSHANA. What do you see?

KING. I see that the darkness of the infinite heavens, whirled into life and being by the power of my love, has drawn the light of a myriad stars into itself, and incarnated itself in a form of flesh and blood. And in that form, what aeons of thought and striving, untold yearnings of limitless skies, the countless gifts of unnumbered seasons!

SUDARSHANA. Am I so wonderful, so beautiful? When I hear you speak so, my heart swells with gladness and pride. But how can I believe the wonderful things you tell me? I cannot find them in myself!

KING. Your own mirror will not reflect them-it lessens you, limits you, makes you look small and insignificant. But could you see yourself mirrored in my own mind, how grand would you appear! In my own heart you are no longer the daily individual which you think you are-you are verily my second self.

SUDARSHANA. Oh, do show me for an instant how to see with your eyes! Is there nothing at all like darkness to you? I am afraid when I think of this. This darkness which is to me real and strong as death-is this simply nothing to you? Then how can there be any union at all between us, in a place like this? No, no-it is impossible: there is a barrier betwixt us two: not here, no, not in this place. I want to find you and see you where I see trees and animals, birds and stones and the earth

KING. Very well, you can try to find me-but none will point me out to you. You will have to recognise me, if you can, yourself. And even if anybody professes to show me to you, how can you be sure he is speaking the truth?

SUDARSHANA. I shall know you; I shall recognise you. I shall find you out among a million men. I cannot be mistaken.

KING. Very well, then, to-night, during the festival of the full moon of the spring, you will try to find me out from the high turret of my palace-search for me with your own eyes amongst the crowd of people.

SUDARSHANA. Wilt thou be there among them?

KING. I shall show myself again and again, from every side of the crowd. Surangama!
(Enter SURANGAMA)

SURANGAMA. What is thy pleasure, lord?

KING. To-night is the full moon festival of the spring.

SURANGAMA. What have I to do to-night?

KING. To-day is a festive day, not a day of work. The pleasure gardens are in their full bloom-you will join in my festivities there.

SURANGAMA. I shall do as thou desirest, lord.

KING. The Queen wants to see me to-night with her own eyes.

SURANGAMA. Where will the Queen see you?

KING. Where the music will play at its sweetest, where the air will be heavy with the dust of flowers-there in the pleasure grove of silver light and mellow gloom.

SURANGAMA. What can be seen in the hide-and-seek of darkness and light? There the wind is wild and restless, everything is dance and swift movement-will it not puzzle the eyes?

KING. The Queen is curious to search me out.

SURANGAMA. Curiosity will have to come back baffled and in tears!

## SONG.

Ah, they would fly away, the restless vagrant eyes, the wild
birds of the forest!
But the time of their surrender will come, their flights hither
and thither will be ended when
The music of enchantment will pursue them and pierce their
hearts.
Alas, the wild birds would fly to the wilderness!

## III

(Before the Pleasure Gardens. Enter AVANTI, KOSHALA, KANCHI, and other KINGS)

AVANTI. Will the King of this place not receive us?

KANCHI. What manner of governing a country is this? The King is having a festival in a forest, where even the meanest and commonest people can have easy access!

KOSHALA. We ought to have had a separate place set apart and ready for our reception.

KANCHI. If he has not prepared such a place yet, we shall compel him to have one erected for us.

KOSHALA. All this makes one naturally suspect if these people have really got any King at all-it looks as if an unfounded rumour has led us astray.

AVANTI. It may be so with regard to the King, but the Queen Sudarshana of this place isn't at all an unfounded rumour.

KOSHALA. It is only for her sake that I have cared to come at all. I don't mind omitting to see one who never makes himself visible, but it would be a stupid mistake if we were to go away without a sight of one who is eminently worth a visit.

KANCHI. Let us make some definite plan, then.

AVANTI. A plan is an excellent thing, so long as you are not yourself entangled in it.

KANCHI. Hang it, who are these vermin swarming this way? Here! who are you?
(Enter GRANDFATHER and the boys)

GRANDFATHER. We are the Jolly Band of Have-Nothings.

AVANTI. The introduction was superfluous. But you will take yourselves away a little further and leave us in peace.

GRANDFATHER. We never suffer from a want of space: we can afford to give you as wide a berth as you like. What little suffices for us is never the bone of contention between any rival claimants. Is not that so, my little friends? (They sing.)

## SONG.

We have nothing, indeed we have nothing at all!
We sing merrily fol de rol de rol!
Some build high walls of their houses
On the bog of the sands of gold.
We stand before them and sing
Fol de rol de rol.
Pickpockets hover about us
And honour us with covetous glances.
We shake our empty pockets and sing
Fol de rol de rol.
When death, the old hag, steals to our doors
We snap our fingers at her face,
And we sing in a chorus with gay flourishes
Fol de rol de rol.

KANCHI. Look over there, Koshala, who are those coming this way?
A pantomime? Somebody is out masquerading as a King.

KOSHALA. The King of this place may tolerate all this tomfoolery, but we won't.

AVANTI. He is perhaps some rural chief.

(Enter GUARDS on foot)

KANCHI. What country does your King come from?

FIRST SOLDIER. He is the King of this country. He is going to command the festivities.
(They go out.)

KOSHALA. What! The King of this country come out for the festivities!

AVANTI. Indeed! We shall then have to return with a sight of him only-leaving the
delectable Queen unseen.

KANCHI. Do you really think that fellow spoke the truth?
Anybody can pass himself off as the King of this kingless
country. Can you not see that the man looks like a dressed-up
King-much too over-dressed?

AVANTI. But he looks handsome-his appearance is not without a certain pleasing attractiveness.

KANCHI. He may be pleasing to your eye, but if you look at him closely enough there can
be no mistaking him . You will see how I expose him before you all.

(Enter the trumped-up "KING".)

"KING". Welcome, princes, to our kingdom! I trust your reception has been properly looked
after by my officials?

KINGS. (with feigned courtesy) Oh yes-nothing was lacking in the reception.

KANCHI. If there was any shortcoming at all, it has been made up by the honour of our
sight of your Majesty.

"KING". We do not show ourselves to the general public, but your great devotion and loyalty
to us has made it a pleasure for us not to deny ourselves to you.

KANCHI. It is truly hard for us, your Majesty, to bear the weight of your gracious favours.

"KING". We are afraid we shall not be able to stop here long.

KANCHI. I have thought so, already: you do not quite look up to it.

"KING". In the meantime if you have any favours to ask of us

KANCHI. We have: but we would like to speak a little more in private.

"KING". (to his attendants) Retire a little from our presence. (They retire.) Now you can
express your desires without any reserve.

KANCHI. There will be no reserve on our part-our only fear is that you might think restraint necessary for yourself.

"KING". Oh no, you need have no scruples on that score.

KANCHI. Come, then, do us homage by placing your head on the ground before us.

"KING". It seems my servants have distributed the Varuni spirits too liberally in the reception camps.

KANCHI. False pretender, it is you who are suffering from an overdose of arrogant spirits. Your head will soon kiss the dust.

"KING". Princes, these heavy jokes are not worthy of a king.

KANCHI. Those who will jest properly with you are near at hand.
General!

"KING". No more, I entreat you. I can see plainly I owe homage to you all. The head is bowing down of itself-there is no need for the application of any sharp methods to lay it low. So here I do my obeisance to you all. If you kindly allow me to escape I shall not inflict my presence long on you.

KANCHI. Why should you escape? We will make you king of this place-let us carry our joke to its legitimate finish. Have you got any following?

"KING". I have. Every one who sees me in the streets flocks after me. When I had a meagre retinue at first every one regarded me with suspicion, but now with the increasing crowd their doubts are waning and dissolving. The crowd is being hypnotised by its own magnitude. I have not got to do anything now.

KANCHI. That's excellent! From this moment we all promise to help and stand by you. But you will have to do us one service in return.

"KING". Your commands and the crown you are putting on my head will be equally binding and sacred to me.

KANCHI. At present we want nothing more than a sight of the
Queen Sudarshana. You will have to see to this.

"KING". I shall spare no pains for that.

KANCHI. We cannot put much faith on your pains-you will be solely directed by our instructions. But now you can go and join the festivities in the royal arbour with all possible splendour and magnificence.(They go out.)
(Enter GRANDFATHER and a band of people)

FIRST CITIZEN. Grandfather, I cannot help saying-yes, and repeating it five hundred times-that our King is a perfect fraud.

GRANDFATHER. Why only five hundred times? There is no need to practise such heroic self-control —you can say it five thousand times if that adds to your pleasure.

SECOND CITIZEN. But you cannot keep up a dead lie forever.

GRANDFATHER. It has made me alive, my friend.

THIRD CITIZEN. We shall proclaim to the whole world that our
King is a lie, the merest and emptiest shadow!

FIRST CITIZEN. We shall all shout from our housetops that we have no King-let him do whatever he likes if he exists.

GRANDFATHER. He will do nothing at all.

SECOND CITIZEN. My son died untimely at twenty-five of raging fever in seven days. Could such a calamity befall me under the rule of a virtuous King?

GRANDFATHER. But you still have got two sons left: while I have lost all my five children one after another.

THIRD CITIZEN. What do you say now?

GRANDFATHER. What then? Shall I lose my King too because I have lost my children? Don't take me for such a big fool as that.

FIRST CITIZEN. It is a fine thing to argue whether there is a King or not when one is simply starving for want of food! Will the King save us?

GRANDFATHER. Brother, you are right. But why not *find* the King who owns all the food? You certainly will not find by your wailings at home.

SECOND CITIZEN. Look at the justice of our King! That Bhadrasen-you know what a touching sight he is when he is speaking of his King-the sentimental idiot! He is reduced to such a state of penury that even the bats that infest his house find it a too uncomfortable place.

GRANDFATHER. Why, look at me! I am toiling and slaving night and day for my King, but I have not yet received so much as a brass farthing for my pains.

THIRD CITIZEN. Now, what do you think of that?

GRANDFATHER. What should I think? Does any one reward his friends? Go, my friends, and say if you like that our King exists nowhere. That is also a part of our ceremony in celebrating this festival.

# IV

(Turret of the Royal Palace. SUDARSHANA and her friend ROHINI)

SUDARSHANA. You may make mistakes, Rohini, but I cannot be mistaken: am I not the Queen? That, of course, must be my King.

ROHINI. He who has conferred such high honour upon you cannot be long in showing himself to you.

SUDARSHANA. His very form makes me restless like a caged bird.
Did you try well to ascertain who he is?

ROHINI. Yes, I did. Every one I asked said that he was the King.

SUDARSHANA. What country is he the King of?

ROHINI. Our country, King of this land.

SUDARSHANA. Are you sure that you are speaking of him who has a sunshade made of flowers held over his head?

ROHINI. The same: he whose flag has the *Kimshuk* flower painted on it.

SUDARSHANA. I recognised him at once, of course, but it is you who had your doubts.

ROHINI. We are apt to make mistakes, my Queen, and we are afraid to offend you in case we are wrong.

SUDARSHANA. Would that Surangama were here! There would remain no room for doubt then.

ROHINI. Do you think her cleverer than any of us?

SUDARSHANA. Oh no, but she would recognise him instantly.

ROHINI. I cannot believe that she would. She merely pretends to know him. There is none to test her knowledge if she professes to know the King. If we were as shameless as she is, it would not have been difficult for us to boast about our acquaintance with the King.

SUDARSHANA. But no, she never boasts.

ROHINI. It is pure affectation, the whole of it: which often goes a longer way than open boasting. She is up to all manner of tricks: that is why we could never like her.

SUDARSHANA. But whatever you may say, I should have liked to ask her if she were here.

ROHINI. Very well, Queen. I shall bring her here. She must be lucky if she is indispensable for the Queen to know the King.

SUDARSHANA. Oh no-it isn't for that-but I would like to hear it said by every one.

ROHINI. Is not every one saying it? Why, just listen, the acclamations of the people mount up even to this height!

SUDARSHANA. Then do one thing: put these flowers on a lotus leaf, and take them to him.

ROHINI. And what am I to say if he asks who sends them?

SUDARSHANA. You will not have to say anything-he will know. He thought that I would not be able to recognise him: I cannot let him off without showing that I have found him out. (ROHINI goes out with the flowers.)

SUDARSHANA. My heart is all a-quiver and restless to-night: I have never felt like this before. The white, silver light of the full moon is flooding the heavens and brimming over on every side like the bubbling foam of wine,... It seizes on me like a yearning, like a mantling intoxication. Here, who is here?

(Enter a SERVANT)

SERVANT. What is your pleasure, your Majesty?

SUDARSHANA. Do you see those festive boys singing and moving through the alleys and avenues of the mango trees? Call them hither, bring them to me: I want to hear them sing. (SERVANT goes out and enters with the boys.) Come, living emblems of youthful spring, begin your festive song! All my mind and body is song and music to-night —but the ineffable melody escapes my tongue: do you then sing for my sake!

## SONG.

My sorrow is sweet to me in this spring night.
My pain smites at the chords of my love and softly sings.
Visions take birth from my yearning eyes and flit in the
moonlit sky.
The smells from the depths of the woodlands have lost their way
in my dreams.
Words come in whispers to my ears, I know not from where,
And bells in my anklets tremble and jingle in time with my
heart thrills.

SUDARSHANA. Enough, enough —I cannot bear it any more! Your song has filled my eyes with tears.... A fancy comes to me-that desire can never attain its object-it need never attain it. What sweet hermit of the woods has taught you this song? Oh that my eyes could see him whose song my ears have heard! Oh, how I wish —I wish I could wander rapt and lovely in the thick woodland arbours of the heart! Dear boys of the hermitage! how shall I reward you? This necklace is but made of jewels, hard stones — its hardness will give you pain —I have got nothing like the garlands of flowers you have on. (The boys bow and go out.)

(Enter ROHINI)

SUDARSHANA. I have not done well —I have not done well, Rohini. I feel ashamed to ask you what happened. I have just realised that no hand can really give the greatest of gifts. Still, let me hear all.

ROHINI. When I gave the King those flowers, he did not appear to understand anything.

SUDARSHANA. You don't say so? He did not understand

ROHINI. No; he sat there like a doll, without uttering a single word. I think he did not want to show that he understood nothing, so he just held his tongue.

SUDARSHANA. Fie on me! My shamelessness has been justly punished. Why did you not bring back my flowers?

ROHINI. How could I? The King of Kanchi, a very clever man, who was sitting by him, took in everything at a glance, and he just smiled a bit and said, "Emperor, the Queen Sudarshana sends your Majesty her greetings with these blossoms-the blossoms that belong to the God of Love, the friend of Spring." The King seemed to awake with a start, and said, "This is the crown of all my regal glory to-night." I was coming back, all out of countenance, when the King of Kanchi took off this necklace of jewels from the King's person, and said to me, "Friend, the King's garland gives itself up to you, in return for the happy fortune you have brought."

SUDARSHANA. What, Kanchi had to make the King understand all this! Woe is me, to-night's festival has opened wide for me the doors of ignominy and shame! What else could I expect? Leave me alone, Rohini; I want solitude for a time. (ROHINI goes out.) A great blow has shattered my pride to atoms to-day, and yet...I cannot efface from my mind that beautiful, fascinating figure! No pride is left me —I am beaten, vanquished, utterly helpless.... I cannot even turn away from him. Oh, how the wish comes back to me again and again-to ask that garland of Rohini! But what would she think! Rohini!

(Enter ROHINI)

ROHINI. What is your wish?

SUDARSHANA. What reward do you deserve for your services to-day?

ROHINI. Nothing from you-but I had my reward from the King as it should be.

SUDARSHANA. That is no free gift, but an extortion, of reward. I do not like to see you put on what was given in so indifferent a manner. Take it off—I give you my bracelets if you leave it here. Take these bracelets, and go now. (ROHINI goes out.) Another defeat! I should have thrown this necklace away, —but I could not! It is pricking me as if it were a garland of thorns — but I cannot throw it away. This is what the god of the festival has brought me to-night —this necklace of ignominy and shame!

## V

(GRANDFATHER near the door of the Pleasure House. A Company of MEN)

GRANDFATHER. Have you had enough of it, friends?

FIRST MAN. Oh, more than that, Grandpa. Just see, they have made me red all over. None has escaped.

(Author's note: During the spring festival in India people throw red powder on each other. In this play this red powder has been taken to be the symbol of the passion of love.)

GRANDFATHER. No? Did they throw the red dust on the Kings too?

SECOND MAN. But who could approach them? They were all secure inside the enclosures.

GRANDFATHER. So they have escaped you! Could you not throw the least bit of colour on them? You should have forced your way there.

THIRD MAN. My dear old man, they have a different sort of red specially to themselves. Their eyes are red: the turbans of their guards and retinue are red too. And the latter flourished their swords about so much that a little more nearness on our part would have meant a lavish display of the fundamental red colour.

GRANDFATHER. Well done, friends-always keep them at a distance. They are the exiles of the Earth-and we have got to keep them so.

THIRD MAN. I am going home, Grandpa; it is past midnight.(Goes out.)
(Enter a BAND of SINGERS, singing.)

All blacks and whites have lost their distinction
And have become red-red as the tinge of your feet.
Red is my bodice and red are my dreams,
My heart sways and trembles like a red lotus.

GRANDFATHER. Excellent, my friends, splendid! So you had a really enjoyable time!

SINGERS. Oh, grand! Everything was red, red! Only the moon in the sky gave us the slip-it remained white.

GRANDFATHER. He only looks so innocent from the outside. If you had only taken off his white disguise, you would have seen his trickery. I have been watching what red colours he is throwing on the Earth to-night. And yet, fancy his remaining white and colourless all the while!


## SONG.

With you is my game, love, my love!
My heart is mad, it will never own defeat,
Do you think you will escape stainless yourself reddening me
with red powder?
Could I not colour your robe with the red pollens of the
blossom of my heart?

(They go out.)
(Enter the "KING" and KANCHI.)

KANCHI. You must do exactly as I have told you. Let there be no mistake of any kind.

"KING". There shall be no mistake.

KANCHI. The Queen Sudarshana's mansions are in the...

"KING". Yes, sire, I have seen the place well.

KANCHI. What you have got to do is to set fire to the garden, and then you will take advantage of the bustle and confusion to accomplish your object straightway.

"KING". I shall remember.

KANCHI. Look here, Sir Pretender, I cannot help thinking that a needless fear is troubling us-there is really no King in this country.

"KING". My sole aim is to rid this country of this anarchy. Your common man cannot live without a King, whether a real one or a fraud! Anarchy is always a source of danger.

KANCHI. Pious benefactor of the people, your wonderful self- sacrifice should really be an example to all of us. I am thinking of doing this extraordinary service to the people myself. (They go out.)

## VI

ROHINI. What is the matter? I cannot make out what is all this!
(To the GARDENERS.) Where are you all going away in such a hurry?

FIRST GARDENER. We are going out of the garden.

ROHINI. Where?

SECOND GARDENER. We do not know where-the King has called us.

ROHINI. Why, the King is in the garden. Which King has called you?

FIRST GARDENER. We cannot say.

SECOND GARDENER. The King we have been serving all our life, of course.

ROHINI. Will you all go?

FIRST GARDENER. Yes, all-we have to go instantly. Otherwise we might get into trouble.
(They go out.)

ROHINI. I cannot understand their words.... I am afraid. They are scampering off like wild animals that fly just before the bank of a river breaks down into the water.
(Enter KING OF KOSHALA)

KOSHALA. Rohini, do you know where your King and Kanchi have gone?

ROHINI. They are somewhere in the garden, but I could not tell you where.

KOSHALA. I cannot really understand their intentions. I have not done well to put my trust in Kanchi. (Exit.)

ROHINI. What is this dark affair going on amongst these kings? Something dreadful is going to happen soon. Shall I too be drawn into this affair? (Enter AVANTI)

AVANTI. Rohini, do you know where the other princes are?

ROHINI. It is difficult to say which of them is where. The King of Koshala just passed by in this direction.

AVANTI. I am not thinking of Koshala. Where are your King and
Kanchi?

ROHINI. I have not seen them for a long time.

AVANTI. Kanchi is always avoiding us. He is certainly planning to deceive us all. I have not done well to put my hand in this imbroglio. Friend, could you kindly tell me any way out of this garden?

ROHINI. I have none.

AVANTI. Is there no man here who will show me the way out?

ROHINI. The servants have all left the garden.

AVANTI. Why did they do so?

ROHINI. I could not exactly understand what they meant. They said the King had commanded them to leave the garden at once.

AVANTI. King? Which King? Rohini They could not say exactly.

AVANTI. This does not sound well. I shall have to find a way out at any cost. I cannot stay here a single moment more. (Goes out hurriedly.)

ROHINI. Where shall I find the King? When I gave him the flowers the Queen had sent, he did not seem much interested in me at the time; but ever since that hour he has been showering gifts and presents on me. This causeless generosity makes me more afraid.... Where are the birds flying at such an hour of the night? What has frightened them all of a sudden? This is not the usual time of their flight, certainly,... Why is the Queen's pet deer running that way? Chapata! Chapata! She does not even hear my call. I have never seen a night like this! The horizon on every side suddenly becomes red, like a madman's eye! The sun seems to be setting at this untimely hour on all sides at the same time. What madness of the Almighty is this!... Oh, I am frightened!... Where shall I find the King?

# VII

(At the Door of the QUEEN'S Palace)

"KING". What is this you have done, Kanchi?

KANCHI. I wanted to fire only this part of the garden near the palace. I had no idea that it would spread so quickly on all sides. Tell me, quick, the way out of this garden.

"KING". I can tell you nothing about it. Those who brought us here have all fled away.

KANCHI. You are a native of this country-you must know the way.

"KING". I have never entered these inner royal gardens before.

KANCHI. I won't hear of it-you must show me the way, or I shall split you into halves.

"KING". You may take my life by that means, but it would be a very precarious method of finding the way out of this garden.

KANCHI. Why were you, then, going about saying that you were the King of this country?

"KING". I am not the King —I am not the King. (Throwing himself on the ground with folded hands.) Where art thou, my King? Save me, oh, save me! I am a rebel-punish me, but do not kill me!

KANCHI. What is the use of shouting and cringing to the empty air? It is a much better way of spending the time to search for the way.

"KING". I shall lie down here —I shall not move an inch. Come what will, I shall not complain.

KANCHI. I will not allow all this nonsense. If I am to be burnt to death, you will be my companion to the very end.

FROM THE OUTSIDE. Oh, save us, save us, our King! The fire is on all sides of us!

KANCHI. Fool, get up, lose no more time.

SUDARSHANA. (entering) King, O my King! save me, save me from death! I am surrounded by fire.

"KING". Who is the King? I am no King.

SUDARSHANA. You are not the King?

"KING". No, I am a hypocrite, I am a scoundrel. (Flinging his crown on the ground.) Let my deception and hypocrisy be shattered into dust! (Goes out with KANCHI.)

SUDARSHANA. No King! He is not the King? Then, O thou God of fire, burn me, reduce me to ashes! I shall throw myself into thy hands, O thou great purifier; burn to ashes my shame, my longing, my desire.

ROHINI. (entering) Queen, where are you going? All your inner chambers are shrouded in raging fire-do you not enter there.

SUDARSHANA. Yes! I will enter those burning chambers! It is the fire of my death! (Enters the Palace.)

# VIII

(The Dark Room. The KING and SUDARSRANA)

KING. Do not be afraid-you have no cause for fear. The fire will not reach this room.

SUDARSHANA. I have no fear-but oh, shame has accompanied me like a raging fire. My face, my eyes, my heart, every part of my body is being scorched and burnt by its flames.

KING. It will be some time before you get over this burning.

SUDARSHANA. This fire will never cease-will never cease!

KING. Do not be despondent, Queen!

SUDARSHANA. O King, I shall not hide anything from you.... I have another's garland round my neck.

KING. That garland, too, is mine-how else could he get it? He stole it from my room.

SUDARSHANA. But it is *his* gift to me: yet I could not fling this garland away! When the fire came roaring on all sides of me, I thought of throwing this garland into the fire. But no, I could not. My mind whispered, "Let that garland be on you in your death.".... What fire is this, O King, into which I, who had come out to see you, leaped like a moth that cannot resist the flame? What a pain is this, oh, what agony! The fire keeps burning as fiercely as ever, but I go on living within its flames!

KING. But you have seen me at last-your desire has been fulfilled.

SUDARSHANA. But did I seek to see you in the midst of this fearful doom? I know not what I saw, but my heart is still beating fast with fear.

KING. What did you see?

SUDARSHANA. Terrible, —oh, it was terrible! I am afraid even to think of it again. Black, black-oh, thou art black like the everlasting night! I only looked on thee for one dreadful instant. The blaze of the fire fell on your features-you looked like the awful night when a comet swings fearfully into our ken — oh, then I closed my eyes —I could not look on you any more. Black as the threatening storm-cloud, black as the shoreless sea with the spectral red tint of twilight on its tumultuous waves!

KING. Have I not told you before that one cannot bear my sight unless one is already prepared for me? One would want to run away from me to the ends of the earth. Have I not seen this times without number? That is why I wanted to reveal myself to you slowly and gradually, not all too sudden.

SUDARSHANA. But sin came and destroyed all your hopes-the very possibility of a union with you has now become unthinkable to me.

KING. It will be possible in time, my Queen. The utter and bleak blackness that has to-day shaken you to your soul with fear will one day be your solace and salvation. What else can my love exist for?

SUDARSHANA. It cannot be, it is not possible. What will your love only do? *My* love has now turned away from you. Beauty has cast its spell on me-this frenzy, this intoxication will never leave me-it has dazzled and fired my eyes, it has thrown its golden glamour over my very dreams! I have told you all now-punish me as you like.

KING. The punishment has already begun.

SUDARSHANA. But if you do not cast me off. I will leave you

KING. You have the utmost liberty to do as you like.

SUDARSHANA. I cannot bear your presence! My heart is angry at you. Why did you-but what have you done to me?...Why are you like this? Why did they tell me you were fair and handsome? Thou art black, black as night —I shall never, I can never, like you. I have seen what I love-it is soft as cream, delicate as the *shirisha* flower, beautiful as a butterfly.

KING. It is false as a mirage, empty as a bubble.

SUDARSHANA. Let it be-but I cannot stand near you —I simply cannot! I must fly away from here. Union with you, it cannot be possible! It cannot be anything but a false union-my mind must inevitably turn away from you.

KING. Will you not even try a little?

SUDARSHANA. I have been trying since yesterday-but the more I try, the more rebellious does my heart become. If I stay with you I shall constantly be pursued and hounded by the thought that I am impure, that I am false and faithless.

KING. Well then, you can go as far from me as you like.

SUDARSHANA. I cannot fly away from you-just because you do not prevent my going. Why do you not hold me back, hold me by the hair, saying, "You shall not go"? Why do you not strike me? Oh, punish me, strike me, beat me with violent hands! But your unresisting silence makes me wild-oh, I cannot bear it!

KING. How do you think that I am really silent? How do you know that I am not trying to keep you back?

SUDARSHANA. Oh, no, no ! —I cannot bear this-tell me aloud, command me with the voice of thunder, compel me with words that will drown everything else in my ears-do not let me off so easily, so mildly!

KING. I shall leave you free, but why should I let you break away from me?

SUDARSHANA. You will not let me? Well then, I must go!

KING. Go then!

SUDARSHANA. Then I am not to blame at all. You could have held me back by force, but you did not! You have not hindered me-and now I shall go away. Command your sentinels to prevent my going.

KING. No one will stand in your way. You can go as free as the broken storm-cloud driven by the tempest.

SUDARSHANA. I can resist no more-something in me is impelling me forward —I am breaking away from my anchor! Perhaps I shall sink, but I shall return no more. (She rushes out.)

(Enter SURANGAMA, who sings)

SURANGAMA. What will of thine is this that sends me afar! Again shall I come back at thy feet from all my wanderings. It is thy love that feigns this neglect-thy caressing hands are pushing me away-to draw me back to thy arms again! O my King, what is this game that thou art playing throughout thy kingdom?

SUDARSHANA. (re-entering) King, O King!

SURANGAMA. He has gone away.

SUDARSHANA. Gone away? Well then,…then he has cast me off for good! I have come back, but he could not wait a single instant for me! Very well, then, I am now perfectly free. Surangama, did he ask you to keep me back?

SURANGAMA. No, he said nothing.

SUDARSHANA. Why should he say anything? Why should he care for me?…I am then free, perfectly free. But, Surangama, I wanted to ask one thing of the King, but could not utter it in his presence. Tell me if he has punished the prisoners with death.

SURANGAMA. Death? My King never punishes with death.

SUDARSHANA. What has he done to them, then?

SURANGAMA. He has set them at liberty. Kanchi has acknowledged his defeat and gone back to his kingdom.

SUDARSHANA. Ah, what a relief!

SURANGAMA. My Queen, I have one prayer to make to you.

SUDARSHANA. You will not have to utter your prayer in words, Surangama. Whatever jewellery and ornaments the King gave me, I leave to you —I am not worthy to wear them now.

SURANGAMA. No, I do not want them, my Queen. My master has never given me any ornaments to wear-my unadorned plainness is good enough for me. He has not given me anything of which I can boast before people.

SUDARSHANA. What do you want of me then?

SURANGAMA. I too shall go with you, my Queen.

SUDARSHANA. Consider what you are saying; you are wanting to leave your master. What a prayer for you to make!

SURANGAMA. I shall not go far from him-when you are going out unguarded he will be with you, close by your side.

SUDARSHANA. You are talking nonsense, my child. I wanted to take Rohini with me, but she would not come. What gives you courage enough to wish to come with me?

SURANGAMA. I have got neither courage nor strength. But I shall go-courage will come of itself, and strength too will come.

SUDARSHANA. No, I cannot take you with me; your presence will constantly remind me of my shame; I shall not be able to endure that.

SURANGAMA. O my Queen, I have made all your good and all your evil my own as well; will you treat me as a stranger still? I must go with you.

## IX

(The KING OF KANYA KUBJA, father of SUDARSHANA, and his MINISTER)

KING OF KANYA KUBJA. I heard everything before her arrival.

MINISTER. The princess is waiting alone outside the city gates on the bank of the river. Shall I send people to welcome her home?

KING OF KANYA KUBJA. What! She who has faithlessly left her husband-do you propose trumpeting her infamy and shame to every one by getting up a show for her?

MINISTER. Shall I then make arrangements for her residence at the palace?

KING OF KANYA KUBJA. You will do nothing of the sort. She has left her place as the Empress of her own accord-here she will have to work as a maid-servant if she wants to stay in my house.

MINISTER. It will be hard and bitter to her, Your Highness.

KING OF KANYA KUBJA. If I seek to save her from her sufferings, then I am not worthy to be her father.

MINISTER. I shall arrange everything as you wish, Your Highness.

KING OF KANYA KUBJA. Let it be kept a secret that she is my daughter; otherwise we shall all be in an awful trouble.

MINISTER. Why do you fear such disaster, Your Highness?

KING OF KANYA KUBJA. When woman swerves from the right path, then she appears fraught with the direst calamity. You do not know with what deadly fear this daughter of mine has inspired me-she is coming to my home laden with peril and danger.

# X

(Inner Apartments of the Palace. SUDARSHANA and SURANGAMA)

SUDARSHANA. Go away from me, Surangama! A deadly anger rages within me —I cannot bear anybody-it makes me wild to see you so patient and submissive.

SURANGAMA. Whom are you angry with?

SUDARSHANA. I do not know; but I wish to see everything destroyed and convulsed in ruin and disaster! I left my place on the throne as the Empress in a moment's time. Did I lose my all to sweep the dust, to sweat and slave in this dismal hole? Why do the torches of mourning not flare up for me all over the world? Why does not the earth quake and tremble? Is my fall but the unobserved dropping of the puny bean-flower? Is it not more like the fall of a glowing star, whose fiery blazon bursts the heavens asunder?

SURANGAMA. A mighty forest only smokes and smoulders before it bursts into a conflagration: the time has not come yet.

SUDARSHANA. I have thrown my queen's honour and glory to the dust and winds-but is there no human being who will come out to meet my desolate soul here? Alone-oh, I am fearfully, terribly alone!

SURANGAMA. You are not alone.

SUDARSHANA. Surangama, I shall not keep anything from you. When he set the palace on fire, I could not be angry with him. A great inward joy set my heart a-flutter all the while. What a stupendous crime! What glorious prowess! It was this courage that made me strong and fired my own spirits. It was this terrible joy that enabled me to leave everything behind me in a moment's time. But is it all my imagination only? Why is there no sign of his coming anywhere?

SURANGAMA. He of whom you are thinking did not set fire to the palace-it is the King of Kanchi who did it.

SUDARSHANA. Coward! But is it possible? So handsome, so bewitching, and yet no manhood in him! Have I deceived myself for the sake of such a worthless creature? O shame! Fie on me!...But, Surangama, don't you think that your King should yet have come to take me back? (SURANGAMA remains silent.) You think I am anxious to go back? Never! Even if the King really came I should not have returned. Not even once did he forbid me to come away, and I found all the doors wide open to let me out! And the stony and dusty road over which I walked-it was nothing to it that a queen was treading on it. It is hard and has no feelings, like your King; the meanest beggar is the same to it as the highest Empress. You are silent! Well, I tell you, your King's behaviour is-mean, brutal, shameful!

SURANGAMA. Every one knows that my King is hard and pitiless-no one has ever been able to move him.

SUDARSHANA. Why do you, then, call him day and night?

SURANGAMA. May he ever remain hard and relentless like rock-may my tears and prayers never move him! Let my sorrows be ever mine only-and may his glory and victory be for ever!

SUDARSHANA. Surangama, look! A cloud of dust seems to rise over the eastern horizon across the fields.

SURANGAMA. Yes, I see it.

SUDARSHANA. Is that not like the banner of a chariot?

SURANGAMA. Indeed, a banner it is.

SUDARSHANA. Then he is coming. He has come at last!

SURANGAMA. Who is coming?

SUDARSHANA. Our King-who else? How could he live without me?
It is a wonder how he could hold out even for these days.

SURANGAMA. No, no, this cannot be the King.

SUDARSHANA. "No," indeed! As if you know everything! Your King is hard, stony,
pitiless, isn't he? Let us see how hard he can be. I knew from the beginning that he would
come-that he would have to rush after me. But remember, Surangama, I never for a single
moment asked him to come. You will see how I make your King confess his defeat to me!
Just go out, Surangama, and let me know everything. (SURANGAMA goes out.) But
shall I go if he comes and asks me to return with him? Certainly not! I will not go! Never!

(Enter SURANGAMA)

SURANGAMA. It is not the King, my Queen.

SUDARSHANA. Not the King? Are you quite sure? What! he has not come yet?

SURANGAMA. No, my King never raises so much dust when he comes.
Nobody can know when he comes at all.

SUDARSHANA. Then this is —

SURANGAMA. The same: he is coming with the King of Kanchi.

SUDARSHANA. Do you know his name?

SURANGAMA. His name is Suvarna.

SUDARSHANA. It is he, then. I thought, "I am lying here like waste refuse and offal,
which no one cares even to touch." But my hero is coming now to release me. Did you
know Suvarna?

SURANGAMA. When I was at my father's home, in the gambling den

SUDARSHANA. No, no, I won't hear anything of him from you. He is my own hero,
my only salvation. I shall know him without your telling stories about him. But just see, a
nice man your King is! He did not care to come to rescue me from even this degradation.
You cannot blame me after this. I could not have waited for him all my life here, toiling
ignominiously like a bondslave. I shall never have *your* meekness and submissiveness.

## XI

(Encampment)

KANCHI. (To KANYA KUBJA'S MESSENGER.) Tell your King that he need not receive us exactly as his guests. We are on our way back to our kingdoms, but we are waiting to rescue Queen Sudarshana from the servitude and degradation to which she is condemned here.

MESSENGER. Your Highness, you will remember that the princess is in her father's house.

KANCHI. A daughter may stay in her father's home only so long as she remains unmarried.

MESSENGER. But her connections with her father's family remain intact still.

KANCHI. She has abjured all such relations now.

MESSENGER. Such relationship can never be abjured, Your Highness, on this side of death: it may remain in abeyance at times, but can never be wholly broken up.

KANCHI. If the King chooses not to give up his daughter to me on peaceful terms, our *Kshatriya* code of righteousness will oblige me to employ force. You may take this as my last word.

MESSENGER. Your Highness, do not forget that our King too is bound by the same code. It is idle to expect that he will deliver up his daughter by merely hearing your threats.

KANCHI. Tell your King that I have come prepared for such an answer. (MESSENGER goes out.)

SUVARNA. King of Kanchi, it seems to me that we are daring too much.

KANCHI. What pleasure would there be in this adventure if it were otherwise?

SUVARNA. It does not cost much courage to challenge Kanya Kubja-but...

KANCHI. If you once begin to be afraid of "but," you will hardly find a place in this world safe enough for you.

(Enter a SOLDIER)

SOLDIER. Your Highness! I have just received the news that the Kings of Koshala, Avanti, and Kalinga are coming this way with their armies. (Exit.)

KANCHI. Just what I was afraid of! The report of Sudarshana's flight has spread abroad-now we are going to be in for a general scramble which is sure to end in smoke.

SUVARNA. It is useless now, Your Highness. These are not good tidings. I am perfectly certain that it is our Emperor himself who has secretly spread the report everywhere.

KANCHI. Why, what good will it bring him?

SUVARNA. The greedy ones will tear one another to pieces in the general rivalry and scramble-and he will take advantage of the situation to go back with the booty.

KANCHI. Now it becomes clear why your King never shows himself. His trick is to multiply himself on every side-fear makes him visible everywhere. But I will still maintain that your King is but an empty fraud from top to bottom.

SUVARNA. But, please Your Highness, will you have the kindness to let me off?

KANCHI. I cannot let you go —I have some use for you in this affair.

(Enter a SOLDIER)

SOLDIER. Your Highness, Virat, Panchal, and Vidarbha too have come. They have en-camped on the other side of the river.(Exit.)

KANCHI. In the beginning we must all fight together. Let the battle with Kanya Kubja first be over, then we shall find some way out of the difficulty.

SUVARNA. Please do not drag me into your plans —I shall be happy if you leave me alone —I am a poor, mean creature-nothing can —

KANCHI. Look here, king of hypocrites, ways and means are never of a very exalted order-roads and stairs and so forth are always to be trodden under our feet. The advantage of utilising men like you in our plans is that we have to make use of no mask or illusion. But if I were to consult my prime minister, it would be absurd for me to call theft by any name less dignified than public benefit. I will go now, and move the princes about like pawns on the chessboard; the game cannot evidently go on if all the chessmen propose moving like kings!

## XII

(Interior of the Palace)

SUDARSHANA. Is the fight still going on?

SURANGAMA. As fiercely as ever.

SUDARSHANA. Before going out to the battle my father came to me and said, "You have come away from one King, but you have drawn seven Kings after you: I have a mind to cut you up into seven pieces and distribute them among the princes. It would have been well if he did so. Surangama!

SURANGAMA. Yes?

SUDARSHANA. If your King had the power to save me, could my present state have left him unmoved?

SURANGAMA. My Queen, why do you ask me? Have I the power to answer for my King? I know my understanding is dark; that is why I never dare to judge him.

SUDARSHANA. Who have joined in this fight?

SURANGAMA. All the seven princes.

SUDARSHANA. No one else?

SURANGAMA. Suvarna attempted to escape-in secret before the fight began-but Kanchi has kept him a prisoner in his camps.

SUDARSHANA. Oh, I should have been dead long ago! But, O King, my King, if you had come and helped my father, your fame would have been none the less! It would have become brighter and higher. Are you quite sure, Surangama, that he has not come?

SURANGAMA. I know nothing for certain.

SUDARSHANA. But since I came here I have felt suddenly many a time as if somebody were playing on a *vina* below my window.

SURANGAMA. There is nothing impossible in the idea that somebody indulges his taste for music there.

SUDARSHANA. There is a deep thicket below my window —I try to find out who it is every time I hear the music, but I can see nothing distinctly.

SURANGAMA. Perhaps some wayfarer rests in the shade and plays on the instrument.

SUDARSHANA. It may be so, but my old window in the palace comes back to my memory. I used to come after dressing in the evening and stand at my window, and out of the blank darkness of our lampless meeting-place used to stream forth strains and songs and melodies, dancing and vibrating in endless succession and overflowing profusion, like the passionate exuberance of a ceaseless fountain!

SURANGAMA. O deep and sweet darkness! the profound and mystic darkness whose servant I was!

SUDARSHANA. Why did you come away with me from that room?

SURANGAMA. Because I knew he would follow us and take us back.

SUDARSHANA. But no, he will not come-he has left us for good. Why should he not?

SURANGAMA. If he can leave us like that, then we have no need of him. Then he does not exist for us: then that dark chamber is totally empty and void-no vina ever breathed its music there — none called you or me in that chamber; then everything has been a delusion and an idle dream.

(Enter the DOORKEEPER)

SUDARSHANA. Who are you?

DOORKEEPER. I am the porter of this palace.

SUDARSHANA. Tell me quickly what you have got to say.

DOORKEEPER. Our King has been taken prisoner.

SUDARSHANA. Prisoner? O Mother Earth! (Faints.)

## XIII

(KING OF KANCHI and SUVARNA)

SUVARNA. You say, then, that there will be no more necessity of any fight amongst yourselves?

KANCHI. No, you need not be afraid. I have made all the princes agree that he whom the Queen accepts as her husband will have her, and the others will have to abandon all further struggle.

SUVARNA. But you must have done with me now, Your Highness-so I beg to be let off now. Unfit as I am for anything, the fear of impending danger has unnerved me and stunned my intellect. You will therefore find it difficult to put me to any use.

KANCHI. You will have to sit there as my umbrella-holder.

SUVARNA. Your servant is ready for anything; but of what profit will that be to you?

KANCHI. My man, I see that your weak intellect cannot go with a high ambition in you. You have no notion yet with what favour the Queen looked upon you. After all, she cannot possibly throw the bridal garland on an umbrella-bearer's neck in a company of princes, and yet, I know, she will not be able to turn her mind away from you. So on all accounts this garland will fall under the shade of my regal umbrella.

SUVARNA. Your Highness, you are entertaining dangerous imaginings about me. I pray you, please do not implicate me in the toils of such groundless notions. I beg Your Highness most humbly, pray set me at liberty.

KANCHI. As soon as my object is attained, I shall not keep you one moment from your liberty. Once the end is attained, it is futile to burden oneself with the means.

(SUDARSHANA and SURANGAMA at the Window)

SUDARSHANA. Must I go to the assembly of the princes, then? Is there no other means of saving father's life?

SURANGAMA. The King of Kanchi has said so.

SUDARSHANA . Are these the words worthy of a King? Did he say so with his own lips?

SURANGAMA. No, his messenger, Suvarna, brought this news.

SUDARSHANA. Woe, woe is me!

SURANGAMA. And he produced a few withered flowers and said, "Tell your Queen that the drier and more withered these souvenirs of the Spring Festival become, the fresher and more blooming do they grow within in my heart."

SUDARSHANA. Stop! Tell me no more. Do not torment me any more.

SURANGAMA. Look! There sit all the princes in the great assembly. He who has no ornament on his person, except a single garland of flowers round his crown-he is the King of Kanchi. And he who holds the umbrella over his head, standing behind him-that is Suvarna.

SUDARSHANA. Is that Suvarna? Are you quite certain?

SURANGAMA. Yes, I know him well.

SUDARSHANA. Can it be that it is this man that I saw the other day? No, no, —I saw something mingled and transfused and blended with light and darkness, with wind and perfume, —no, no, it cannot be he; that is not he.

SURANGAMA. But every one admits that he is exceedingly beautiful to look at.

SUDARSHANA. How could that beauty fascinate me? Oh, what shall I do to purge my eyes of their pollution?

SURANGAMA. You will have to wash them in that bottomless darkness.

SUDARSHANA. But tell me, Surangama, why does one make such mistakes?

SURANGAMA. Mistakes are but the preludes to their own destruction.

MESSENGER. (entering) Princess, the Kings are waiting for you in the hall. (Exit.)

SUDARSHANA. Surangama, bring me the veil. (SURANGAMA goes out.) O King, my only King! You have left me alone, and you have been but just in doing so. But will you not know the inmost truth within my soul? (Taking out a dagger from within her bosom.) This body of mine has received a stain —I shall make a sacrifice of it to-day in the dust of the hall, before all these princes! But shall I never be able to tell you that I know of no stain of faithlessness within the hidden chambers of my heart? That dark chamber where you would come to meet me lies cold and empty within my bosom to-day —but, O my Lord! none has opened its doors, none has entered it but you, O King! Will you never come again to open those doors? Then, let death come, for it is dark like yourself, and its features are beautiful as yours . It is you-it is yourself, O King!

(The Gathering of the PRINCES)

VIDARBHA. King of Kanchi, how is it that you have not got a single piece of ornament on your person?

KANCHI. Because I entertain no hopes at all, my friend.
Ornaments would but double the shame of my defeat.

KALINGA. But your umbrella-bearer seems to have made up for that, —he is loaded with gold and jewellery all over.

VIRAT. The King of Kanchi wants to demonstrate the futility and inferiority of outer beauty and grandeur. Vanity of his prowess has made him discard all outer embellishments from his limbs.

KOSLIALA. I am quite up to his trickery; he is seeking to prove his own dignity, maintaining a severe plainness among the bejewelled princes.

PANCHALA. I cannot commend his wisdom in this matter. Every one knows that a woman's eyes are like a moth in that they fling themselves headlong on the glare and glitter of jewel and gold.

KALINGA. But how long shall we have to wait more?

KANCHI. Do not grow impatient, King of Kalinga-sweet are the fruits of delay.

KALINGA. If I were sure of the fruit I could have endured it. It is because my hopes of tasting the fruit are extremely precarious that my eagerness to have a sight of her breaks through all bounds.

KANCHI. But you are young still-abandoned hope comes back to you again and again like a shameless woman at your age: we, however, have long passed that stage.

KOSHALA. Kanchi, did you feel as if something shook your seat just now? Is it an earthquake?

KANCHI. Earthquake? I do not know.

VIDARBHA. Or perhaps some other prince is coming with his army.

KALINGA. There is nothing against your theory except that we should have first heard the news from some herald or messenger in that case.

VIDARBHA. I cannot regard this as a very auspicious omen.

KANCHI. Everything looks inauspicious to the eye of fear.

VIDARBHA. I fear none except Fate, before which courage or heroism is as futile as it is absurd.

PANCHALA. Vidarbha, do not darken to-day's happy proceedings with your unwelcome prognostications.

KANCHI. I never take the unseen into account till it has become "seen."

VIDARBHA. But then it might be too late to do anything.

PANCHALA. Did we not all of us start at a specially auspicious moment?

VIDARBHA. Do you think you insure against every possible risk by starting at auspicious moments? It looks as if —

KANCHI. You had better let the "as if" alone: though our own creation, it often proves our ruin and destruction.

KALINGA. Isn't that music somewhere outside?

PANCHALA. Yes, it sounds like music, sure enough.

KANCHI. Then at last it must be the Queen Sudarshana who is approaching near. (Aside to SUVARNA.) Suvarna, you must not hide and cower behind me like that. Mind, the umbrella in your hand is shaking!

(Enter GRANDFATHER, dressed as a warrior)

KALINGA. Who is that? —Who are you?

PANCHALA. Who is this that dares to enter this hall without being invited?

VIRAT. Amazing impudence! Kalinga, just prevent the fellow from advancing further.

KALINGA. You are all my superiors in age-you are fitter to do that than myself.

VIDARBHA. Let us hear what he has to say.

GRANDFATHER. The KING has come.

VIDARBHA. (starting) King?

PANCHALA. Which King?

KALINGA. Where does he come from?

GRANDFATHER. My King!

VIRAT. Your King?

KALINGA. Who is he?

KOSHALA. What do you mean?

GRANDFATHER. You all know whom I mean. He has come.

VIDARBHA. He has come?

KOSHALA. With what intention?

GRANDFATHER. He has summoned you all to come to him.

KANCHI. Summoned us, indeed? In what terms has he been pleased to summon us?

GRANDFATHER. You can take his call in any way you like-there is none to prevent you-he is prepared to make all kinds of welcome to suit your various tastes.

VIRAT. But who are you?

GRANDFATHER. I am one of his generals.

KANCHI. Generals? It is a lie! Do you think of frightening us? Do you imagine that I cannot see through your disguise? We all know you well-and you pose as a "general" before us!

GRANDFATHER. You have recognised me to perfection. Who is so unworthy as I to bear my King's commands? And yet it is he who has invested me with these robes of a general and sent me here: he has chosen me before greater generals and mightier warriors.

KANCHI. All right, we shall go to observe the proprieties and amenities on a fitting occasion-but at present we are in the midst of a pressing engagement. He will have to wait till this little function is over.

GRANDFATHER. When he sends out his call he does not wait.

KOSHALA. I shall obey his call; I am going at once.

VIDARBHA. Kanchi, I cannot agree with you in your proposal to wait till this function is over. I am going.

KALINGA. You are older than I am —I shall follow you.

PANCHALA. Look behind you, Prince of Kanchi, your regal umbrella is lying in the dust: you have not noticed when your umbrella-holder has stolen away.

KANCHI. All right, general. I too am going-but not to do him homage. I go to fight him on the battle-ground.

GRANDFATHER. You will meet my King in the field of battle: that is no mean place for your reception.

VIRAT. Look here, friends, perhaps we are all flying before an imagined terror-it looks as if the King of Kanchi will have the best of it.

PANCHALA. Possibly, when the fruit is so near the hand, it is cowardly and foolish to go away without plucking it.

KALINGA. It is better to join the King of Kanchi. He cannot be without a definite plan and purpose when he is doing and daring so much.

## XVI

(SUDARSHANA and SURANGAMA)

SUDARSHANA. The fight is over now. When will the King come?

SURANGAMA. I do not know myself: I am also looking forward to his coming.

SUDARSHANA. I feel such a throb of joy, Surangama, that my breast is positively aching. But I am dying with shame too; how shall I show my face to him?

SURANGAMA. Go to him in utmost humility and resignation, and all shame will vanish in a moment.

SUDARSHANA. I cannot help confessing that I have met with my uttermost defeat for all the rest of my life. But pride made me claim the largest share in his love so long. Every one used to say I had such wonderful beauty, such graces and virtues; every one used to say that the King showed unlimited kindness towards me-this is what makes it difficult for me to bend my heart in humility before him.

SURANGAMA. This difficulty, my Queen, will pass off.

SUDARSHANA. Oh, yes, it will pass-the day has arrived for me to humble myself before the whole world. But why does not the King come to take me back? What more is he waiting for yet?

SURANGAMA. Have I not told you my King is cruel and hard-very hard indeed?

SUDARSHANA. Go out, Surangama, and bring me news of him.

SURANGAMA. I do not know where I should go to get any news of him. I have asked Grandfather to come; perhaps when he comes we shall hear something from him.

SUDARSHANA. Alack, my evil fate! I have been reduced to asking others to hear about my own King!
    (Transciber's note: Alack should probably be replaced with Alas.)
    (Enter GRANDFATHER)

SUDARSHANA. I have heard that you are my King's friend, so accept my obeisance and give me your blessings.

GRANDFATHER. What are you doing, Queen? I never accept anybody's obeisance. My relation with every one is only that of comradeship.

SUDARSHANA. Smile on me, then-give me good news. Tell me when the King is coming to take me back.

GRANDFATHER. You ask me a hard question, indeed! I hardly understand yet the ways of my friend. The battle is over, but no one can tell where he is gone.

SUDARSHANA. Is he gone away, then?

GRANDFATHER. I cannot find any trace of him here.

SUDARSHANA. Has he gone? And do you call such a person your friend?

GRANDFATHER. That is why he gets people's abuse as well as suspicion. But my King simply does not mind it in the least.

SUDARSHANA. Has he gone away? Oh, oh, how hard, how cruel, how cruel! He is made of stone, he is hard as adamant! I tried to move him with my own bosom-my breast is torn and bleeding-but him I could not move an inch! Grandfather, tell me, how can you manage with such a friend?

GRANDFATHER. I have known him now—I have known him through my griefs and joys-he can make me weep no more now.

SUDARSHANA. Will he not let me know him also?

GRANDFATHER. Why, he will, of course. Nothing else will satisfy him.

SUDARSHANA. Very well, I shall see how hard he can be! I shall stay here near the window without saying a word; I shall not move an inch; let me see if he will not come!

GRANDFATHER. You are young still-you can afford to wait for him; but to me, an old man, a moment's loss is a week. I must set out to seek him whether I succeed or not.(Exit.)

SUDARSHANA. I do not want him —I will not seek him! Surangama, I have no need of your King! Why did he fight with the princes? Was it for me at all? Did he want to show off his prowess and strength? Go away from here —I cannot bear your sight. He has humbled me to the dust, and is not satisfied still!

## XVII

### (A Band of CITIZENS)

FIRST CITIZEN. When so many Kings met together, we thought we were going to have some big fun; but somehow everything took such a turn that nobody knows what happened at all!

SECOND CITIZEN. Did you not see, they could not come to an agreement among themselves? —every one distrusted every one else.

THIRD CITIZEN. None kept to their original plans; one wanted to advance, another thought it better policy to recede; some went to the right, others made a rush to the left: how can you call that a fight?

FIRST CITIZEN. They had no eye to real fighting-each had his eye on the others.

SECOND CITIZEN. Each was thinking, "Why should I die to enable others to reap the harvest?"

THIRD CITIZEN. But you must all admit that Kanchi fought like a real hero.

FIRST CITIZEN. He for a long time after his defeat seemed loth to acknowledge himself beaten.

SECOND CITIZEN. He was at last fixed in the chest by a deadly missile.

THIRD CITIZEN. But before that he did not seem to realise that he had been losing ground at every step.

FIRST CITIZEN. As for the other Kings-well, nobody knows where they fled, leaving poor Kanchi alone in the field.

SECOND CITIZEN. But I have heard that he is not dead yet.

THIRD CITIZEN. No, the physicians have saved him-but he will carry the mark of his defeat on his breast till his dying day.

FIRST CITIZEN. None of the other Kings who fled has escaped; they have all been taken prisoners. But what sort of justice is this that was meted out to them?

SECOND CITIZEN. I heard that every one was punished except Kanchi, whom the judge placed on his right on the throne of justice, putting a crown on his head.

THIRD CITIZEN. This beats all mystery hollow.

SECOND CITIZEN. This sort of justice, to speak frankly, strikes us as fantastic and capricious.

FIRST CITIZEN. Just so. The greatest offender is certainly the King of Kanchi; as for the others, greed of gain now pressed them to advance, now they drew back in fear.

THIRD CITIZEN. What kind of justice is this, I ask? It is as if the tiger got scot-free, while his tail got cut off.

SECOND CITIZEN. If I were the judge, do you think Kanchi would be whole and sound at this hour? There would be nothing left of him altogether.

THIRD CITIZEN. They are great, high justices, my friends; their brains are of a different stamp from ours.

FIRST CITIZEN. Have they got any brains at all, I wonder? They simply indulge their sweet whims as there are none to say anything to them from above.

SECOND CITIZEN. Whatever you may say, if we had the governing power in our hands we should certainly have carried on the government much better than this.

THIRD CITIZEN. Can there be any real doubts about that? That of course goes without saying.

## XVIII

(The Street. GRANDFATHER and KANCHI)

GRANDFATHER. What, Prince of Kanchi, you here!

KANCHI. Your King has sent me on the road.

GRANDFATHER. That is a settled habit with him.

KANCHI. And now, no one can get a glimpse of him.

GRANDFATHER. That too is one of his amusements.

KANCHI. But how long more will he elude me like this? When nothing could make me acknowledge him as my King, he came all of a sudden like a terrific tempest-God knows from where-and scattered my men and horses and banners in one wild tumult: but now, when I am seeking the ends of the earth to pay him my humble homage, he is nowhere to be seen.

GRANDFATHER. But however big an Emperor he may be, he has to submit to him that yields. But why have you come out at night, Prince?

KANCHI. I still cannot get rid of the feeling of a secret dread of being laughed at by people when they see me meekly doing my homage to your King, acknowledging my defeat.

GRANDFATHER. Such indeed is the people. What would move others to tears only serves to move their empty laughter.

KANCHI. But you too are on the road, Grandfather.

GRANDFATHER. This is my jolly pilgrimage to the land of losing everything.

## SINGS.

I am waiting with my all in the hope of losing everything.
I am watching at the roadside for him who turns one out into
the open road,
Who hides himself and sees, who loves you unknown to you,
I have given my heart in secret love to him,
I am waiting with my all in the hope of losing everything.

## XIX

(A Road. SUDARSHANA and SURANGAMA)

SUDARSHANA. What a relief, Surangama, what freedom! It is my defeat that has brought me freedom. Oh, what an iron pride was mine! Nothing could move it or soften it. My darkened mind could not in any way be brought to see the plain truth that it was not the King who was to come, it was I who ought to have gone to him. All through yesternight I lay alone on the dusty floor before that window-lay there through the desolate hours and wept! All night the southern winds blew and shrieked and moaned like the pain that was biting at my heart; and all through it I heard the plaintive "Speak, wife!" of the nightbird echoing in the tumult outside!...It was the helpless wail of the dark night, Surangama!

SURANGAMA. Last night's heavy and melancholy air seemed to hang on for an eternity-oh, what a dismal and gloomy night!

SUDARSHANA. But would you believe it —I seemed to hear the soft strains of the *vina* floating through all that wild din and tumult! Could he play such sweet and tender tunes, he who is so cruel and terrible? The world knows only my indignity and ignominy-but none but my own heart could hear those strains that called me through the lone and wailing night. Did you too, Surangama, hear the *vina*? Or was that but a dream of mine?

SURANGAMA. But it is just to hear that same *vina*'s music that I am always by your side. It is for this call of music, which I knew would one day come to dissolve all the barriers of love, that I have all along been listening with an eager ear.

SUDARSHANA. He did at last send me on the open road —I could not withstand his will. When I shall find him, the first words that I shall tell him will be, "I have come of my own will —I have not awaited your coming." I shall say, "For your sake have I trodden the hard and weary roads, and bitter and ceaseless has been my weeping all the way." I shall at least have this pride in me when I meet him.

SURANGAMA. But even that pride will not last. He came before you did-who else could have sent you on the road?

SUDARSHANA. Perhaps he did. As long as a sense of offended pride remained with me, I could not help thinking that he had left me for good; but when I flung my dignity and pride to the winds and came out on the common streets, then it seemed to me that he too had come out: I have been finding him since the moment I was on the road. I have no misgivings now. All this suffering that I have gone through for his sake, the very bitternesss of all this is giving me his company. Ah! yes, he has come-he has held me by the hand, just as he used to do in that chamber of darkness, when, at his touch, all my body would start with a sudden thrill: it is the same, the same touch again! Who says that he is not here? —Surangama, can you not see that he has come, in silence and secret?...Who is that there? Look, Surangama, there is a third traveller of this dark road at this hour of the night.

SURANGAMA. I see, it is the King of Kanchi, my Queen.

SUDARSHANA. King of Kanchi!

SURANGAMA. Don't be afraid, my Queen!

SUDARSHANA. Afraid! Why should I be afraid? The days of fear are gone for ever for me.

KANCHI. (entering) Queen-mother, I see you two on this road! I am a traveller of the same path as yourself. Have no fear of me, O Queen!

SUDARSHANA. It is well, King of Kanchi, that we should be going together, side by side-this is but right. I came on your way when I first left my home, and now I meet you again on my way back. Who could have dreamed that this meeting of ours would augur so well?

KANCHI. But, Queen-mother, it is not meet that you should walk over this road on foot. Will you permit me to get a chariot for you?

SUDARSHANA. Oh, do not say so: I shall never be happy if I could not on my way back home tread on the dust of the road that led me away from my King. I would be deceiving myself if I were now to go in a chariot.

SURANGAMA. King, you too are walking in the dust to-day: this road has never known anybody driving his horse or chariot over it.

SUDARSHANA. When I was the Queen, I stepped over silver and gold —I shall have now to atone for the evil fortune of my birth by walking over dust and bare earth. I could not have dreamed that thus I would meet my King of common earth and dust at every step of mine to-day.

SURANGAMA. Look, my Queen, there on the eastern horizon comes the dawn. We have not long to walk: I see the spires of the golden turrets of the King's palace.

(Enter GRANDFATHER)

GRANDFATHER. My child, it is dawn-at last!

SUDARSHANA. Your benedictions have given me Godspeed, and here I am, at last.

GRANDFATHER. But do you see how ill-mannered our King is? He has sent no chariot, no music band, nothing splendid or grand.

SUDARSHANA. Nothing grand, did you say? Look, the sky is rosy and crimson from end to end, the air is full of the welcome of the scent of flowers.

GRANDFATHER. Yes, but however cruel our King may be, we cannot seek to emulate him: I cannot help feeling pain at seeing you in this state, my child. How can we bear to see you going to the King's palace attired in this poor and wretched attire? Wait a little —I am running to fetch you your Queen's garments.

SUDARSHANA. Oh no, no, no! He has taken away those regal robes from me for ever-he has attired me in a servant's dress before the eyes of the whole world: what a relief this has been to me! I am his servant now, no longer his Queen. To-day I stand at the feet of all those who can claim any relationship with him.

GRANDFATHER. But your enemies will laugh at you now: how can you bear their derision?

SUDARSHANA. Let their laughter and derision be immortal-let them throw dust at me in the streets: this dust will to-day be the powder with which I shall deck myself before meeting my lord.

GRANDFATHER. After this, we shall say nothing. Now let us play the last game of our Spring Festival-instead of the pollen of flowers let the south breeze blow and scatter dust of lowliness in every direction! We shall go to the lord clad in the common grey of the dust. And we shall find him too covered with dust all over. For do you think the people spare him? Even he cannot escape from their soiled and dusty hands, and he does not even care to brush the dirt off his garments.

KANCHI. Grandfather, do not forget me in this game of yours! I also will have to get this royal garment of mine soiled till it is beyond all recognition.

GRANDFATHER. That will not take long, my brother. Now that you have come down so far-you will change your colour in no time. Just look at our Queen-she got into a temper with herself and thought that she could spoil her matchless beauty by flinging away all her ornaments: but this insult to her beauty has made it shine forth in tenfold radiance, and now it is in its unadorned perfection. We hear that our King is all innocent of beauty — that is why he loves all his manifold beauty of form which shines as the very ornament of his breast. And that beauty has to-day taken off its veil and cloak of pride and vanity! What could I not give to be allowed to hear the wonderful music and song that has filled my King's palace to-day!

SURANGAMA. Lo, there rises the sun!

# XX

(The Dark Chamber)

SUDARSHANA. Lord, do not give me back the honour which you once did turn away from me! I am the servant of your feet —I only seek the privilege of serving you.

KING. Will you be able to bear me now?

SUDARSHANA. Oh yes, yes, I shall. Your sigh repelled me because I had sought to find you in the pleasure garden, in my Queen's chambers: there even your meanest servant looks handsomer than you. That fever of longing has left my eyes for ever. You are not beautiful, my lord-you stand beyond all comparisons!

KING. That which can be comparable with me lies within yourself.

SUDARSHANA. If this be so, then that too is beyond comparison.
Your love lives in me-you are mirrored in that love, and you see
your face reflected in me: nothing of this mine, it is all yours,
O lord!

KING. I open the doors of this dark room to-day —the game is finished here! Come, come with me now, come outside —*into the light*!

SUDARSHANA. Before I go, let me bow at the feet of my lord of darkness, my cruel, my terrible, my peerless one!

THE END

# SANYASI, OR THE ASCETIC

"Lead us from the unreal to the real."

TO DR. JAGADISH CHANDRA ROSE

I

*Sanyasi, outside the cave*

The division of days and nights is not for me, nor that of months and years. For me, the stream of time has stopped, on whose waves dances the world, like straws and twigs. In this dark cave I am alone, merged in myself, —and the eternal night is still, like a mountain lake afraid of its own depth. Water oozes and drips from the cracks, and in the pools float the ancient frogs. I sit chanting the incantation of nothingness. The world's limits recede, line after line. — The stars, like sparks of fire, flown from the anvil of time, are extinct; and that joy is mine which comes to the God Shiva, when, after aeons of dream, he wakes up to find himself alone in the heart of the infinite annihilation. I am free, I am the great solitary One. When I was thy slave, O Nature, thou didst set my heart against itself, and madest it carry the fierce war of suicide through its world. Desires, that have no other ends, but to feed upon themselves and all that comes to their mouths, lashed me into fury. I ran about, madly chasing my shadow. Thou drovest me with thy lightning lashes of pleasure into the void of satiety. And the hungers, who are thy decoys, ever led me into the endless famine, where food turned into dust, and drink into vapour.

Till, when my world was spotted with tears and ashes, I took my oath, that I would have revenge upon thee, interminable Appearance, mistress of endless disguises. I took shelter in the darkness, —the castle of the Infinite, —and fought the deceitful light, day after day, till it lost all its weapons and lay powerless at my feet. Now, when I am free of fear and desires, when the mist has vanished, and my reason shines pure and bright, let me go out into the kingdom of lies, and sit upon its heart, untouched and unmoved.

## II

*Sanyasi, by the roadside*

How small is this earth and confined, watched and followed by the persistent horizons. The trees, houses, and crowd of things are pressing upon my eyes. The light, like a cage, has shut out the dark eternity; and the hours hop and cry within its barriers, like prisoned birds. But why are these noisy men rushing on, and for what purpose? They seem always afraid of missing something, —the something that never comes to their hands.

(The crowd passes.

#### Enter a Village Elder and Two Women

FIRST WOMAN. O my, O my! You do make me laugh.

SECOND WOMAN. But who says you are old?

VILLAGE ELDER. There are fools who judge men by their outside.

FIRST WOMAN. How sad! We have been watching your outside from our infancy. It is just the same all through these years.

VILLAGE ELDER. Like the morning sun.

FIRST WOMAN. Yes, like the morning sun in its shining baldness.

VILLAGE ELDER. Ladies, you are overcritical in your taste. You notice things that are unessential.

SECOND WOMAN. Leave off your chatter, Ananga. Let us hasten home, or my man will be angry.

FIRST WOMAN. Good bye, sir. Please judge us from our outside, we won't mind that.

VILLAGE ELDER. Because you have no inside to speak of.

(They go.

#### Enter Three Villagers

FIRST VILLAGER. Insult me? the scoundrel! He shall regret it.

SECOND VILLAGER. He must be taught a thorough lesson.

FIRST VILLAGER. A lesson that will follow him to his grave.

THIRD VILLAGER. Yes, brother, set your heart upon it. Never give him quarter.

SECOND VILLAGER. He has grown too big.

First Villager Big enough to burst at last.

THIRD VILLAGER. The ants, when they begin to grow wings, perish.

SECOND VILLAGER. But have you got a plan?

FIRST VILLAGER. Not one, but hundreds. I will drive my plough-share over his household. —I will give him a donkey-ride through the town, with his cheeks painted white and black. I will make the world too hot for him, and—

(They go.

Enter Two Students

FIRST STUDENT. I am sure Professor Madhab won in the debate.

SECOND STUDENT. No, it was Professor Janardan.

FIRST STUDENT. Professor Madhab maintained his point to the last. He said that the subtle is the outcome of the gross.

SECOND STUDENT. But Professor Janardan conclusively proved that the subtle is the origin of the gross.

FIRST STUDENT. Impossible.

SECOND STUDENT. It is clear as the day-light.

FIRST STUDENT. Seeds come from the tree.

SECOND STUDENT. The tree comes from the seed.

FIRST STUDENT. Sanyasi, which of these is true? Which is the original, the subtle or the gross?

SANYASI. Neither.

SECOND STUDENT. Neither. Well, that sounds satisfactory.

SANYASI. The origin is the end, and the end is the origin. It is a circle. —The distinction between the subtle and gross is in your ignorance.

FIRST STUDENT. Well, it sounds very simple —^and I think this was what my master meant.

SECOND STUDENT. Certainly this agrees more with what my master teaches.

(They go out.

SANYASI. These birds are word-peckers. When they pick up some wriggling nonsense, which can fill their mouth, they are happy.

Enter Two Flower-Girls, singing

## SONG

> The weary hours pass by.
> The flowers that blossom in the light
> Fade and drop in the shadow.
> I thought I would weave a garland
>
> In the cool of the morning for my love.
> But the morning wears on.
> The flowers are not gathered.
> And my love is lost.

A WAYFARER. Why such regret, my darlings? When the garlands are ready, the necks will not be wanting.

FIRST FLOWER-GIRL. Nor the halter.

SECOND FLOWER-GIRL. You are bold. Why do you come so close?

WAYFARER. You quarrel for nothing, my girl. I am far enough from you to allow an elephant to pass between us.

SECOND FLOWER-GIRL. Indeed. Am I such a fright? I wouldn't have eaten you, if you had come.

(They go out laughing.)

Comes an old Beggar

BEGGAR. Kind sirs, have pity on me. May God prosper you. Give me one handful from your plenty.

Enters a Soldier

SOLDIER. Move away. Don't you see the Minister's son is coming.?

(They go out

SANYASI. It is midday. The sun is growing strong. The sky looks like an overturned burning copper bowl. The earth breathes hot sighs, and the whirling sands dance by. What sights of man have I seen! Can I ever again shrink back into the smallness of these creatures, and become one of them? No, I am free. I have not this obstacle, this world round me. I live in a pure desolation.

Enter the girl Vasanti and a Woman

WOMAN. Girl, you are Raghu's daughter, aren't you? You should keep away from this road. Don't you know it goes to the temple?

VASANTI. I am on the farthest side. Lady.

WOMAN. But I thought my cloth-end touched you. I am taking my offerings to the goddess, —I hope they are not polluted.

VASANTI. I assure you, your cloth did not touch me. (The Woman goes,) I am Vasanti, Raghu's daughter. May I come to you, father?

SANYASI. Why not, child?

VASANTI. I am a pollution, as they call me.

SANYASI. But they are all that, —a pollution. They roll in the dust of existence. Only he is pure who has washed away the world from his mind. But what have you done, daughter?

VASANTI. My father, who is dead, had defied their laws and their gods. He would not perform their rites.

SANYASI. Why do you stand away from me?

VASANTI. Will you touch me?

SANYASI. Yes, because nothing can touch me truly. I am ever away in the endless. You can sit here, if you wish.

VASANTI. (Breaking into a sob.) Never tell me to leave you, when once you have taken me near you.

SANYASI. Wipe away your tears, child. I am a Sanyasi. I have neither hatred, nor attachment in my heart, —I never claim you as mine; therefore I can never discard you. You are to me as this blue sky is, —you are, —yet you are not.

VASANTI. Father, I am deserted by gods and men alike.

SANYASI. So am I. I have deserted both gods and men.

VASANTI. You have no mother?

SANYASI. No.

VASANTI. Nor father?

SANYASI. No.

VASANTI. Nor any friend?

SANYASI. No.

VASANTI. Then I shall be with you. —You won't leave me?

SANYASI. I have done with leaving. You can stay near me, yet never coming near me.

VASANTI. I do not understand you, father. Tell me, is there no shelter for me in the whole world .f^

SANYASI. Shelter? Don't you know this world is a bottomless chasm? The swarm of creatures, coming out from the hole of nothingness, seeks for shelter, and enters into the gaping mouth of this emptiness, and is lost. These are the ghosts of lies around you, who hold their market of illusions, —and the foods which they sell are shadows. They only deceive your hunger, but do not satisfy. Come away from here, child, come away.

VASANTI. But, father, they seem so happy in this world. Can we not watch them from the roadside?

SANYASI. Alas, they do not understand. They cannot see that this world is death spread out to eternity. —It dies every moment, yet never comes to the end. —And we, the creatures of this world, live by feeding upon death.

VASANTI. Father, you frighten me.

Enters a Traveller

TRAVELLER. Can I get a shelter near this place?

SANYASI. Shelter there is nowhere, my son, but in the depth of one's self. —Seek that; hold to it fast, if you would be saved.

TRAVELLER. But I am tired, and want shelter.

VASANTI. My hut is not far from here. Will you come?

Traveller But who are you?

Vasanti Must you know me? I am Raghu's daughter.

TRAVELLER. God bless you, child, but I cannot stay.

(Goes,

Men come bearing somebody on a bed

FIRST BEARER. He is still asleep.

SECOND BEARER. How heavy the rascal is!

A TRAVELLER. (outside their group) Whom do you carry?

THIRD BEARER. Binde, the weaver, was sleeping as one dead, and we have taken him away.

SECOND BEARER. But I am tired, brothers. Let us give him a shake, and waken him up.

BINDE. (wakes up) Ee, a, u —

THIRD BEARER. What's that noise?

BINDE. I say. Who are you? Where am I being carried?

                    (They put down the bed from their shoulders.

THIRD BEARER. Can't you keep quiet, like all decent dead people?

SECOND BEARER. The cheek of him! He must talk, even though he is dead.

THIRD BEARER. It would be more proper of you, if you kept still.

BINDS. I am sorry to disappoint you, gentlemen, you have made a mistake. —I was not dead, but fast asleep.

SECOND BEARER. I admire this fellow's impudence. Not only must he die, but argue.

THIRD BEARER. He won't confess the truth. Let us go, and finish the rites of the dead.

BINDE. I swear by your beard, my brother, I am as alive as any of you.

                    (They take him away, laughing.

SANYASI.
The girl has fallen asleep, with her arm beneath her little head; I think I must leave her now, and go. But, coward, must you run away, —run away from this tiny thing? These are nature's spiders' webs, they have danger merely for moths, and not for a Sanyasi like me.

VASANTI. (awaking with a start) Have you left me. Master? —Have you gone away?

SANYASI. Why should I go away from you? What fear have I? Afraid of a shadow?

VASANTI. Do you hear the noise in the road?

SANYASI. But stillness is in my soul.
                    Enters a young Woman, followed by Men

WOMAN. Go now. Leave me. Don't talk to me of love.

FIRST MAN. Why, what has been my crime?

WOMAN. You men have hearts of stone.

FIRST MAN. Incredible. If our hearts were of stone, how could Cupid's darts make damage there?

OTHER MAN. Bravo. Well said.

SECOND MAN. Now, what is your answer to that, my dear?

148

WOMAN. Answer! You think you have said something very fine, —don't you? It is perfect rubbish.

FIRST MAN. I leave it to your judgment, gentlemen. What I said was this, that if our hearts be of stone, how can —

THIRD MAN. Yes, yes, it has no answer at all.

FIRST MAN. Let me explain it to you. She said we men have hearts of stone, didn't she? Well, I said, in answer, if our hearts were truly of stone, how could Cupid's darts damage them? You understand?

SECOND MAN. Brother, I have been selling molasses in the town for the last twenty-four years, —do you think I cannot understand what you say?

(They go out.

SANYASI. What are you doing, my child?

VASANTI. I am looking at your broad palm, father. My hand is a little bird that finds its nest here. Your palm is great, like the great earth which holds all. These lines are the rivers, and these are hills.

(Puts her cheek upon it.

SANYASI. Your touch is soft, my daughter, like the touch of sleep. It seems to me this touch has something of the great darkness, which touches one's soul with the wand of the eternal. —But, child, you are the moth of the daylight. You have your birds and flowers and fields-what can you find in me, who have my centre in the One and my circumference nowhere?

VASANTI. I do not want anything else. Your love is enough for me.

SANYASI. The girl imagines I love her, —foolish heart. She is happy in that thought. Let her nourish it. For they have been brought up in illusions, and they must have illusions to console them,

VASANTI. Father, this creeper trailing on the grass, seeking some tree to twine itself round, is my creeper. I have tended it and watered it from the time when it had pushed up only two little leaves into the air, like an infant's cry. This creeper is me, —it has grown by the road-side, it can be so easily crushed. Do you see these beautiful little flowers, pale blue with white spots in their hearts, —these white spots are their dreams. Let me gently brush your forehead with these flowers. To me, things that are beautiful are the keys to all that I have not seen and not known.

SANYASI. No, no, the beautiful is mere phantasy. To him who knows, the dust and the flower are the same. —But what languor is this that is creeping into my blood and drawing before my eyes a thin mist veil of all the rainbow colours.? Is it nature herself weaving her dreams round me, clouding my senses.? {Suddenly he tears the creeper, and rises up.) No more of this; for this is death. What game of yours is this with me, little girl? I am a sanyasi, I have cut all my knots, I am free. —No, no, not those tears. I cannot bear them. —But where was hidden in my heart this snake, this anger, that hissed out of its dark with its fang.? No, they are not dead, —they outlive starvation. These hell-creatures clatter their skeletons and dance in my heart, when their mistress, the great witch, plays upon her magic flute. —Weep not, child, come to me. You seem to me like a cry of a lost world, like the song of a wandering star. You bring to my mind something, which is infinitely more than this Nature, — more than the sun and stars. It is as great as the darkness. I understand it not. I have never known it, therefore I fear it. I must leave you. —Go back whence you came, —the messenger of the unknown.

VANSATI. Leave me not, father, —I have none else but you.

SANYASI. I must go, I thought that I had known, —but I do not know. Yet I must know. I leave you, to know who you are.

VASANTI. Father, if you leave me, I shall die.

SANYASI. Let go my hand. Do not touch me. I must be free. —
(He runs away.

## III

*The Sanyasi is seen, sitting upon a boulder in a mountain path*

(A shepherd boy passes by, singing.

## THE SONG

*Do not turn aivay your face, my love.*
*The spring has bared open its breast.*
*The flowers breathe their secrets in the dark.*
*The rustle of the forest leaves comes across the shy.*
*Like the sobs of the night.*
*Come, love, show me your face.*

SANYASI. The gold of the evening is melting in the heart of the blue sea. The forest, on the hillside, is drinking the last cup of the daylight. On the left, the village huts are seen through the trees with their evening lamps lighted, like a veiled mother watching by her sleeping children. Nature, thou art my slave. Thou hast spread thy many-coloured carpet in the great hall where I sit alone, like a king, and watch thee dance with thy starry necklace twinkling on thy breast.

(Shepherd girls pass by, singing.

Song of the shepherd girls
The music comes from across the dark river and calls me.
I was in the house and happy.
But the flute sounded in the still air of night.
And a pain pierced my heari.
Oh, tell me the way who know it, —
Tell me the way to him.
I will go to him with my one little flower.
And leave it at his feet.
And tell him that his music is one with my love.

(They go.

SANYASI. I think such an evening had come to me only once before in all my births. Then its cup overbrimmed with love and music, and I sat with someone, the memory of whose face is in that setting star of the evening. —But where is my Httle girl, with her dark sad eyes, big with tears? Is she there, sitting outside her hut, watching that same star through the immense loneHness of the evening? But the star must set, the evening close her eyes in the night, and tears must cease and sobs be stilled in sleep. No, I will not go back. Let the world-dreams take their own shape. Let me not trouble its course and create new phantasies. I will see, and think, and know.

Enters a ragged Girl Girl Are you there, father?

SANYASI. Come, child, sit by me. I wish I could own that call of yours. Someone did call me father, once, and the voice was somewhat like yours. The father answers now, —but where is that call?

GIRL. Who are you?

SANYASI. I am a sanyasi. Tell, me child, what is your father?

GIRL. He gathers sticks from the forest.

SANYASI. And you have a mother?

GIRL. No. She died when I was young.

SANYASI. Do you love your father?

GIRL. I love him more than anything else in the world. I have no one else but him.

SANYASI. I understand you. Give me your little hand, —let me hold it in my palm, —in this big palm of mine.

GIRL. Sanyasi, do you read palms? Can you read in my palm all that I am and shall be?

SANYASI. I think I can read, but dimly know its meaning. One day, I shall know it.

GIRL. Now I must go to meet my father.

SANYASI. Where?

GIRL. Where the road goes into the forest. He will miss me, if he does not find me there.

SANYASI. Bring your head near to me, child. Let me give you my kiss of blessing, before you go.

(Girl goes.

A Mother enters, with two children

MOTHER. How stout and chubby Misri's children are. They are something to look at. But the more I feed you, the more you seem to grow thin every day.

FIRST GIRL. But why do you always blame us for that, mother? Can we help it?

MOTHER. Don't I tell you to take plenty of rest? But you must always be running about.

SECOND GIRL. But, mother, we run about on your errands.

MOTHER. How dare you answer me like that?

SANYASI. Where are you going, daughter?

MOTHER. My salutation, father. We are going home.

SANYASI. How many are you?

MOTHER. My mother-in-law, and my husband and two other children, beside these.

SANYASI. How do you spend your days?

MOTHER. I hardly know how my days pass. My man goes to the field, and I have my house to look after. Then, in the evening, I sit to spin with my elder girls. (To the girls.) Go and salute the sanyasi. Bless them, father.

(They go.

Enter Two Men

FIRST MAN. Friend, go back from here. Do not come any further.

SECOND MAN. Yes, I know. Friends meet in this earth by chance, and the chance carries us on together some portion of the way, and then comes the moment when we must part.

SECOND FRIEND. Let us carry away with us the hope that we part to meet again.

FIRST FRIEND. Our meetings and partings belong to all the movements of the world. Stars do not take special notice of us.

SECOND FRIEND. Let us salute those stars which did throw us together. If for a moment, still it has been much.

FIRST FRIEND. Look back for a minute before you go. Can you see that faint glimmer of the water in the dark, and those casuarina trees on the sandy bank? Our village is all one heap of dark shadows. You can only see the lights. Can you guess which of those lights are ours?

SECOND FRIEND. Yes, I think I can.

FIRST FRIEND. That light is the last farewell look of our past days upon their parting guest. A little further on, and there will remain one blot of darkness.

(They go away.

SANYASI. The night grows dark and desolate. It sits like a woman forsaken, —those stars are her tears, turned into fire. O my child, the sorrow of your little heart has filled, for ever, all the nights of my life with its sadness. Your dear caressing hand has left its touch in this night air, — I feel it on my forehead, —it is damp with your tears. My darling, your sobs that pursued me, when I fled away, have clung to my heart. I shall carry them to my death.

# IV

*Sanyasi, in the village path*

Let my vows of sanyasi go. I break my staff and my alms-bowl. This stately ship, this world, which is crossing the sea of time, —let it take me up again, let me join once more the pilgrims. O the fool, who wanted to seek safety in swimming alone and gave up the light of the sun and stars, to pick his way with his glow-worm's lamp! The bird flies in the sky, not to fly away into the emptiness, but to come back again to this great earth. —I am free. I am free from the bodiless chain of the Nay. I am free among things, and forms and purpose. The finite is the true infinite, and love knows its truth. My girl, you are the spirit of all that is, —I can never leave you.

Enters a Village Elder

SANYASI. Do you know, brother, where Raghu's daughter is?

ELDER. She has left her village, and we are glad.

SANYASI. Where has she gone?

ELDER. Do you ask where? It is all one to her where she goes.

(Goes out.

SANYASI. My darling has gone to seek a somewhere in the emptiness of nowhere. She must find me.

A crowd of Villagers enter

FIRST MAN. So our King's son is going to be married to-night.

SECOND MAN. Can you tell me, when is the wedding hour?

THIRD MAN. The wedding hour is only for the bridegroom and the bride. What have we got to do with it?

A WOMAN. But won't they give us cakes for the happy day?

FIRST MAN. Cakes? You are silly. My uncle lives in the town —I have heard from him that we shall have curds and parched rice.

SECOND MAN. Grand.

FOURTH MAN. But we shall have a great deal more water than curds. You may be sure of that.

FIRST MAN. Moti, you are a dull fellow. Water in the curds at a prince's wedding!

FOURTH MAN. But we are not princes ourselves, Panchu. For us, poor people, the curds have the trick of turning into water most parts.

FIRST MAN. Look there. That son of the charcoalburner is still busy with his work. We mustn't allow that.

SECOND MAN. We shall burn him into charcoal, if he does not come out.

SANYASI. Do you know, any of you, where is Raghu's daughter.?

THE WOMAN. She has gone away.

SANYASI. Where?

WOMAN. That we don't know.

FIRST MAN. But we are sure that she is not the bride for our prince.

(They laugh and go out.

Enters a Woman, with a child

WOMAN. My obeisance to you, father. Let my child touch your feet with his head. He is sick. Bless him, father.

SANYASI. But, daughter, I am no longer a sanyasi. Do not mock me with your salutation.

WOMAN. Then who are you? What are you doing?

SANYASI. I am seeking.

WOMAN. Seeking whom?

SANYASI. Seeking my lost world back. —Do you know Raghu's daughter? Where is she?

WOMAN. Raghu's daughter? She is dead.

SANYASI. No, she cannot be dead. No. No.

WOMAN. But what is her death to you, Sanyasi?

SANYASI. Not only to me; it would be death to all.

WOMAN. I do not understand you.

SANYASI. She can never be dead.

**MALINI**

TO MY NIECE INDIRA DEVI

## ACT I

*The Balcony of the Palace facing the street*

MALINI. The moment has come for me, and my life, hke the dew drop upon a lotus leaf, is trembling upon the heart of this great time. I shut my eyes and seem to hear the tumult of the sky, and there is an anguish in my heart, I know not for what.

Enters Queen

QUEEN. My child, what is this? Why do you forget to put on dresses that befit your beauty and youth? Where are your ornaments? My beautiful dawn, how can you absent the touch of gold from your limbs?

MALINI. Mother, there are some who are born poor, even in a king's house. Wealth does not cling to those whose destiny it is to find riches in poverty.

QUEEN. That the child whose only language was the baby cry should talk to me in such riddles! —My heart quakes in fear when I listen to you. Where did you pick up your new creed, which goes against all our holy books? My child, they say that the Buddhist monks, from whom you take your lessons, practice black arts; that they cast their spells upon men's minds, confounding them with lies. But I ask you, is religion a thing that one has to find by seeking ? Is it not like sunlight, given to you for all days? I am a simple woman. I do not understand men's creeds and dogmas. I only know that women's true objects of worship come to their own arms, without asking, in the shape of their husbands and their children.

Enters King

KINIG. My daughter, storm clouds are gathering over the King's house. Go no farther along your perilous path. Pause, if only for a short time.

QUEEN. What dark words are these?

KING. My foolish child, if you must bring your new creed into this land of the old, let it not come like a sudden flood threatening those who dwell on the bank. Keep your faith to your own self. Rake not up public hatred and mockery against it.

QUEEN. Do not chide my girl, and teach her the crookedness of your diplomacy. If my child should choose her own teachers and pursue her own path, I do not know who can blame her.

KING. Queen, my people are agitated, they clamour for my daughter's banishment.

QUEEN. Banishment? Of your own daughter?

KING. The Brahmins, frightened at her heresy, have combined, and —

QUEEN. Heresy indeed. Are all truths confined only in their musty, old books? Let them fling away their worm-eaten creeds, and come and take their lessons from this child. I tell you, King, she is not a common girl, —she is a pure flame of fire. Some divine spirit has taken birth in her. Do not despise her, lest some day you strike your forehead, and weep, and find her no more.

MALINI. Father, grant to your people their request. The great moment has come. Banish me.

KING. Why, child? What want do you feel in your father's house?

MALINI. Listen to me, father. Those, who cry for my banishment, cry for me. Mother, I have no words in which to tell you what I have in my mind. Leave me without regret, like the tree that sheds its flowers unheeding. Let me go out to all men, — for the world has claimed me from the King's hands.

KING. Child, I do not understand you.

MALINI. Father, you are a King. Be strong and fulfil your mission.

QUEEN. Child, is there no place for you here, where you were born? Is the burden of the world waiting for your little shoulders?

MALINI. I dream, while I am awake, that the wind is wild, and the water is troubled; the night is dark, and the boat is moored in the haven. Where is the captain, who shall take the wanderers home? I feel I know the path, and the boat will thrill with life at my touch, and speed on.

QUEEN. Do you hear. King? Whose words are these? Do they come from this little girl? Is she your daughter, and have I borne her?

KING. Yes, even as the night bears the dawn, — the dawn that is not of the night, but of all the world.

QUEEN. King, have you nothing to keep her bound to your house, —this image of light? — My darling, your hair has come loose on your shoulders. Let me bind it up. —Do they talk of banishment. King? If this be a part of their creed, then let come the new religion, and let those Brahmins be taught afresh what is truth.

KING. Queen, let us take away our child from this balcony. Do you see the crowd gathering in the street?

[They all go out

Enter a crowd of Brahmins, in the street, before the palace balcony.

[They shout

BRAHMINS. Banishment of the King's daughter!

KEMANKAR. Friends, keep your resolution firm. The woman, as an enemy, is to be dreaded more than all others. For reason is futile against her and forces are ashamed; man's power gladly surrenders itself to her powerlessness, and she takes her shelter in the strongholds of our own hearts.

1ST BRAHMIN. We must have audience with our King, to tell him that a snake has raised its poisonous hood from his own nest, and is aiming at the heart of our sacred religion.

SUPRIYA. Religion? I am stupid. I do not understand you. Tell me, sir, is it your religion that claims the banishment of an innocent girl?

1ST BRAHMIN. You are a marplot, Supriya, you are ever a hindrance to all our enterprises.

2ND BRAHMIN. We have united in defence of our faith, and you come like a subtle rift in the wall, like a thin smile on the compressed lips of contempt.

SUPRIYA. You think that, by the force of numbers, you will determine truth, and drown reason by your united shouts?

1ST BRAHMIN. This is rank insolence, Supriya.

SUPRIYA. The insolence is not mine but theirs who shape their scripture to fit their own narrow hearts.

2ND BRAHMIN. Drive him out. He is none of us.

1ST BRAHMIN. We have all agreed upon the banishment of the Princess. —He who thinks differently, let him leave this assembly.

SUPRIYA. Brahmins, it was a mistake on your part to elect me as one of your league. I am neither your shadow, nor an echo of your texts. I never admit that truth sides with the shrillest voice and I am ashamed to own as mine a creed that depends on force for its existence. (To Kemankar.) Dear friend, let me go.

KEMANKAR. No, I will not. I know you are firm in your action, only doubting when you debate. Keep silence, my friend; for the time is evil.

SUPRIYA. Of all things the blind certitude of stupidity is the hardest to bear. To think of saving your religion by banishing a girl from her home! But let me know what is her offence. Does she not maintain that truth and love are the body and soul of religion? If so, is that not the essence of all creeds?

KEMANKAR. Religion is one in its essence, but different in its forms. The water is one, yet by its different banks it is bounded and preserved for different peoples. What if you have a well-spring of your own in your heart, spurn not your neighbours who must go for their draught of water to their ancestral pond with the green of its gradual slopes mellowed by ages and its ancient trees bearing eternal fruit.

SUPRIYA. I shall follow you, my friend, as I have ever done in my life, and not argue.

Enters third Brahmin

3RD BRAHMIN. I have good news. Our words have prevailed, and the King's army is about to take our side openly.

2ND BRAHMIN. The army? —I do not quite like it.

1ST BRAHMIN. Nor do I. It smells of rebellion.

2nd Brahmin; Kemankar, I am not for such extreme measures.

1ST BRAHMIN. Our faith will give us victory, not our arms. Let us make penance, and recite sacred verses. Let us call on the names of our guardian gods.

2ND BRAHMIN. Come, Goddess, whose wrath is the sole weapon of thy worshippers, deign to take form and crush even to dust the blind pride of unbelievers. Prove to us the strength of our faith, and lead us to victory.

ALL. We invoke thee. Mother, descend from thy heavenly heights and do thy work among mortals.

Enters Malini

MALINI. I have come. (They all bow to her, except Kemankar and Supriya, who stand aloof and watch.)

2ND BRAHMIN. Goddess. —Thou hast come at last, as a daughter of man, withdrawing all thy terrible power into the tender beauty of a girl. Whence hast thou come. Mother? What is thy wish?

MALINI.

I have come down to my exile at your call,

2ND BRAHMIN. To exile from heaven, because thy children of earth have called thee?

1ST BRAHMIN. Forgive us, Mother. Utter ruin threatens this world and it cries aloud for thy help.

MALINI. I will never desert you. I always knew that your doors were open for me. The cry went from you for my banishment and I woke up, amidst the wealth and pleasure of the King's house.

KEMANKAR. The Princess.

ALL. The King's daughter.

MALINI. I am exiled from my home, so that I may make your home my own. Yet tell me truly, have you need of me? When I lived in seclusion, a lonely girl, did you call to me from the outer world? Was it no dream of mine?

1ST BRAHMIN. Mother, you have come, and taken your seat in the heart of our hearts.

MALINI. I was born in a King's house, never once looking out from my window. I had heard that it was a sorrowing world, —the world out of my reach. But I did not know where it felt its pain. Teach me to find this out.

1ST BRAHMIN. Your sweet voice brings tears to our eyes.

MALINI. The moon has just come out of those clouds. Great peace is in the sky. It seems to gather all the world in its arms, under the fold of one vast moonlight. There goes the road, losing itself among the solemn trees with their still shadows. There are the houses, and there the temple; the river bank in the distance looks dim and desolate. I seem to have come down, like a sudden shower from a cloud of dreams, into this world of men, by the roadside.

1ST BRAHMIN. You are the divine soul of this world.

2ND BRAHMIN. Why did not our tongues burst in pain, when they shouted for your banishment?

1ST BRAHMIN. Come, Brahmins, let us restore our Mother to her home.
                    (They shout.

Victory to the Mother of the world! Victory to the Mother in the heart of the Man's daughter!
                    (Malini goes, surrounded by them.

KEMANKAR. Let the illusion vanish. Where are you going, Supriya, like one walking in his sleep?

SUPRIYA. Leave hold of me, let me go.

KEMANKAR. Control yourself. Will you, too, fly into the fire with the rest of the blinded swarm?

SUPRIYA. Was it a dream, Kemankar?

KEMANKAR. It was nothing but a dream. Open your eyes, and wake up.

SUPRIYA. Your hope of heaven is false, Kemankar. Vainly have I wandered in the wilderness of doctrines, —I never found peace. The God, who belongs to the multitude, and the God of the books are not my own God. These never answered my questions and never consoled me. But, at last, I have found the divine breathing and alive in the living world of men.

KEMANKAR. Alas, my friend, it is a fearful moment when a man's heart deceives him. Then blind desire becomes his gospel and fancy usurps the dread throne of his gods. Is yonder moon, lying asleep among soft fleecy clouds, the true emblem of everlasting reality? The naked day will come to-morrow, and the hungry crowd begin again to drag the sea of existence with their thousand nets. And then this moonlight night will hardly be remembered, but as a thin film of unreality made of sleep and shadows and delusions. The magic web, woven of the elusive charms of a woman, is like that, —and can it take the place of highest truth? Can any creed, born of your fancy, satisfy the gaping thirst of the midday, when it is wide awake in its burning heat?

SUPRIYA. Alas, I know not.

KEMANKAR. Then shake yourself up from your dreams, and look before you. The ancient house is on fire, whose nurslings are the ages. The spirits of our forefathers are hovering over the impending ruins, like crying birds over their perishing nests. Is this the time for vacillation, when the night is dark, the enemies knocking at the gate, the citizens asleep, and men drunken with delusions laying their hands upon their brothers' throats?

SUPRIYA. I will stand by you.

KEMANKAR. I must go away from here.

SUPRIYA. Where? And for what?

KEMANKAR. To foreign lands. I shall bring soldiers from outside. For this conflagration cries for blood, to be quenched.

SUPRIYA. But our own soldiers are ready.

KEMANKAR. Vain is all hope of help from them. They, like moths, are already leaping into the fire. Do you not hear how they are shouting like fools? The whole town has gone mad, and is lighting her festival lamps at the funeral pyre of her own sacred faith.

SUPRIYA. If you must go, take me with you.

KEMANKAR. No. You remain here, to watch and keep me informed. But, friend, let your heart be not drawn away from me by the novelty of the falsehood.

SUPRIYA. Falsehood is new, but our friendship is old. We have ever been together from our childhood. This is our first separation.

KEMANKAR. May it prove our last! In evil times the strongest bonds give way. Brothers strike brothers and friends turn against friends. I go out into the dark, and in the darkness of night I shall come back to the gate. Shall I find my friend watching for me, with the lamp lighted? I take away that hope with me.

(They go.

Enter King, with the Prince, in the balcony.

KING. I fear I must decide to banish my daughter.

PRINCE. Yes, Sire, delay will be dangerous.

KING. Gently, my son, gently. Never doubt that I will do my duty. Be sure I will banish her.

(Prince goes.

Enters Queen

QUEEN. Tell me. King, where is she? Have you hidden her, even from me?

KING. Whom?

QUEEN. My Malini.

KING. What? Is she not in her room?

QUEEN. No, I cannot find her. Go with your soldiers and search for her through all the town, from house to house. The citizens have stolen her. Banish them all. Empty the whole town, till they return her.

KING. I will bring her back, —even if my Kingdom goes to ruin.

(The Brahmins and soldiers bring Malini, with torches lighted.

QUEEN. My darling, my cruel child. I never keep my eyes off you, —how could you evade me, and go out?

2ND BRAHMIN. Do not be angry with her, Queen. She came to our home to give us her blessings.

1ST BRAHMIN. Is she only yours? And does she not belong to us as well?

2ND BRAHMIN. Our little mother, do not forget us. You are our star, to lead us across the pathless sea of life.

MALINI. My door has been opened for you. These walls will nevermore separate us.

BRAHMINS. Blessed are we, and the land where we were born.

(They go.

MALINI. Mother, I have brought the outer world into your house. I seem to have lost the bounds of my body. I am one with the life of this world.

QUEEN. Yes, child. Now you shall never need to go out. Bring in the world to you, and to your mother. —It is close upon the second watch of the night. Sit here. Calm yourself. This flaming life in you is burning out all sleep from your eyes.

MALINI. (Embracing her mother.) Mother, I am tired. My body is trembling. So vast is this world. —Mother dear, sing me to sleep. Tears come to my eyes, and a sadness descends upon my heart.

## ACT II

MALINI. What can I say to you? I do not know how to argue. I have not read your books.

SUPRIYA. I am learned only among the fools of learning. I have left all arguments and books behind me. Lead me, princess, and I shall follow you, as the shadow follows the lamp.

MALINI. But, Brahmin, when you question me, I lose all my power and do not know how to answer you. It is a wonder to me to see that even you, who know everything, come to me with your questions.

SUPRIYA. Not for knowledge I come to you. Let me forget all that I have ever known. Roads there are, without number, but the light is missing.

MALINI. Alas, sir, the more you ask me, the more I feel my poverty. Where is that voice in me, which came down from heaven, like an unseen flash of lightning, into my heart? Why did you not come that day, but keep away in doubt.? Now that I have met the world face to face my heart has grown timid, and I do not know how to hold the helm of the great ship that I must guide. I feel I am alone, and the world is large, and ways are many, and the light from the sky comes of a sudden to vanish the next moment. You who are wise and learned, will you help me?

SUPRIYA. I shall deem myself fortunate, if you ask my help.

MALINI. There are times when despair comes to choke all the life-currents; when suddenly, amidst crowds of men, my eyes turn upon myself and I am frightened. Will you befriend me in those moments of blankness, and utter me one word of hope that will bring me back to life?

SUPRIYA. I shall keep myself ready. I shall make my heart simple and pure, and my mind peaceful, to be able truly to serve you.

Enters Attendant

ATTENDANT. The citizens have come, asking to see you.

MALINI. Not to-day. Ask their pardon for me. I must have time to fill my exhausted mind, and have rest to get rid of weariness.

(Attendant goes.

Tell me again about Kemankar, your friend. I long to know what your life has been and its trials.

SUPRIYA. Kemankar is my friend, my brother, my master. His mind has been firm and strong, from early days, while my thoughts are always flickering with doubts. Yet he has ever kept me close to his heart, as the moon does its dark spots. But, however strong a ship may be, if it harbours a small hole in its bottom, it must sink. — That I would make you sink, Kemankar, was in the law of nature.

MALINI. You made him sink?

SUPRIYA. Yes, I did. The day when the rebellion slunk away in shame before the light in your face and the music in the air that touched you, Kemankar alone was unmoved. He left me behind him, and said that he must go to the foreign land to bring soldiers, and uproot the new creed from the sacred soil of Kaslii. —You know what followed. You made me live again in a new land of birth. "Love for all life" was a mere word, waiting from the old time to be made real, —and I saw that truth in you in flesh. My heart cried for my friend, but he was away, out of my reach; then came his letter, in which he wrote that he was coming with a foreign army at his back, to wash away the new faith in blood, and to punish you with death. —I could wait no longer. I showed the letter to the King.

MALINI. Why did you forget yourself, Supriya? Why did fear overcome you? Have I not room enough in my house for him and his soldiers?

Enters King

KING. Come to my arms, Supriya, I went at a fit time to surprise Kemankar and to capture him. An hour later, and a thunder-bolt would have burst upon my house in my sleep. You are my friend, Supriya, come —

SUPRIYA. God forgive me.

KING. Do you not know, that a King's love is not unsubstantial? I give you leave to ask for any reward that comes to your mind. Tell me, what do you want.?

SUPRIYA. Nothing, Sire, nothing. I shall live, begging from door to door.

KING. Only ask me, and you shall have provinces worthy to tempt a king.

SUPRIYA. They do not tempt me.

KING. I understand you. I know towards what moon you raise your hands. Mad youth, be brave to ask even that which seems so impossible. Why are you silent? Do you remember the day when you prayed for my Malini's banishment? Will you repeat that prayer to me, to lead my daughter to exile from her father's house? — My daughter, do you know that you owe your life to this noble youth? And is it hard for you to pay off that debt with your —?

SUPRIYA. For pity's sake, Sire, no more of this. Worshippers there are many who by lifelong devotion have gained the highest fulfilment of their desire. Could I be counted one of them I should be happy. But to accept it from the King's hands as the reward of treachery? Lady mine, you have the plenitude and peace of your greatness; you know not the secret cravings of a poverty-stricken soul. I dare not ask from you an atom more than that pity of love which you have for every creature in the world.

MALINI. Father, what is your punishment for the captive?

KING. He shall die.

MALINI. On my knees I beg from you his pardon.

KING. But he is a rebel, my child.

SUPRIYA. Do you judge him. King? He also judged you, when he came to punish you, not to rob your kingdom.

MALINI. Spare him his life, father. Then only will you have the right to bestow on him your friendship, who has saved you from a great peril.

KING. What do you say, Supriya? Shall I restore a friend to his friend's arms?

SUPRIYA. That will be king-like in its grace.

KING. It will come in its time, and you will find back your friend. But a King's generosity must not stop there. I must give you something which exceeds your hope,—yet not as a mere reward. You have won my heart, and my heart is ready to offer you its best treasure. — My child, where was this shyness in you before now? Your dawn had no tint of rose,—its light was white and dazzling. But to-day a tearful mist of tenderness sweetly tempers it for mortal eyes. (To Supriya.) Leave my feet, rise up and come to my heart. Happiness is pressing it like pain. Leave me now for a while. I want to be alone with my Malini. (Supriya goes.) I feel I have found back my child once again, — not the bright star of the sky, but the sweet flower that blossoms on earthly soil. She is my daughter, the darling of my heart.

Enters Attendant

ATTENDANT. The captive, Kemankar, is at the door.

KING. Bring him in. Here comes he, with his eyes fixed, his proud head held high, a brooding shadow on his forehead, Hke a thunder cloud motionless in a suspended storm.

MALINI. The iron chain is shamed of itself upon those limbs. The insult to greatness is its own insult. He looks like a god defying his captivity.

Enters Kemankar in chains

KING. What punishment do you expect from my hands?

KEMANKAR. Death.

KING. But if I pardon you?

KEMANKAR. Then I shall have time again to complete the work I began.

KING. You seem out of love with your life. Tell me your last wish, if you have any.

KEMANKAR. I want to see my friend, Supriya, before I die.

KING. (To the attendant.) Ask Supriya to come.

MALINI. There is a power in that face that frightens me. Father, do not let Supriya come.

KING. Your fear is baseless, child.

(Supriya enters, and walks towards Kemankar, with arms extended.)

KEMANKAR. No, no, not yet. First let us have our say, and then the greeting of love. — Come closer to me. You know I am poor in words,—and my time is short. My trial is over, but not yours. Tell me, why have you done this?

SUPRIYA. Friend, you will not understand me. I had to keep my faith, even at the cost of my love.

KEMANKAR. I understand you, Supriya. I have seen that girl's face, glowing with an inner light, looking like a voice becoming visible. You offered, to the fire of those eyes, the faith in your fathers' creed, the faith in your country's good, and built up a new one on the foundation of a treason.

SUPRIYA. Friend, you are right. My faith has come to me perfected in the form of that woman. Your sacred books were dumb to me. I have read, by the help of the light of those eyes, the ancient book of creation, and I have known that true faith is there, where there is man, where there is love. It comes from the mother in her devotion, and it goes back to her from her child. It descends in the gift of a giver and it appears in the heart of him who takes it. I accepted the bond of this faith which reveals the infinite in man, when I set my eyes upon that face full of light and love and peace of hidden wisdom.

KEMANKAR. I also once set my eyes on that face, and for a moment dreamt that religion had come at last, in the form of a woman, to lead man's heart to heaven. For a moment, music broke out from the very ribs of my breast and all my life's hopes blossomed in their fulness. Yet did not I break through these meshes of illusion to wander in foreign lands? Did not I suffer humiliation from unworthy hands in patience, and bear the pain of separation from you, who have been my friend from my infancy? And what have you been doing meanwhile? You sat in the shade of the King's garden, and spent your sweet leisure in idly weaving a lie to condone your infatuation and calling it a religion.

SUPRIYA. My friend, is not this world wide enough to hold men whose natures are widely different? Those countless stars of the sky, do they fight for the mastery of the One? Cannot faiths hold their separate lights in peace for the separate worlds of minds that need them?

KEMANKAR. Words, mere words. To let falsehood and truth live side by side in amity, the infinite world is not wide enough. That the corn ripening for the food of man should make room for thorny weeds, love is not so hatefully all-loving. That one should be allowed to sap the sure ground of friendship with betrayal of trust, could tolerance be so traitorously wide as that? That one should die like a thief to defend his faith and the other live in honour and wealth who betrayed it-no, no, the world is not so stony-hard as to bear without pain such hideous contradictions in its bosom.

SUPRIYA. (To Malini.) All these hurts and insults I accept in your name, my lady. Kemankar, you are paying your life for your faith, —I am paying more. It is your love, dearer than my life.

KEMANKAR. No more of this prating. All truths must be tested in death's court. My friend, do you remember our student days when we used to wrangle the whole night through, to come at last to our teacher, in the morning, to know in a moment which of us was right.? Let that morning break now. Let us go there to that land of the final, and stand before death with all our questions, where the changing mist of doubts will vanish at a breath, and the mountain peaks of eternal truth will appear, and we two fools will look at each other and laugh. —Dear friend, bring before death that which you deem your best and immortal.

SUPRIYA. Friend, let it be as you wish.

KEMANKAR. Then come to my heart. You had wandered far from your comrade, in the infinite distance, —now, dear friend, come eternally close to me, and accept from one, who loves you, the gift of death. (Strikes SupRiYA with his chains, and Supriya falls.)

KEMANKAR. (Embracing the dead body of Supriya.) Now call your executioner.

KING. (Rising up.) Where is my sword?

MALINI. Father, forgive Kemankar!

**SACRIFICE**

*A temple of the Goddess Kali in Tripura.*
Enters Gunavati, the Queen

## SACRIFICE

GUNAVATI. Have I offended thee, dread Mother? Thou grantest children to the beggar woman, who sells them to live, and to the adulteress, who kills them to save herself from infamy, and here I am, the Queen, with all the world lying at my feet, hankering in vain for the baby-touch at my bosom, to feel the stir of a dearer life within my life. What sin have I committed. Mother, to merit this, to be banished from the mothers' heaven?
(Enters Raghupati, the priest)

O Master, have I ever been remiss in my worship? and my husband, is he not godlike in his

purity? Then why has the Goddess, who weaves the web of this world-illusion, assigned my place in the barren waste of childlessness?

RAGHUPATI. Our Mother is all caprice, she knows no law, our sorrows and joys are mere freaks of her mind. Have patience, daughter, to-day we shall offer special sacrifice in your name to please her.

GUNAVATI. Accept my grateful obeisance, father. My offerings are already on their way to the temple, —red bunches of hybiscus and beasts of sacrifice.

(They go out.

Enter Govinda, the King; Jaising, the servant of temple; and Aparna, the beggar girl.

JAISING. What is your wish, Sire?

GOVINDA. Is it true that this poor girl's pet goat has been brought by force to the temple to be killed? Will Mother accept such a gift with grace?

JAISING. King, how are we to know whence the servants collect our daily offerings of worship? But, my child, why is this weeping? Is it worthy of you to shed tears for that which Mother herseK has taken?

APARNA. Mother! I am his mother. If I return late to my hut, he refuses his grass, and bleats, with his eyes on the road. I take him up in my arms, when I come, and share my food with him. He knows no mother but me.

JAISING. Sire, could I make the goat live again, by giving up a portion of my life, gladly would I do it. But how can I restore that which Mother herself has taken?

AJPARNA. Mother has taken? It is a lie. Not mother, but demon.

JAISING. O, the blasphemy!

APARNA. Mother, art thou there to rob a poor girl of her love? Then where is the throne, before which to condemn thee? Tell me, King.

GOVINDA. I am silent, my child. I have no answer.

APARNA. This blood-streak running down the steps, is it his? O my darling, when you trembled and cried for dear life, why did your call not reach my heart through the whole deaf world?

JAISING. (To the image.) I have served thee from my infancy. Mother Kali, yet I understand thee not. Does pity only belong to weak mortals, and not to gods? Come with me, my child, let me do for you what I can. Help must come from man, when it is denied from gods.
(All go out hut the King)

Enter Raghupati; Nakshatra, who is the King's brother; and the courtiers


ALL. Victory be to the King!

GOVINDA. Know you all, that I forbid shedding of blood in the temple from to-day for ever.

MINISTER. You forbid sacrifice to the Goddess?

GENERAL. Nay an Rai Forbid sacrifice?

NAKSHATRA. How terrible! Forbid sacrifice?

RAGHUPATI. Is it a dream?

GOVINDA. No dream, father. It is awakening. Mother came to me, in a girl's disguise, and told me that blood she cannot suffer.

RAGHUPATI. She has been drinking blood for ages. Whence comes this loathing all of a sudden?

GOVINDA. No, she never drank blood, she kept her face averted.

RAGHUPATI. I warn you, think and consider. You have no power to alter laws laid down in scriptures.

GOVINDA. God's words are above all laws.

RAGHUPATI. Do not add pride to your folly. Do you have the effrontery to say that you alone have heard God's words, and not I?

NALCSHATRA. It is strange, that the King should have heard from gods and not the priest.

GOVINDA. God's words are ever ringing in the world, and he who is wilfully deaf cannot hear them.

RAGHUPATI. Atheist! Apostate!

GOVINDA. Father, go to your morning service, and declare to all worshippers that henceforward they will be punished with banishment who shed creatures' blood in their worship of the Mother of all creatures.

RAGHUPATI. Is this your last word?

GOVINDA. Yes.

RAGHUPATI. Then curse upon you! Do you, in your enormous pride, imagine that the Goddess, dwelling in your land, is your subject? Do you presume to bind her with your laws and rob her of her dues? You shall never do it. I declare it, —I who am her servant.

[Goes.

NAY AN RAI. Pardon me, Sire, but have you the right?

MINISTER. King, is it too late to revoke your order?

GOVINDA. We dare not delay to uproot sin from our realm.

MINISTER. Sin can never have such a long lease of life. Could they be sinful, —the rites that have grown old at the feet of the Goddess?

(The King is silent.

NAKSHATRA. Indeed they could not be.

MINISTER. Our ancestors have performed these rites with reverence; can you have the heart to insult them?

(The King remains silent

NAYAN RAI. That which has the sanction of ages, do you have the right to remove it?

GOVINDA. No more doubts and disputes. Go and spread my order in all my lands.

MINISTER. But, Sire, the Queen has offered her sacrifice for this morning's worship; it is come near the temple gate.

GOVINDA. Send it back. (He goes.)

MINISTER. What is this?

NAKSHATRA. Are we, then, to come down to the level of Buddhists, and treat animals as if they have their right to live? Preposterous!

(They all go out

Enters Raghupati, —Jaising following him with ajar of water to wash his feet.

JAISING. Father.

RAGHUPATI. Go!

JAISING. Here is some water.

RAGHUPATI. No need of it!

JAISING. Your clothes.

RAGHUPATI. Take them away!

JAISING. Have I done anything to offend you?

RAGHUPATI. Leave me alone. The shadows of evil have thickened. The King's throne is raising its insolent head above the temple altar. Ye Gods of these degenerate days, are ye ready to obey the King's laws with bowed heads, fawning upon him like his courtiers?

JAISING. Whatever has happened, father?

RAGHUPATI. I cannot find words to say. Ask the Mother Goddess who has been defied.

JAISING. Defied? By whom?

RAGHUPATI. By King Govinda.

JAISING. King Govinda defied Mother Kali?

RAGHUPATI. Defied you and me, all scriptures, all countries, all time, defied Mahakali, the Goddess of the endless stream of time, —sitting upon that puny little throne of his.

JAISING. King Govinda?

RAGHUPATI. Yes, yes, your King Govinda, the darling of your heart. Ungrateful! I have given all my love to bring you up, and yet King Govinda is dearer to you than I am.

JAISING. The child raises its arms to the full moon, sitting upon his father's lap. You are my father and my full moon is King Govinda. Then is it true, what I hear from people, that our King forbids all sacrifice in the temple? But in this we cannot obey him.

RAGHUPATI. Banishment is for him who does not obey.

JAISING. It is no calamity to be banished from a land where Mother's worship remains incomplete. No, so long as I live, the service of the temple shall be fully performed.

(They go out.

Enter Gunavati and her attendant

GUNAVATI. What is it you say? The Queen's sacrifice turned away from the temple gate? Is there a man in this land who carries more than one head on his shoulders, that he could dare think of it? Who is that doomed creature?

ATTENDANT. I am afraid to name him.

GUNAVATI. Afraid to name him, when I ask you? Whom do you fear more than me?

ATTENDANT. Pardon me.

GUNAVATI. Give my salutation to the priest, and ask him to come.

(Attendant goes out.

Enters Govinda

GUNAVATI. Have you heard, King? My offerings have been sent back from Mother's temple.

GOVINDA. I know it.

GUNAVATI. You know it, and yet bear the insult?

GOVINDA. I beg to ask your pardon for the culprit.

GUNAVATI. I know, King, your heart is merciful, but this is no mercy. It is feebleness. If your kindness hampers you, leave the punishment in my hand. Only, tell me, who is he?

GOVINDA. It is I, my Queen. My crime is in nothing else but having given you pain.

GUNAVATI. I do not understand you.

GOVINDA. From to day shedding of blood in gods' temples is forbidden in my land.

GUNAVATI. Who forbids it?

GOVINDA. Mother herself.

GUNAVATI. Who heard it?

GOVINDA. I.

GUNAVATI. You! That makes me laugh. The Queen of all the world comes to the gate of Tripura's King with her petition.

GOVINDA. Not with her petition, but with her sorrow.

GUNAVATI. Your dominion is outside the temple limit. Do not send your commands there, where they are impertinent.

GOVINDA. The command is not mine, it is Mother's.

GUNAVATI. If you have no doubt in your decision, do not cross my faith. Let me perform my worship according to my light.

GOVINDA. I promised my Goddess to prevent sacrifice of life in her temple, and I must carry it out.

GUNAVATI. I also promised my Goddess the blood of three hundred kids and one hundred buffaloes, and I will carry it out. You may leave me now.

GOVINDA. As you wish.

(He goes out

Enters Raghupati

GUNAVATI. My offerings have been turned back from the temple, father.

RAGHUPATI. The worship offered by the most ragged of all beggars is not less precious than yours. Queen. But the misfortune is that Mother has been deprived.

GUNAVATI. What will come of all this, father?

RAGHUPATI. That is only known to her who fashions this world with her dreams. But this is certain, that the throne which casts its shadow upon Mother's shrine will burst like a bubble, vanishing in the void.

GUNAVATI. Have mercy and save us, father.

RAGHUPATI. Ha, ha I I am to save you, —you, the consort of a King who boasts of his kingdom on the earth and in heaven as well, before whom the gods and the Brahmins must-Oh, shame! Oh, the evil age, when the Brahmin's futile curse recoils upon himself, to sting him into madness. (About to tear his sacrificial thread.)

GUNAVATI. (Preventing him.) Have mercy upon me.

Raghupati Then give back to Brahmins what is theirs by right.

Gunavati Yes, I will. Go, master, to your worship, and nothing will hinder you.

RAGHUPATI. Indeed your favour overwhelms me. At the merest glance of your eyes gods are saved from ignominy and the Brahmin is restored to his sacred offices. Thrive and grow fat and sleek till the dire day of judgment comes. (Goes out.)

Re-enters King Govinda

GOVINDA. My Queen, the shadow of your angry brows hides all light from my heart.

GUNAVATI. Go! Do not bring a curse upon this house.

GOVINDA. Woman's smile removes all curse from the house, her love is God's grace.

GUNAVATI. Go, and never show your face to me vagain.

GOVINDA. I shall come back, my Queen, when you remember me.

GUNAVATI. (Clinging to the King's feet.) Pardon me. King. Have you become so hard, that you forget to respect woman's pride? Do you not know, beloved, that thwarted love takes the disguise of anger?

GOVINDA. I would die, if I lost my trust in you. I know, my love, that clouds are for moments only, and the sun is for all days.

GUNAVATI. Yes, the clouds will pass by, God's thunder will return to his armoury, and the sun of all days will shine upon the traditions of all time. Yes, my King, order it so, that Brahmins be restored to their rights, the Goddess to her offerings, and the King's authority to its earthly limits.

GOVINDA. It is not the Brahmin's right to violate the eternal good. Creature's blood is not the offering for gods. And it is within the rights of the King and the peasant alike to maintain truth and righteousness.

GUNAVATI. I prostrate myself on the ground before you; I beg at your feet. The custom that comes through all ages is not the King's own. Like the heaven's air, it belongs to all men. Yet your Queen begs it of you, with clasped hands, in the name of your people. Can you still remain silent, proud man, refusing entreaties of love in favour of duty which is doubtful? Then go, go, go from me.

(They go.

Enter Raghupati, Jaising and Nayan Rai

RAGHUPATI. General, your devotion to Mother is well known.

NAYAN RAI. It runs through generations of my ancestors.

RAGHUPATI. Let this sacred love give you indomitable courage. Let it make your sword-blade mighty as God's thunder, and win its place above all powers and positions of this world.

NAYAN RAI. The Brahmin's blessings will never be in vain.

RAGHUPATI. Then I bid you collect your soldiers and strike Mother's enemy down to the dust.

NAYAN RAI. Tell me, father, who is the enemy?

RAGHUPATI. Govinda.

NAYAN RAI. Our King?

RAGHUPATI. Yes, attack him with all your force.

NAYAN RAI. It is evil advice. Father, is this to try me?

RAGHUPATI. Yes, it is to try you, to know for certain whose servant you are. Give up all hesitation. Know that the Goddess calls, and all earthly bonds must be severed.

NAYAN RAI. I have no hesitation in my mind. I stand firm in my post, where my Goddess has placed me.

RAGHUPATI. You are brave.

NAYAN RAI. Am I the basest of Mother's servants, that the order should come for me to turn traitor? She herself stands upon the faith of man's heart. Can she ask me to break it? Then to-day comes to dust the King, and to-morrow the Goddess herself.

JAISING. Noble words.

RAGHUPATI. The King, who has turned traitor to Mother, has lost all claims to your allegiance.

NAYAN RAI. Drive me not, father, into a wilderness of debates. I know only one path, — the straight path of faith and truth. This stupid servant of Mother shall never swerve from that highway of honour.

(Goes out.

JAISING. Let us be strong in our faith as he is, master. Why ask the aid of soldiers.? We have the strength within ourselves for the task given to us from above. Open the temple gate wide, father. Sound the drum. Come, come, O citizens, to worship her, who takes all fear away from our hearts. Come, Mother's children.

(Citizens come.

FIRST CITIZEN. Come, come, we are called.

ALL. Victory to Mother!

(They sing and dance.

The dread Mother dances naked in the battlefield.
Her lolling tongue hums like a red flame of fire,
Her dark tresses fly in the sky, sweeping away the sun and stars.
Red streams of blood run from her cloudblack limbs.
And the world trembles and cracks under her tread.

JAISING. Do you see the beasts of sacrifice coming towards the temple, driven by the Queen's attendants?

(They cry.

Victory to Mother! Victory to our Queen!

RAGHUPATI. Jaising, make haste and get ready for the worship.

JAISING. Everything is ready, father.

RAGHUPATI. Send a man to call Prince Nakshatra in my name.

(Citizens sing and dance.)
Enters King Govinda Silence, Raghupati! Do you dare to disregard my order?

RAGHUPATI. Yes, I do.

GOVINDA. Then you are not for my land.

RAGHUPATI. No, my land is there, where the King's crown kisses the dust. Ho! Citizens! Let Mother's offerings be brought in here.

(They heat drums

GOVINDA. Silence! (To his attendants.) Ask my General to come. Raghupati, you drive me to call soldiers to defend God's right. I feel the shame of it; for the force of arms only reveals man's weakness.

Enter General Nayan Rai and Chandpal, who is the second in comviand of the army.

GOVINDA. Stand here with your soldiers to prevent sacrifice of life in the temple.

NAYAN. Pardon me, Sire. The King's servant is powerless in the temple of God.

GOVINDA. General, it is not for you to question my order. You are to carry out my words. Their merits and demerits belong only to me.

NAYAN. I am your servant, my King, but I am a man above all. I have reason and my religion. I have my King, —and also my God.

GOVINDA. Then surrender your sword to Chandpal. He will protect the temple from pollution of blood.

NAYAN RAI. Why to Chandpal? This sword was given to my forefathers by your royal ancestors. If you want it back, I will give it up to you. Be witness, my fathers, who are in the heroes' paradise, the sword that you made sacred with your loyal faith and bravery, I surrender to my King.

(Goes out.

RAGHUPATI. The Brahmin's curse has begun its work already.

Enters Jaising

JAISING. The beasts have been made ready for the sacrifice.

GOVINDA. Sacrifice?

JAISING. (On his knees.) King, listen to my earnest entreaties. Do not stand in the way, hiding the Goddess, man as you are.
Raghupati Shame, Jaising. Rise up and ask my pardon. I am your Master. Your place is at

my feet, not the King's. Fool! Do you ask King's sanction to do God's service? Leave alone the worship and the sacrifice. Let us wait and see how his pride prevails in the end. Come away.

[They go out

Enters Aparna, the beggar girl

APARNA. Where is Jaising? He is not here, but only you, —the image whom nothing can move. You rob us of all our best without uttering a word. We pine for love, and die beggars for want of it. Yet it comes to you unasked, though you need it not. Like a grave, you hoard it under your miserly stone, keeping it from the use of the yearning world. Jaising, what happiness do you find from her? What can she speak to you? O my heart, my famished heart!

Enters Raghupati

RAGHUPATI. Who are you?

APARNA. I am a beggar girl. Where is Jaising?

RAGHUPATI. Leave this place at once. I know you are haunting this temple, to steal Jaising's heart from the Goddess.

APARNA. Has the Goddess anything to fear from me? I fear her.

[She goes out.

Enter Jaising and Prince Nakshatea

NAKSHATRA. Why have you called me?

RAGHUPATI. Last night the Goddess told me in a dream, that you shall become king withm a week.

NAKSHATRA. Ha, ha, this is news indeed.

RAGHUPATI. Yes, you shall be King.

NAKSHATRA. I cannot beUeve it.

RAGHUPATI. You doubt my words?

NAKSHATRA. I do not want to doubt them. But suppose, by chance, it never comes to pass.

RAGHUPATI. No, it shall be true.

NAKSHATRA. But, tell me, how can it ever become true?

RAGHUPATI. The Goddess thirsts for King's blood.

NAKSHATRA. King's blood.?

RAGHUPATI. You must offer it to her before you can be king.

NAKSHATRA. I know not where to get it.

RAGHUPATI. There is King Govinda. —Jaising, keep still. —Do you understand? Kill him in secret. Bring his blood, while warm, to the altar. —Jaising, leave this place, if you cannot remain still, —

NAKSHATRA. But he is my brother, and I love him.

RAGHUPATI. Your sacrifice will be all the more precious.

NAKSHATRA. But, father, I am content to remain as I am. I do not want the kingdom.

RAGHUPATI. There is no escape for you, because the Goddess commands it. She is thirsting for blood from the King's house. If your brother is to hve, then you must die.

NAKSHATRA. Have pity on me, father.

RAGHUPATI. You shall never be free in life, or in death, until her bidding is done.

NAKSHATRA. Advise me, then, how to do it.

RAGHUPATI. Wait in silence. I will tell you what to do, when the time comes. And now, go.

(Nakshatra goes.

JAISING. What is it that I heard? Merciful Mother, is it your bidding? To ask brother to kill brother.? Master, how could you say that it was Mother's own wish?

RAGHUPATI. There was no other means but this to serve my Goddess.

JAISING. Means? Why means? Mother, have you not your own sword to wield with your own hand? Must your wish burrow underground, like a thief, to steal in secret? Oh, the sin!

RAGHUPATI. What do you know about sin?

JAISING. What I have learnt from you.

RAGHUPATI. Then come and learn your lesson once again from me. Sin has no meaning in reality. To kill is but to kill, it is neither sin nor anything else. Do you not know that the dust of this earth is made of countless killings? Old Time is ever writing the chronicle of the transient life of creatures in letters of blood. Killing is in the wilderness, in the habitations of man, in birds' nests, in insects' holes, in the sea, in the sky; there is killing for life, for sport, for nothing whatever. The world is ceaselessly killing; and the great Goddess Kali, the spirit of ever changing time, is standing with her thirsty tongue hanging down from her mouth, with her cup in hand, into which is running the red life-blood of the world, like juice from the crushed cluster of grapes.

JAISING. Stop, master. Is then love a falsehood and mercy a mockery, and the one thing true, from the beginning of time, the lust for destruction? Would it not have destroyed itself long ago? You are playing with my heart, my master. Look there, she is gazing at me. My blood-thirsty Mother, wilt thou accept my blood? Is it so delicious to thee? Master, did you call me? The Mother, who is thirsting for our love, you accuse of blood-thirstiness!

RAGHUPATI. Then let the sacrifice be stopped in the temple.

JAISING. Yes, let it be stopped. —No, no, master, you know what is right and what is wrong. The heart's laws are not the laws of scripture. Eyes cannot see with their own light, —the light must come from the outside. Tell me, father, is it true that the Goddess seeks King's blood?

RAGHUPATI. Alas, child, have you lost your faith in me?

JAISING. My world stands upon my faith in you. If the Goddess must have King's blood, let me bring it to her. I will never allow a brother to kill his brother.

RAGHUPATI. But there can be no evil in carrying out God's wishes.

JAISING. No, it must be good, and I will earn the merit of it.

RAGHUPATI. But, my boy, I have reared you from your childhood, and you have grown close to my heart. I can never bear to lose you, by any chance.

JAISING. I will not let your love for me be soiled with sin. Release Prince Nakshatra from his promise.

RAGHUPATI. I will think, and decide to-morrow.

(He goes.

JAISING. Deeds are better, however cruel they may be, than the hell of thinking and doubting. You are true, my master, to kill is no sin, to kill a brother is no sin, to kill a king is no sin. —Where do you go, my brothers? To the fair at Nishipur? There the women are to dance? Oh, this world is pleasant! And the dancing limbs of the girls are beautiful. In what careless merriment the crowds flow through the roads, making the sky ring with their laughter and song. I will follow them.

Enters Raghupati

RAGHUPATI. Jaising.

JAISING. I do not know you. I drift with the crowd. Why ask me to stop? Go your own way.

RAGHUPATI. Jaising.

JAISING. The road is straight before me. With an alms bowl in hand and the beggar girl as my sweetheart I shall walk on. Who says that the world's ways are devious? Anyhow we reach the end, —the end where all laws and rules are no more, where the errors and hurts of life are forgotten. What is the use of all these scriptures, and the teacher and his instructions? —My master, my father, what wild words are these of mine? I was living in a dream. There stands the temple, cruel and immovable as truth. What was your order, my teacher? I have not forgotten it. (Bringing out the knife.) I am sharpening your words in my mind, till they become one with this knife in keenness. Have you any other order to give me?

RAGHUPATI. My boy, my darling, how can I tell you how deep is my love for you?

JAISING. No, master, do not tell me of love. Let me think only of duty. Love, like the green grass and the trees and life's music, is only for the surface of the world. It comes and vanishes like a dream. But underneath is duty, like the rude layers of stone, like a huge load that nothing can move.

(They go out.

Enter King Govinda and Chandpal

CHANDPAL. Sire, I warn you to be careful.

GOVINDA. Why? What do you mean?

CHANDPAL. I have overheard a conspiracy to take away your life.

GOVINDA. Who wants my life?

CHANDPAL. I am afraid to tell you, lest the news become to you more deadly than the knife itself. It was Prince Nakshatra, who —

GOVINDA. Nakshatra?

CHANDPAL. He has promised to Raghupati to bring your blood to the Goddess.

GOVINDA. To the Goddess? Then I cannot blame him. For a man loses his humanity when it concerns his gods. You go to your work and leave me alone.
(Chandpal goes out.)

(Addressing the image.) Accept these flowers, Goddess, and let your creatures live in peace.

Mother, those who are weak in this world are so helpless, and those who are strong are so cruel. Greed is pitiless, ignorance blind, and pride takes no heed when it crushes the small under its foot. Mother, do not raise your sword and lick your lips for blood; do not set brother against brother, and woman against man. If it is your desire to strike me by the hand of one I love, then let it be fulfilled. For the sin has to ripen to its ugliest limits, before it can burst and die a hideous death.

(Jaising rushes in.

JAISING. Tell me, Goddess, dost thou truly want King's blood? Ask it in thine own voice, and thou shalt have it.

A VOICE. I want King's blood.

JAISING. King, say your last prayer, for your time has come.

GOVINDA. What makes you say it, Jaising?

JAISING. Did you not hear what the Goddess said?

GOVINDA. It was not the Goddess. I heard the familiar voice of Raghupati.

JAISING. Drive me not from doubt to doubt. It is all the same, whether the voice comes from the Goddess, or from my master. —
(He unsheathes his knife, and then throws it away.

Listen to the cry of thy children. Mother. Let there be only flowers for thy offerings, —no

more blood. They are red even as blood, —these bunches of hybiscus. They have come out of the heart-burst of the earth, pained at the slaughter of her children. Accept this. Thou must accept this. I defy thy anger. Blood thou shalt never have. Redden thine eyes. Raise thy sword. Bring thy furies of destruction. I do not fear thee. King, leave this temple to its Goddess, and go to your men.
(Govinda goes.

Alas, alas, in a moment I gave up all that I had, my master, my Goddess.

(Raghupati comes.

RAGHUPATI. I have heard all. Traitor, you have betrayed your master.

JAISING. Punish me, father.

RAGHUPATI. What punishment will you have?

JAISING. Punish me with my life.

RAGHUPATI. No, that is nothing. Take your oath touching the feet of the Goddess.

JAISING. I touch her feet.

RAGHUPATI. Say, I will bring kingly blood to the altar of the Goddess, before it is midnight.

JAISING. I will bring kingly blood to the altar of the Goddess, before it is midnight.

(They go out.

Enters Gunavati

GUNAVATI. I failed. I had hoped that, if I remained hard and cold for some days, he would surrender. Such faith I had in my power, vain woman that I am. I showed my sullen anger, and remained away from him; but it was fruitless. Woman's anger is like a diamond's glitter; it only shines, but cannot burn. I would it were like thunder, bursting upon the King's house, startling him up from his sleep, and dashing his pride to the ground.

Enters the boy Druva

GUNAVATI. Where are you going?

DRUVA. I am called by the King. (Goes out)

GUNAVATI. There goes the darling of the King's heart. He has robbed my unborn children of their father's love, usurped their right to the first place in the King's breast. O Mother Kali, your creation is infinite and full of wonders, only send a child to my arms in merest wliim, a tiny little warm living flesh to fill my lap, and I shall offer you whatever you wish. (Enters Nakshatra.) Prince Nakshatra, why are you so excited?

NAKSHATRA. Tell me what you want of me.

GUNAVATI. The thief that steals the crown awaiting you, —remove him. Do you understand?

NAKSHATRA. Yes, except who the thief is.

GUNAVATI. That boy, Druva. Do you not see how he is growing in the King's lap, till one day he reaches the crown?

NAKSHATRA. Yes, I have often thought of it. I have seen my brother putting his crown on the boy's head in play.

GUNAVATI. Playing with the crown is a dangerous game. If you do not remove the player, he will make a game of you.

NAKSHATRA. Yes, I like it not.

GUNAVATI. Offer him to Kali. Have you not heard that Mother is thirsting for blood?

NAKSHATRA. But, sister, this is not my business.

GUNAVATI. Fool, can you feel yourself safe, so long as Mother is not appeased? Blood she must have; save your own, if you can.

NAKSHATRA. But she wants King's blood.

GUNAVATI. Who told you that.?

NAHSHATRA. I know it from one to whom the Goddess herself sends her dreams.

GUNAVATI. Then that boy must die for the King. His blood is more precious to your brother than his own, and the King can only be saved by paying the price, which is more than his life.

NAHSHATRA. I understand.

GUNAVATI. Then lose no time. Run after him. He is not gone far. But remember. Offer him in my name.

NAHSHATRA. Yes, I will.

GUNAVATI. The Queen's offerings have been turned back from Mother's gate. Pray to her that she may forgive me.

(They go out.

Enters Jaising

JAISING. Goddess, is there any little thing, that yet remains, out of the wreck of thee? If there be but a faintest spark of thy light in the remotest of the stars of evening, answer my cry, though thy voice be the feeblest. Say to me, " Child, here I am." — No, she is nowhere. She is naught. But take pity upon Jaising, O Illusion! Art thou so irredeemably false, that not even my love can send the slightest tremor of life through thy nothingness? O fool, for whom have you upturned your cup of life, emptying it to the last drop? for this unanswering void, —truthless, merciless, and motherless?
(Enters Aparna)

Aparna, they drive you away from the temple; yet you come back over and over again. For

you are true, and truth cannot be banished. We enshrine falsehood in our temple, with all devotion; yet she is never there. Leave me not, Aparna. Sit here by my side. Why are you so sad, my darling? Do you miss some god, who is god no longer? But is there any need of God in this little world of ours? Let us be fearlessly godless and come closer to each other. They want our blood. And for this, they have come down to the dust of our earth, leaving their magnificence of heaven. For in their heaven there are no men, no creatures, who can suffer. No, my girl, there is no Goddess.

APARNA. Then leave this temple, and come away with me.

JAISING. Leave this temple? Yes, I will leave. Alas, Aparna, I must leave. Yet I cannot leave it, before I have paid my last dues to the —. But let that be. Come closer to me, my love. Whisper something to my ears, which will overflow this life with sweetness, flooding death itself.

APARNA. Words do not flow when the heart is full.

JAISING. Then lean your head on my breast. Let the silence of two eternities, life and death, touch each other. —But no more of this. I must go.

APARNA. Jaising, do not be cruel. Can you not feel what I have suffered?

JAISING. Am I cruel? Is this your last word to me? Cruel, as that block of stone, whom I called Goddess? Aparna, my beloved, if you were the Goddess, you would know what fire is this that burns my heart. But you are my Goddess. Do you know how I know it?

APARNA. Tell me.

JAISING. You bring to me your sacrifice every moment, as a mother does to her child. God must be all sacrifice, pouring out his life in all creation.

APARNA. Jaising, come, let us leave this temple and go away together.

JAISING. Save me, Aparna, have mercy upon me and leave me. I have only one object in my life. Do not usurp its place.

(Rushes out

APARNA. Again and again I have suffered. But my strength is gone. My heart breaks.

(She goes out

Enter Raghupati and Prince Nakshatra

RAGHUPATI. Prince, where have you kept the boy?

NAKSHATRA. He is in the room where the vessels for worship are kept. He has cried himself to sleep. I think I shall never be able to bear it, when he wakes up again.

RAGHUPATI. Jaising was of the same age when he came to me. And I remember how he cried till he slept at the feet of the Goddess, —the temple lamp dimly shining on his tear-stained child-face. It was a stormy evening like this.

NAKSHATRA. Father, delay not. I wish to finish it all, while he is sleeping. His cry pierces my heart like a knife.

RAGHUPATI. I will drug him to sleep, if he wakes up.

NAKSHATRA. The King will soon find it out, if you are not quick. For, in the evening, he leaves the care of his kingdom to come to this boy.

RAGHUPATI. Have more faith in the Goddess. The victim is now in her own hands and it shall never escape.

NAKSHATRA. But Chandpal is so watchful.

RAGHUPATI. Not more so than our Mother.

NAKSHATRA. I thought I saw a shadow pass by.

RAGHUPATI. The shadow of your own fear.

NAKSHATRA. Do we not hear the sound of a cry?

RAGHUPATI. The sound of your own heart. Shake off your despondency, Prince. Let us drink this wine duly consecrated. So long as the purpose remains in the mind, it looms large and fearful. In action it becomes small. The vapour is dark and diffused. It dissolves into water drops that are small and sparkling. Prince, it is nothing. It takes only a moment, — not more than it does to snuff a candle.

NAKSHATRA. I think we should not be too rash. Leave this work till to-morrow night.

RAGHUPATI. To-night is as good as to-morrow night, perhaps better.

NAKSHATRA. Listen to the sound of footsteps.

RAGHUPATI. I do not hear it.

NAKSHATRA. See there, —the light.

RAGHUPATI. The King comes. I fear we have delayed too long.

King comes with attendants

GOVINDA. Make them prisoners. (To Raghupati.) Have you anything to say?

RAGHUPATI. Nothing.

GOVINDA. Do you admit your crime?

RAGHUPATI. Crime? Yes, my crime was that, in my weakness, I delayed in carrying out Mother's service. The punishment comes from the Goddess. You are merely her instrument.

GOVINDA. According to my law, my soldiers shall escort you to exile, Raghupati, where you shall spend eight years of your life.

RAGHUPATI. King, I never bent my knees to any mortal in my life. I am a Brahmin. Your caste is lower than mine. Yet, in all humility, I pray to you, give 'me only one day's time.

GOVINDA. I grant it.

RAGHUPATI. (Mockingly.) You are the King of all kings. Your majesty and mercy are alike immeasurable. Whereas I am a mere worm, hiding in the dust. (He goes out)

GOVINDA. Nakshatra, admit your guilt.

NAKSHATRA. I am guilty. Sire, and I dare not ask for your pardon.

GOVINDA. Prince, I know you are tender of heart. Tell me, who beguiled you with evil counsel?

NAKSHATRA. I will not take other names, King. My guilt is my own. You have pardoned your foolish brother more than once, and once more he begs to be pardoned. Govinda Nakshatra, leave my feet. The judge is still more bound by his laws than his prisoner.

ATTENDANTS. Sire, remember that he is your brother, and pardon him.

GOVINDA. Let me remember that I am a king. Nakshatra shall remain in exile for eight years, in the house we have built, by the sacred river, outside the limits of Tripura. (Taking Nakshatra's hands.) The punishment is not yours only, brother, but also mine, —the more so because I cannot share it bodily.

(They all go out.

Enter Raghupati and Jaising

RAGHUPATI. My pride wallows in the mire. I have shamed my Brahminhood. I am no longer your master, my child. Yesterday I had the authority to command you. To-day I can only beg your favour. Life's days are mere tinsel, most trifling of God's gifts, and I had to beg for one of those days from the King with bent knees. Let that one day be not in vain. Let its infamous black brows be red with King's blood before it dies. Why do you not speak, my boy? Though I forsake my place as your master, yet have I not the right to claim your obedience as your father, —I who am more than a father to you, because father to an orphan? You are still silent, my child? Then let my knees bend to you, who were smaller than my knees when you first came to my arms.

JAISING. Father, do not torture the heart that is already broken. If the Goddess thirsts for kingly blood, I will bring it to her before to-night. I will pay all my debts, yes, every farthing. Keep ready for my return. I will delay not.

(Goes out.

(Storm outside.)

RAGKUPATI. She is awake at last, the Terrible. Her curses go shrieking through the town. The hungry furies are shaking the cracking branches of the world tree with all their might, for the stars to break and drop. My Mother, why didst thou keep thine own people in doubt and dishonour so long? Leave it not for thy servant to raise thy sword. Let thy mighty arm do its own work! —I hear steps.

Enters Aparna

APARNA. Where is Jaising?

RAGHUPATI. Away evil omen (Aparna goes out) But if Jaising never comes back? No, he will not break his promise. Victory to thee, Great Kali, the giver of all success! — But if he meet with obstruction? If he be caught and lose his life at the guards' hands? —Victory to thee, watchful Goddess, Mother invincible! Do not allow thy repute to be lost, and thine enemies to laugh at thee. If thy children must lose their pride and faith in their Mother, and bow down their heads in shame before the rebels, who then shall remain in this orphaned world to carry thy banner? — I hear his steps. But so soon? Is he coming back foiled in his purpose? No, that cannot be. Thy miracle needs not time, O Mistress of all time, terrible with thy necklace of human skulls.
(Rushes in Jaising.

Jaising, where is the blood?

JAISING. It is with me. Let go my hands. Let me offer it myself (Eritering the temple.) Must thou have kingly blood. Great Mother, who nourishest the world at thy breast with life? —I am of the royal caste, a Kshatriya. My ancestors have sat upon thrones, and there are rulers of men in my mother's line. I have kingly blood in my veins. Take it, and quench thy thirst for ever.

(Stabs himself f and falls,

RAGHUPATI. Jaising! O cruel, ungrateful! You have done the blackest crime. You kill your father! Jaising, forgive me, my darling. Come back to my heart, my heart's one treasure! Let me die in your place.

Enters Aparna

APARNA. It will madden me. Where is Jaising? Where is he?

RAGHUPATI. Come, Aparna, come, my child, call him with all your love. Call him back to life. Take him to you, away from me, only let him live.
(Aparna enters the temple and swoons.)

(Beating his forehead on the temple floor.) Give him, give him, give him. —Give him back

to me! (Stands up addressing the image.) Look how she stands there, the silly stone, — deaf, dumb, blind, —the whole sorrowing world weeping at her door, — the noblest hearts wrecking themselves at her stony feet. Give me back my Jaising. Oh, it is all in vain. Our bitterest cries wander in emptiness, —the emptiness that we vainly try to fill with these stony images of delusion. Away with them! Away with these our impotent dreams, that harden into stones, burdening our world.
(He throws away the image, and comes out into ihe courtyard.

Enters Gunavati

GUNAVATI. Victory to thee, great Goddess! —But, where is the Goddess?

RAGHUPATI. Goddess there is none.

GUNAVATI. Bring her back, father. I have brought her my offerings. I have come at last, to appease her anger with my own heart s blood. Let her know that the Queen is true to her promise. Have pity on me, and bring back the Goddess only for this night. Tell me, —where is she? Raghupati She is nowhere, —neither above, nor below.

GUNAVATI. Master, was not the Goddess here in the temple?

RAGHUPATI. Goddess? —If there were any true Goddess anywhere in the world, could she bear this thing to usurp her name?

GUNAVATI. Do not torture me. Tell me truly. Is there no Goddess?

RAGHUPATI. No, there is none.

GUNAVATI. Then who was here?

RAGHUPATI. Nothing, nothing.

Aparna comes out from the temple.

APARNA. Father.

RAGHUPATI. My sweet child! "Father," —did you say? Do you rebuke me with that name? My son, whom I have killed, has left that one dear call behind him in your sweet voice.

APARNA. Father, leave this temple. Let us go away from here.

Enters the King

GOVINDA. Where is the Goddess?

RAGHUPATI. The Goddess is nowhere.

GOVINDA. But what blood-stream is this?

RAGHUPATI. King, Jaising, who loved you so dearly, has killed himself.

GOVINDA. Killed himself? Why?

RAGHUPATI. To kill the falsehood, that sucks the life-blood of man.

GOVINDA. Jaising is great. He has conquered death. My flowers are for him.

GUNAVATI. My King.

GOVINDA. Yes, my love.

GUNAVATI. The Goddess is no more.

GOVINDA. She has burst her cruel prison of stone, and come back to woman's heart.

APARNA. Father, come away.

RAGHUPAT. i Come, child. Come, Mother. I have found thee. Thou art the last gift of Jaising.

# THE KING AND THE QUEEN

# ACT I

*The Palace Garden.*
*King Vikram and Queen Sumitra*

VIKRAM. Why have you delayed in coming to me for so long, my love?

SUMITRA. Do you not know, my King, that I am utterly yours, wherever I am? It was your Louse, and its service, that kept me away from your presence, but not from you.

VIKRAM. Leave the house, and its service, alone. My heart cannot spare you for my world, I am jealous of its claims.

SUMITRA. No, King, I have my place in your heart, as your beloved, and in your world, as your Queen.

VIKRAM. Alas, my darling, where have vanished those days of unalloyed joy, when we first met in love; when our world awoke not, — only the flush of the early dawn of our union broke through our hearts in overflowing silence? You had sweet shyness in your eyelids, like a dew drop on the tip of a flower-petal, and the smile flickered on your lips like a timid evening lamp in the breeze. I remember the eager embrace of your love, when the morning broke and we had to part, and your unwilling steps, heavy with languor, that took you away from me. Where were the house, and its service, and the cares of your world?

SUMITRA. But then we were scarcely more than a boy and a girl; and to-day we are the King and the Queen.

VIKRAM. The King and the Queen? Mere names. We are more than that; we are lovers.

SUMITRA. You are my King, my husband, and I am content to follow your steps. Do not shame me by putting me before your kingship.

VIKRAM. Do you not want my love?

SUMITRA. Love me truly by not making your love extravagant; for truth can afford to be simple.

VIKRAM. I do not understand woman's heart.

SUMITRA. King, if you thriftlessly squander your all upon me, then I shall be deprived.

VIKRAM. No more vain words. Queen. The birds' nests are silent with love. Let lips keep guard upon lips, and allow not words to clamour.

Enters Attendant

ATTENDANT. The minister begs audience, to discuss a grave matter of state.

VIKRAM. No, not now.

(Attendant goes.

SUMITRA. Sire, ask him to come.

VIKRAM. The state and its matter can wait. But sweet leisure comes rarely. It is frail, like a flower. Respite from duty is a part of duty.

SUMITRA. Sire, I beg of you, attend to your work.

VIKRAM. Again, cruel woman. Do you imagine that I always follow you to win your unwilling favour, drop by drop? I leave you and go. (He goes.)

Enter Devadatta, the King's Brahmin friend.

SUMITRA. Tell me, sir, what is that noise outside the gate?

DEVADATTA. That noise? Command me, and with the help of soldiers I shall drive away that noise, ragged and hungry.

SUMITRA. Do not mock me. Tell me what has happened.

DEVADATTA. Nothing. It is merely hunger, —the vulgar hunger of poverty. The famished horde of barbarians is rudely clamouring, making the drowsy cuckoos in your royal garden start up in fear.

Sumitra Tell me, father, who are hungry?

DEVADATTA. It is their ill-fate. The King's poor subjects have been practising long to live upon half a meal a day, but they have not yet become experts in complete starvation. It is amazing.

SUMITRA. But, father, the land is smiling with ripe corn. Why should the King's subjects die of hunger.?

DEVADATTA. The corn is his, whose is the land, —it is not for the poor. They, like intruding dogs at the King's feast, crouch in the corner for their crumbs, or kicks.

SUMITRA. Does it mean, that there is no King in this lamd?

DEVADATTA. Not one, but hundreds.

SUMITRA. Are not the King's officers watchful?

DEVADATTA. Who can blame your officers? They came penniless from the alien land. Is it to bless the King's subjects with their empty hands?

SUMITRA. From the ahen land? Are they my relatives?

DEVADATTA. Yes, Queen.

SUMITRA. What about Jaisen?

DEVADATTA. He rules the province of Singarh with such scrupulous care, that all the rubbish, in the shape of food and raiment, has been cleared away; only the skin and bones remain.

SUMITRA. And Shila?

DEVADATTA. He keeps his eyes upon the trade; he relieves all merchants of their excessive profits, taking the burden upon his own broad shoulders.

SUMITRA. And Ajit?

DEVADATTA. He lives in Vijaykote. He smiles sweetly, strokes the land on its back with his caressing hand, and whatever comes to his touch gathers with care.

SUMITRA. What shame is this. I must remove this refuse from my father's land and save my people. Leave me now, the King comes. (Enters the King.) I am the mother of my people. I cannot bear their cry. Save them, King.

VIKRAM. What do you want me to do?

SUMITRA. Turn those out from your kingdom, who are oppressing the land.

VIKRAM. Do you know who they are?

SUMITRA. Yes, I know.

VIKRAM. They are your own cousins.

SUMITRA. They are not a whit more my own than my people. They are robbers, who, under the cover of your throne, seek for their victims.

VIKRAM. They are Jaisen, Shila, Ajit.

SUMITRA. My country must be rid of them.

Vikram They will not move without fight.

SUMITRA. Then fight them, Sire.

VIKRAM. Fight? But let me conquer you first, and then I shall have time to conquer my enemies.

SUMITRA. Allow me. King, as your Queen. I will save your subjects myself. (Goes.)

VIKRAM. This is how you make my heart distraught. You sit alone upon your peak of greatness, where I do not reach you. You go to attend your own God, and I go seeking you in vain.

Enters Devadatta

DEVADATTA. Where is the Queen, Sire? Why are you alone?

VIKRAM. Brahmin, this is all your conspiracy. You come here to talk of the state news to the Queen?

DEVADATTA. The state is shouting its own news loud enough to reach the Queen's ears. It has come to that pass, when it takes no heed lest your rest be broken. Do not be afraid of me, King. I have come to ask my Brahmin's dues from the Queen. For my wife is out of humour, her larder is empty, and in the house there are a number of empty stomachs. (He goes.)

VIKRAM. I wish all happiness to my people. Why should there be suffering, and injustice? Why should the strong cast his vulture's eyes upon the poor man's comforts, pitifully small? (Enters Minister.) Banish all the foreign robbers from my kingdom, this moment. I must not hear the cry of the oppressed for a day longer.

MINISTER. But, King, the evil that has been slowly growing for long, you cannot uproot in a day.

VIKRAM. Strike at its root with vigour, and fell it with your axe in a day, —the tree that has taken a hundred years to grow.

MINISTER. But we want arms and soldiers.

VIKRAM. Where is my general?

MINISTER. He himself is a foreigner.

VIKRAM. Then invite the hungry people. Open my treasure; stop this cry with food; send them away with money, —And if they want to have my kingdom, let them do so in peace, and be happy. (He goes.)

Enter Sumitra and Devadatta

MINISTER. Queen, my humble salutation to you.

QUEEN. We cannot allow misery to go unchecked in our land.

MINISTER. What are your commands, Queen?

QUEEN. Call immediately, in my name, all our chiefs who are foreigners.

MINISTER. I have done so already. I have taken upon myself to invite them into the capital, in the King's name, without asking for his sanction, for fear of refusal.

QUEEN. When did you send your messengers?

MINISTER. It will soon be a month hence. I am expecting their answers every moment. But I am afraid they will not respond.

QUEEN. Not respond to the King's call?

DEVADATTA. The King has become a piece of wild rumour, which they can believe, or not, as they like.

QUEEN. Keep your soldiers ready, Minister, for these people. They shall have to answer to me, as my relatives.

(The Minister goes.

DEVADATTA. Queen, they will not come.

QUEEN. Then the King shall fight them.

DEVADATTA. The King will not fight.

QUEEN. Then I will.

Devadatta You!

QUEEN. I will go to my brother Kumarsen, Kashmir's King, and with his help fight these rebels, who are a disgrace to Kashmir. Father, help me to escape from this kingdom, and do your duty, if things come to the worst.

DEVADATTA. I salute thee, Mother of the people.

(He goes.

Enters Vikram

VIKRAM. Why do you go away, Queen? My hungry desire is revealed to you in its naked poverty. Do you therefore go away from me in derision?

SUMITRA. I feel shamed to share alone your heart, which is for all men.

VIKRAM. Is it absolutely true, Queen, that you stand on your giddy height, and I grovel in the dust? No. I know my power. There is an unconquerable force in my nature, which I have turned into love for you.

SUMITRA. Hate me, King, hate me. Forget me. I shall bear it bravely,-but do not wreck your manhood against a woman s charms.

VIKRAM. So much love, yet such neglect? Your very indifference, like a cruel knife, cuts into my bosom, laying bare the warm bleeding love, —and then, to fling it into the dust!

SUMITRA. I throw myself at your feet, my beloved. Have you not forgiven your Queen, again and again, for wrongs done? Then why is this wrath, Sire, when I am blameless?

KING. Rise up, my love. Come to my heart. Shut my life from all else for a moment, with your encircling arms, rounding it into a world completely your own.

A VOICE FROM OUTSIDE. Queen.

SUMITRA. It is Devadatta. —Yes, father, what is the message?

Enters Devadatta

DEVADATTA. They have defied the King's call, —the foreign governors of the provinces, —and they are preparing for rebellion.

SUMITRA. Do you hear. King?

VIKRAM. Brahmin, the palace garden is not the council-house.

DEVADATTA. Sire, we rarely meet our King in the council-house, because it is not the palace garden.

QUEEN. The miserable dogs, grown fat upon the King's table sweepings, dare dream of barking against their master.? King, is it time for debating in the council chamber? Is not the course clear before you? Go with your soldiers and crush these miscreants.

VIKRAM. But our general himself is a foreigner.

QUEEN. Go yourself.

VIKRAM. Am I your misfortune, Queen, —a bad dream, a thorn in your flesh? No, I will never move a step from here. I will offer them terms of peace. Who is it that has caused this mischief? The Brahmin and the woman conspired to wake up the sleeping snake from its hole. Those who are too feeble to protect themselves are the most thoughtless in causing disasters to others.

QUEEN. O the unfortunate land, and the unfortunate woman who is the Queen of this land.

VIKRAM. Where are you going?

QUEEN. I am going to leave you.

VIKRAM. Leave me?

QUEEN. Yes. I am going to fight the rebels.

VIKRAM. Woman, you mock me.

QUEEN. I take my farewell.

KING. You dare not leave me.

QUEEN. I dare not stay by your side, when I weaken you.

KING. Go, proud woman. I will never ask you to turn back, —but claim no help from me.

(Queen goes.

DEVADATTA. King, you allow her to go alone.?

KING. She is not going. I do not believe her words.

DEVADATTA. I think she is in earnest.

KING. It is her woman's wiles. She threatens me, while she wants to spur me into action; and I despise her methods. She must not think that she can play with my love. She shall regret it. O my friend, must I learn my lesson at last, that love is not for the King, —and learn it from that woman, whom I love like my doom? Devadatta, you have grown with me from infancy, —can you not forget, for a moment, that I am a king, and feel that I have a man's heart that knows pain?

DEVADATTA. My heart is yours, my friend, which is not only ready to receive your love, but* your anger.

KING. But why do you invite the snake into my nest?

DEVADATTA. Your house was on fire, —I merely brought the news, and wakened you up. Am I to blame for that?

KING. What is the use of waking? When all are mere dreams, let me choose my own little dream, if I can, and then die. Fifty years hence, who will remember the joys and sorrows of this moment? Go, Devadatta, leave me to my kingly loneliness of pain.

Enters a Courtier who is a foreigner

COURTIER. We ask justice from your hands, King, — we, who came to this land with the Queen.

KING. Justice for what?

COURTIER. It has come to our ears, that false accusations against us are brought before you, for no other cause than that we are foreigners.

KING. Who knows, if they are not true? But so long as I trust you, can you not remain silent? Have I ever insulted you with the least suspicion-the suspicions that are bred like maggots in the rotten hearts of cowards? Treason I do not fear. I can crush it under my feet. But I fear to nourish littleness in my own mind. —You can leave me now.

(The courtier goes.

Enter Minister and Devadatta

MINISTER. Sire, the Queen has left the palace, riding on her horse.

KING. What do you say? Left my palace?

MINISTER. Yes, King.

KING. Why did you not stop her?

MINISTER. She left in secret.

KING. Who brought you the news?

MINISTER. The priest. He saw her riding before the palace temple.

KING. Send for him.

MINISTER. But Sire, she cannot be far. She has only just left. You can yet bring her back.

KING. Bringing her back is not important. The great fact is, that she left me. —Left me! And all the King's soldiers and forts, and prisons and iron chains, could not keep fast this little heart of a woman.

MINISTER. Alas, King. Calumny, like a floodburst, when the dyke is broken, will rush in from all sides.

KING. Calumny! Let the people's tongues rot with their own poison.

DEVADATTA. In the days of eclipse, men dare look at the midday sun through their broken pieces of glass, blackened with soot. Great Queen, your name will be soiled, tossed from mouth to mouth, but your light will ever shine far above all soiling.

KING. Bring the priest to me. (Minister goes.) I can yet go to seek her, and bring her back. But is this my eternal task.? That she should always avoid me, and I should ever run after the fugitive heart? Take your flight, woman, day and night, homeless, loveless, without rest and peace. (Enters Priest.) Go, go, I have heard enough, I do not want to know more. (The priest is about to go,) Come back. — Tell me, did she come down to the temple to pray, with tears in her eyes?

PRIEST. No, Sire. Only, for a moment, she checked her horse and turned her face to the temple, bowing her head low, —then rode away fast as lightning. I cannot say, if she had tears in her eyes. The light from the temple was dim.

KING. Tears in her eyes? You could not even imagine such enormity? Enough. You may go. (The Priest goes.) My God, you know that all the wrong that I have done to her, was that I loved her. I was wiUing to lose my heaven and my kingdom for her love. But they have not betrayed me, only she has.

Enters Minister

MINISTER. Sire, I have sent messengers on horseback in pursuit of her.

KING. Call them back. The dream has fled away. Where can your messengers find it? Get ready my army. I will go to war myself, and crush the rebellion.

MINISTER. As you command. (Goes away.)

VIKRAM. Devadatta, why do you sit silent and sad? The thief has fled, leaving the booty behind, and now I pick up my freedom. This is a moment of rejoicing to m.e. False, false friend, false are my words. Cruel pain pierces my heart.

DEVADATTA. You shall have no time for pain, or for love, now, —your life will become one stream of purpose, and carry your kingly heart to its great conquest.

VIKRAM. But I am not yet completely freed in my heart. I still believe she will soon come back to me, when she finds that the world is not her lover, and that man's heart is the only world for a woman. She will know what she has spurned, when she misses it; and my time will come when, her pride gone, she comes back, and jealously begins to woo me.

Enters Attendant

ATTENDANT. A letter from the Queen. (Gives the letter, and goes.)

KING. She relents already. {Reads the letter.) Only this. Just two lines, to say that she is going to her brother in Kashmir, to ask him to help her to quell the rebellion in my kingdom. This is insult! Help from Kashmir!

DEVADATTA. Lose no time to forestall her, —and let that be your revenge.

KING. My revenge? You shall know it.

## ACT II

*Tent in Kashmir*
VIKRAM and the General

GENERAL. Pardon me, King, if I dare offer you advice in the interest of your kingdom.

VIKRAM. Speak to me.

GENERAL. The rebellion in our land has been quelled. The rebels themselves are fighting on your side. Why waste our strength and time in Kashmir, when your presence in your own capital is so urgently needed?

VIKRAM. The fight here is not over yet.

GENERAL. But Kumarsen, tlie Queen's brother, is already punished for his sister's temerity. His army is routed, he is hiding for his Hfe. His uncle, Chandrasen, is only too eager to be seated upon the vacant throne. Make him the king, and leave this unfortunate country to peace.

VIKRAM. It is not for punishment, that I stay here; it is for fight. The fight has become like a picture to a painter. I must add bold lines, blend strong colours, and perfect it every day. My mind grows more and more immersed in it, as it blossoms into forms; and I leave it with a sigh, when it is finished. The destruction is merely its materials, out of which it takes its shape. It is a creation. It is beautiful, as red bunches of palash, that break out like a drunken fury, yet every one of its flowers delicately perfect.

GENERAL. But, Sire, this cannot go on for ever. You have other duties. The minister has been sending me message after message, entreating me to help you to see how this war is ruining your country.

VIKRAM. I cannot see anything else in the world but what is growing under my masterly hands. Oh, the music of swords. Oh, the great battles, that clasp your breast tight like hard embraces of love. Go, General, you have other works to do, —your advices flash out best on the points of your swords. (General goes.) This is deliverance. The bondage has fled of itself, leaving the prisoner free. Revenge is stronger than the thin wine of love. Revenge is freedom, —freedom from the coils of cloying sweetness.

Enters General

GENERAL. I can espy a carriage coming towards our tent, perhaps bringing an envoy of peace. It has no escort of armed soldiers.

KING. Peace must follow the war. The time for it has not yet come.

GENERAL. Let us hear the messenger first, and then, —

KING. And then continue the war.

Enters a Soldier

SOLDIER. The Queen has come asking for your audience.

VIKRAM. What do you say.?

SOLDIER. The Queen has come.

VIKRAM. Which Queen?

SOLDIER. Our Queen, Sumitra.

VIKRAM. Go, General, see who has come.

(The General and the Soldier go.

KING. This is the third time that she has come, vainly attempting to coax me away, since I have carried war into Kashmir. But these are no dreams-these battles. To wake up suddenly, and then find again the same palace gardens, the flowers, the Queen, the long days made of sighs and small favours. No, a thousand times, no. She has come to make me captive, to take me as her trophy from the war-field into her palace hall. She may as well try to capture the thunderstorms.

Enters General

GENERAL. Yes, Sire, it is our own Queen, who wants to see you. It breaks my heart when I cannot allow her to come freely into your presence.

KING. This is neitlier the time, nor the place, to see a woman.

GENERAL. But, Sire.

KING. No, no. Tell my guards to keep a strict watch at my tent door, —not for enemies, but for women.

(General goes.

Enters Shankar

SHANKAR. I am Shankar, —King Kumarsen's servant. You have kept me captive in your tent.

KING. Yes, I know you.

SHANKAR. Your Queen waits outside your tent.

KING. She will have to wait for me farther away.

SHANKAR. It makes me blush to say, that she has come humbly to ask your pardon; or, if that is impossible, to accept her punishment from your hand. For she owns that she alone was to blame, —and she asks you, in the name of all that is sacred, to spare her brother's country and her brother.

KING. But you must know, old man, it is war, —and this war is with her brother, and not herself. I have no time to discuss the rights and wrongs of the question with a woman. But, being a man, you ought to know that when once a war is started, rightly or wrongly, it is our man's pride that must ca ±y it on to the end.

SHANKAR. But do you know. Sire, you are carrying on this war with a woman, and she is your Queen. Our Ejng is merely espousing her cause, being her brother. I ask you, is it king-like, or man-like, to magnify a domestic quarrel into a war, carrying it from country to country?

KING. I warn you, old man, your tongue is becoming dangerous. You may tell the Queen, in my name, that when her brother, Kumarsen, owns his defeat and surrenders himself into our hands, the question of pardoning will then be discussed.

SHANKAR. That is as impossible as for the morning sun to kiss the dust of the western horizon. My King will never surrender himself alive into your hands, and his sister will never suffer it.

KING. Then the war must continue. But do you not think that bravery ceases to be bravery at a certain point, and becomes mere fool-hardiness? Your King can never escape me. I have surrounded him on all sides, and he knows it.

SHANKAR. Yes, he knows it and also knows that there is a great gap.

KING. What do you mean?

SHANKAR. I mean death, —the triumphal gate through which he will escape you, if I know him right. And there waits his revenge. (He goes.)
(Enters Attendant)

Sire, Chandrasen, and his wife Revati, Kumarsen's uncle and aunt, have come to see you.

KING. Ask them in.

Enter Chandrasen and Revati

KING. My obeisance to you both.

CHANDRASEN. May you live long.

REVATI. May you be victorious.

CHANDRASEN. What punishment have you decided for him?

KING. If he surrenders, I shall pardon him.

REVATI. Only this, and nothing more? If tame pardon comes at the end, then why is there such preparation? Kings are not overgrown children, and war is no mere child's play.

VIKRAM. To rob was not my purpose, but to restore my honour. The head that bears the crown cannot bear insult.

CHANDRASEN. My son, forgive him. For he is neither mature in age, nor in wisdom. You may deprive him of his right to the throne, or banish him, but spare him his life.

KING. I never wished to take his life.

REVATI. Then why such an army and arms? You kill the soldiers, who have done you no harm, and spare him who is guilty?

VIKRAM. I do not understand you.

CHANDRASEN. It is nothing. She is angry with Kumarsen for having brought our country into trouble, and for giving you just cause for anger, who are so nearly related to us.

VIKRAM. Justice will be meted out to him, when he is captured.

REVATI. I have come to ask you never to suspect that we are hiding him. It is the people. Burn their crops and their villages, — drive them with hunger, and then they will bring him out.

CHANDRASEN. Gently, wife, gently. Come to the palace, son, the reception of Kashmir awaits you there.

KING. You go there now, and I shall follow you. {They go out.) Oh, the red flame of hell-fire. The greed and hatred in a woman's heart. Did I catch a glimpse of my own face in her face, I wonder? Are there lines like those on my forehead, the burnt tracks made by a hidden fire? Have my lips grown as thin and curved at both ends as hers, like some murderer's knife? No, my passion is for war, —it is neither for greed, nor for cruelty; its fire is like love's fire, that knows no restraint, that counts no cost, that burns itself, and all that it touches, either into a flame, or to ashes.

Enters Attendant

ATTENDANT. The Brahmin, Devadatta, has come, awaiting your pleasure.

KING. Devadatta has come? Bring him in, — No, no, stop. Let me think, —I know him. He has come to turn me back from the battle-field. Brahmin, you undermined the river banks, and now, when the water overflows, you piously pray that it may irrigate your fields, and then tamely go back. Will it not wash away your houses, and ruin the country? The joy of the terrible is blind, —its term of life is short, and it must gather its plunder in fearful haste, like a mad elephant uprooting the lotus from the pond. Wise councils will come, in their turn, when the great force is spent, —No, I must not see the Brahmin.

Enters Amaru, the chieftain of Trichur hills

AMARU. Sire, I have come at your bidding, and I own you as my King.

KING. You are the chief of this place?

AMARU. Yes. I am the chief of Trichur. You are the Kjng of many kings, and I am your servant. I have a daughter, whose name is Ila. She is young and comely. Do not think me vain, when I say that she is worthy to be your spouse. She is waiting outside. Permit me, King, and I shall send her to you as the best greeting of this land of flowers. (He goes out.)

Enters Ila with her Attendant

KING. Ah! She comes, as a surprise of dawn, when the moment before it seemed like a dark night. Come, maiden, you have made the battle-field forget itself. Kashmir has shot her best arrow, at last, to pierce the heart of the war-god. You make me feel that my eyes had been wandering among the wilderness of things, to find at last their fulfilment. But why do you stand so silent, with your eyes on the ground? I can almost see a trembling of pain in your limbs, whose intensity makes it invisible.

ILA. (Kneeling.) I have heard that you are a great King. Be pleased to grant me my prayer.

KING. Rise up, fair maiden. This earth is not worthy to be touched by your feet. Why do you kneel in the dust? There is nothing that I cannot grant you.

ILA. My father has given me to you. I beg myself back from your hands. You have wealth untold, and territories unlimited, — go and leave me behind in the dust; there is nothing that you can want.

KING. Is there, indeed, nothing that I can want? How shall I show you my heart? Where is its wealth? Where are its territories? It is empty. Had I no kingdom, but only you —

ILA. Then first take my life, —as you take that of the wild deer of the forest, piercing her heart with your arrows, —

KING. But why, child, —why such contempt for me? Am I so utterly unworthy of you? I have won kingdoms with the might of my arms. Can I not hope to beg your heart for me?

ILA. But my heart is not mine. I have given it to one who left me months ago, promising to come back and meet me in the shade of our ancient forest. Days pass, and I wait, and the silence of the forest grows wistful. If he find me not, when he comes back! If he go away for ever, and the forest shadows keep their ancient watch for the love-meeting that remains eternally unfulfilled! King, do not take me away, —leave me for him, who has left me, to find me again.

VIKRAM. What a fortunate man is he. But I warn you, girl, gods are jealous of our love. Listen to my secret. There was a time when I despised the whole world, and only loved. I woke up from my dream, and found that the world was there, —only my love burst as a bubble. What is his name, for whom you wait?

ILA. He is Kashmir's King. His name is Kumarsen.

VIKRAM. Kumarsen!

ILA. Do you know him? He is known to all. Kashmir has given its heart to him.

VIKRAM. Kumarsen? Kashmir's King?

ILA. Yes. He must be your friend.

VIKRAM. But do you not know, that the sun of his fortune has set? Give up all hope of him. He is like a hunted animal, running and hiding from one hole to another. The poorest beggar in these hills is happier than he.

ILA. I hardly understand you, King.

VIKRAM. You, women, sit in the seclusion of your hearts, and only love. You do not know how the roaring torrent of the world passes by, and we, men, are carried away in its waves in all directions. With your sad, big eyes, filled with tears, you sit and watch, clinging to flimsy hope. But learn to despair, my child.

ILA. Tell me the truth. King. Do not deceive me. I am so very little and so trivial. But I am all his own. Where, — in what homeless wilds, —is my lover roaming? I will go to seek him, —I, who never have been out of my house. Show me the way, —

VIKRAM. His enemy's soldiers are after him, — he is doomed.

ILA. But are you not his friend? Will you not save him? A king is in danger, and will you suffer it as a King? Are you not honour-bound to succour him? I know that all the world loved him. But where are they, in his time of misfortune? Sire, you are great in power, but what is your power for, if you do not help the great? Can you keep yourself aloof? Then show me the way, —I will offer my life for him, — the one, weak woman.

VIKRAM. Love him, love him with all you have — Love him, who is the King of your precious heart. I have lost my love's heaven myself, —but let me have the happiness to make you happy. I will not covet your love. —The withered branch cannot hope to blossom with borrowed flowers. Trust me. I am your friend. I will bring him to you.

ILA. Noble King. I owe you my life and my heaven of happiness.

VIKRAM. Go, and be ready with your bridal dress. I will change the tune of my music. (Ila goes.) This war is growing tiresome. But peace is insipid. Homeless fugitive, you are more fortunate than I am. Woman's love, like heaven's watchful eyes, follows you wherever you go in this world, making your defeat a triumph and misfortune splendid, like sunset clouds.

Enters Devadatta

DEVADATTA. Save me from my pursuers.

KING. Who are they?

DEVADATTA. They are your guards, King. They kept me under strict watch for this everlasting half-hour. I talked to them of art and letters; they were amused. They thought I was playing the fool to please them. Then I began to recite to them the best lyrics of Kalidas, —and it soothed this pair of yokels to sleep. In perfect disgust, I left their tent to come to you.

KING. These guards should be punished for their want of taste in going off to sleep when the prisoner recited Kalidas.

DEVADATTA. We shall think of the punishment later on. In the meanwhile, we must leave this miserable war and go back home. Once I used to think that only they died of love's separation, who were the favoured of fortune, delicately nurtured. But since I left home to come here, I have discovered that even a poor Brahmin is not too small to fall a victim to angered love.

VIKRAM. Love and death are not too careful in their choice of victims. They are impartial. Yes, friend, let us go back home. Only I have one thing to do, before I leave this place. Try to find out, from the chief of Trichur, Kumarsen's hiding-place. Tell him, when you find him, that I am no longer his enemy. And, friend, if somebody else is there with him, —if you meet her, —

DEVADATTA. Yes, yes, I know. She is ever in our thoughts, yet she is beyond our words. She, who is noble, her sorrow has to be great.

VIKRAM. Friend, you have come to me, like the first sudden breeze of spring. Now my flowers will follow, with all the memories of the past happy years.

[Devadatta goes.

Enters Chandrasen

VIKRAM. I have glad tidings for you. I have pardoned Kumarsen.

CHANDRASEN. You may have pardoned him, —but now that I represent Kashmir, he must await his country's judgment at my hands. He shall have his punishment from me.

VIKRAM. What punishment?

CHANDRASEN. He shall be deprived of his throne.

VIKRAM. Impossible. His throne I will restore to him.

CHANDRASEN. What right have you in Kashmir's throne?

VIKRAM. The right of the victorious. This throne is now mine, and I will give it to him.

CHANDRASEN. You give it to him! Do I not know proud Kumarsen, from his infancy? Do you think he will accept his father's throne as a gift from you? He can bear your vengeance, but not your generosity.

Enters a Messenger

MESSENGER. The news has reached us that Kumarsen is coming in a closed carriage to surrender himself. (Goes out.)

CHANDRASEN. Incredible! The lion comes to beg his chains! Is life so precious?

VIKRAM. But why does he come in a closed carriage?

CHANDRASEN. How can he show himself? The eyes of the crowd in the streets will pierce him, like arrows, to the quick. Ejng, put out the lamp, when he comes, receive him in darkness. Do not let him suffer the insult of the light.

Enters Devadatta

DEVADATTA. I hear that the King, Kumarsen, is coming to see you of his own will.

VIKRAM. I will receive him with solemn rituals, — with you as our priest. Ask my general to employ his soldiers to make preparation for a wedding festival.

Enter the Brahmin Elders

ALL. Victory be to you.

FIRST ELDER. We hear that you have invited our King, to restore him to his throne, — Therefore we have come to bless you for the joy that you have given to Kashmir. (Enters Shankar)

(They bless him, and the King bows to them. The Brahmins go out.

Shankar (To Chandrasen.) Sire, is it true that Kumarsen is coming to surrender himself to

his enemies?

CHANDRASEN. Yes, it is true.

SHANKAR. Worse than a thousand lies. O my beloved King, I am your old servant, I have suffered pain that only God knows, yet never complained. But how can I bear this? That you should travel through all the roads of Kashmir, to enter your cage of prison? Why did not your servant die before this day?

Enters a Soldier

SOLDIER. The carriage is at the door.

KING. Have they no instruments at hand, — flutes and drums? Let them strike a glad tune. (Coming near the door,) I welcome you, my kingly friend, with all my heart.

Enters Sumitra, with a covered tray in her hands.

VIKRAM. Sumitra. My Queen!

SUMITRA. King Vikram, day and night you sought him in hills and forests, spreading devastation, neglecting your people and your honour, and to-day he sends through me to you his coveted head, —the head upon which death sits even more majestic than his crown.

VIKRAM. My Queen.

SUMITRA. Sire, no longer your Queen; for merciful death has claimed me.

(Falls and dies.

SHANKAR. My King, my Master, my darling boy, you have done well. You have come to your eternal throne. God has allowed me to live for so long to witness this glory. And now, my days are done, and your servant will follow you.

Enters Ila, dressed in a bridal dress
ILA. King, I hear the bridal music. Where is my lover? I am ready.

# MY REMINISCENCES – AUTOBIOGRAPHY

## PREFACE

These Reminiscences were written and published by the Author in his fiftieth year, shortly before he started on a trip to Europe and America for his failing health in 1912. It was in the course of this trip that he wrote for the first time in the English language for publication.

In these memory pictures, so lightly, even casually presented by the author there is, nevertheless, revealed a connected history of his inner life together with that of the varying literary forms in which his growing self found successive expression, up to the point at which both his soul and poetry attained maturity.

This lightness of manner and importance of matter form a combination the translation of which into a different language is naturally a matter of considerable difficulty. It was, in any case, a task which the present Translator, not being an original writer in the English language, would hardly have ventured to undertake, had there not been other considerations. The translator's familiarity, however, with the persons, scenes, and events herein depicted made it a temptation difficult for him to resist, as well as a responsibility which he did not care to leave to others not possessing these advantages, and therefore more liable to miss a point, or give a wrong impression.

The Translator, moreover, had the author's permission and advice to make a free translation, a portion of which was completed and approved by the latter before he left India on his recent tour to Japan and America.

In regard to the nature of the freedom taken for the purposes of the translation, it may be mentioned that those suggestions which might not have been as clear to the foreign as to the Bengali reader have been brought out in a slightly more elaborate manner than in the original text; while again, in rare cases, others which depend on allusions entirely unfamiliar to the non-Indian reader, have been omitted rather than spoil by an over-elaboration the simplicity and naturalness which is the great feature of the original.

There are no footnotes in the original. All the footnotes here given have been added by the Translator in the hope that they may be of further assistance to the foreign reader.

**PART I**

# 1

I know not who paints the pictures on memory's canvas; but whoever he may be, what he is painting are pictures; by which I mean that he is not there with his brush simply to make a faithful copy of all that is happening. He takes in and leaves out according to his taste. He makes many a big thing small and small thing big. He has no compunction in putting into the background that which was to the fore, or bringing to the front that which was behind. In short he is painting pictures, and not writing history.

Thus, over Life's outward aspect passes the series of events, and within is being painted a set of pictures. The two correspond but are not one.

We do not get the leisure to view thoroughly this studio within us. Portions of it now and then catch our eye, but the greater part remains out of sight in the darkness. Why the ever-busy painter is painting; when he will have done; for what gallery his pictures are destined-who can tell?

Some years ago, on being questioned as to the events of my past life, I had occasion to pry into this picture-chamber. I had thought to be content with selecting some few materials for my Life's story. I then discovered, as I opened the door, that Life's memories are not Life's history, but the original work of an unseen Artist. The variegated colours scattered about are not reflections of outside lights, but belong to the painter himself, and come passion-tinged from his heart; thereby unfitting the record on the canvas for use as evidence in a court of law.

But though the attempt to gather precise history from memory's storehouse may be fruitless, there is a fascination in looking over the pictures, a fascination which cast its spell on me.

The road over which we journey, the wayside shelter in which we pause, are not pictures while yet we travel-they are too necessary, too obvious. When, however, before turning into the evening resthouse, we look back upon the cities, fields, rivers and hills which we have been through in Life's morning, then, in the light of the passing day, are they pictures indeed. Thus, when my opportunity came, did I look back, and was engrossed.

Was this interest aroused within me solely by a natural affection for my own past? Some personal feeling, of course, there must have been, but the pictures had also an independent artistic value of their own. There is no event in my reminiscences worthy of being preserved for all time. But the quality of the subject is not the only justification for a record. What one has truly felt, if only it can be made sensible to others, is always of importance to one's fellow men. If pictures which have taken shape in memory can be brought out in words, they are worth a place in literature.

It is as literary material that I offer my memory pictures. To take them as an attempt at autobiography would be a mistake. In such a view these reminiscences would appear useless as well as incomplete.

## 2. TEACHING BEGINS

We three boys were being brought up together. Both my companions were two years older than I. When they were placed under their tutor, my teaching also began, but of what I learnt nothing remains in my memory.

What constantly recurs to me is "The rain patters, the leaf quivers."[2] I am just come to anchor after crossing the stormy region of the *kara, khala*[3] series; and I am reading "The rain patters, the leaf quivers," for me the first poem of the Arch Poet. Whenever the joy of that day comes back to me, even now, I realise why rhyme is so needful in poetry. Because of it the words come to an end, and yet end not; the utterance is over, but not its ring; and the ear and the mind can go on and on with their game of tossing the rhyme to each other. Thus did the rain patter and the leaves quiver again and again, the live-long day in my consciousness.

Another episode of this period of my early boyhood is held fast in my mind.

We had an old cashier, Kailash by name, who was like one of the family. He was a great wit, and would be constantly cracking jokes with everybody, old and young; recently married sons-in-law, new comers into the family circle, being his special butts. There was room for the suspicion that his humour had not deserted him even after death. Once my elders were engaged in an attempt to start a postal service with the other world by means of a planchette. At one of the sittings the pencil scrawled out the name of Kailash. He was asked as to the sort of life one led where he was. Not a bit of it, was the reply. "Why should you get so cheap what I had to die to learn?"

This Kailash used to rattle off for my special delectation a doggerel ballad of his own composition. The hero was myself and there was a glowing anticipation of the arrival of a heroine. And as I listened my interest would wax intense at the picture of this world-charming bride illuminating the lap of the future in which she sat enthroned. The list of the jewellery with which she was bedecked from head to foot, and the unheard of splendour of the preparations for the bridal, might have turned older and wiser heads; but what moved the boy, and set wonderful joy pictures flitting before his vision, was the rapid jingle of the frequent rhymes and the swing of the rhythm.

These two literary delights still linger in my memory-and there is the other, the infants' classic: "The rain falls pit-a-pat, the tide comes up the river."

The next thing I remember is the beginning of my school-life. One day I saw my elder brother, and my sister's son Satya, also a little older than myself, starting off to school, leaving me behind, accounted unfit. I had never before ridden in a carriage nor even been out of the house. So when Satya came back, full of unduly glowing accounts of his adventures on the way, I felt I simply could not stay at home. Our tutor tried to dispel my illusion with sound advice and a resounding slap: "You're crying to go to school now, you'll have to cry a lot more to be let off later on." I have no recollection of the name, features or disposition of this tutor of ours, but the impression of his weighty advice and weightier hand has not yet faded. Never in my life have I heard a truer prophecy.

My crying drove me prematurely into the Oriental Seminary. What I learnt there I have no idea, but one of its methods of punishment I still bear in mind. The boy who was unable to repeat his lessons was made to stand on a bench with arms extended, and on his upturned palms were piled a number of slates. It is for psychologists to debate how far this method is likely to conduce to a better grasp of things. I thus began my schooling at an extremely tender age.

My initiation into literature had its origin, at the same time, in the books which were in vogue in the servants' quarters. Chief among these were a Bengali translation of Chanakya's aphorisms, and the Ramayana of Krittivasa.

A picture of one day's reading of the Ramayana comes clearly back to me.

The day was a cloudy one. I was playing about in the long verandah[4] overlooking the road. All of a sudden Satya, for some reason I do not remember, wanted to frighten me by shouting, "Policeman! Policeman!" My ideas of the duties of policemen were of an extremely vague description. One thing I was certain about, that a person charged with crime once placed in a policeman's hands would, as sure as the wretch caught in a crocodile's serrated grip, go under and be seen no more. Not knowing how an innocent boy could escape this relentless penal code, I bolted towards the inner apartments, with shudders running down my back for blind fear of pursuing policemen. I broke to my mother the news of my impending doom, but it did not seem to disturb her much. However, not deeming it safe to venture out again, I sat down on the sill of my mother's door to read the dog-eared Ramayana, with a marbled paper cover, which belonged to her old aunt. Alongside stretched the verandah running round the four sides of the open inner quadrangle, on which had fallen the faint afternoon glow of the clouded sky, and finding me weeping over one of its sorrowful situations my great-aunt came and took away the book from me.

# 3. WITHIN AND WITHOUT

Luxury was a thing almost unknown in the days of my infancy. The standard of living was then, as a whole, much more simple than it is now. Apart from that, the children of our household were entirely free from the fuss of being too much looked after. The fact is that, while the process of looking after may be an occasional treat for the guardians, to the children it is always an unmitigated nuisance.

We used to be under the rule of the servants. To save themselves trouble they had almost suppressed our right of free movement. But the freedom of not being petted made up even for the harshness of this bondage, for our minds were left clear of the toils of constant coddling, pampering and dressing-up.

Our food had nothing to do with delicacies. A list of our articles of clothing would only invite the modern boy's scorn. On no pretext did we wear socks or shoes till we had passed our tenth year. In the cold weather a second cotton tunic over the first one sufficed. It never entered our heads to consider ourselves ill-off for that reason. It was only when old Niyamat, the tailor, would forget to put a pocket into one of our tunics that we complained, for no boy has yet been born so poor as not to have the wherewithal to stuff his pockets; nor, by a merciful dispensation of providence, is there much difference between the wealth of boys of rich and of poor parentage. We used to have a pair of slippers each, but not always where we had our feet. Our habit of kicking the slippers on ahead, and catching them up again, made them work none the less hard, through effectually defeating at every step the reason of their being.

Our elders were in every way at a great distance from us, in their dress and food, living and doing, conversation and amusement. We caught glimpses of these, but they were beyond our reach. Elders have become cheap to modern children; they are too readily accessible, and so are all objects of desire. Nothing ever came so easily to us. Many a trivial thing was for us a rarity, and we lived mostly in the hope of attaining, when we were old enough, the things which the distant future held in trust for us. The result was that what little we did get we enjoyed to the utmost; from skin to core nothing was thrown away. The modern child of a well-to-do family nibbles at only half the things he gets; the greater part of his world is wasted on him.

Our days were spent in the servants' quarters in the south-east corner of the outer apartments. One of our servants was Shyam, a dark chubby boy with curly locks, hailing from the District of Khulna. He would put me into a selected spot and, tracing a chalk line all round, warn me with solemn face and uplifted finger of the perils of transgressing this ring. Whether the threatened danger was material or spiritual I never fully understood, but a great fear used to possess me. I had read in the Ramayana of the tribulations of Sita for having left the ring drawn by Lakshman, so it was not possible for me to be sceptical of its potency.

Just below the window of this room was a tank with a flight of masonry steps leading down into the water; on its west bank, along the garden wall, an immense banyan tree; to the south a fringe of cocoanut palms. Ringed round as I was near this window I would spend the whole day peering through the drawn Venetian shutters, gazing and gazing on this scene as on a picture book. From early morning our neighbours would drop in one by one to have their bath. I knew the time for each one to arrive. I was familiar with the peculiarities of each one's toilet. One would stop up his ears with his fingers as he took his regulation number of dips, after which he would depart. Another would not venture on a complete immersion but be content with only squeezing his wet towel repeatedly over his head. A third would carefully drive the surface impurities away from him with a rapid play of his arms, and then on a sudden impulse take his plunge. There was one who jumped in from the top steps without any preliminaries at all. Another would walk slowly in, step by step, muttering his morning prayers the while. One was always in a hurry, hastening home as soon as he was through with his dip. Another was in no sort of hurry at all, taking his bath leisurely, followed with a good rub-down, and a change from wet bathing clothes into clean ones, including a careful adjustment of the folds of his waist cloth, ending with a turn or two in the outer[5] garden, and the gathering of flowers, with which he would finally saunter slowly homewards, radiating the cool comfort of his refreshed body, as he went. This would go on till it was past noon. Then the bathing places would be deserted and become silent. Only the ducks remained, paddling about after water snails, or busy preening their feathers, the live-long day.

When solitude thus reigned over the water, my whole attention would be drawn to the shadows under the banyan tree. Some of its aerial roots, creeping down along its trunk, had formed a dark complication of coils at its base. It seemed as if into this mysterious region the laws of the universe had not found entrance; as if some old-world dream-land had escaped the divine vigilance and lingered on into the light of modern day. Whom I used to see there, and what those beings did, it is not possible to express in intelligible language. It was about this banyan tree that I wrote later:

> With tangled roots hanging down from your branches, O ancient banyan tree,
> You stand still day and night, like an ascetic at his penances,
> Do you ever remember the child whose fancy played with your shadows?

Alas! that banyan tree is no more, nor the piece of water which served to mirror the majestic forest-lord! Many of those who used to bathe there have also followed into oblivion the shade of the banyan tree. And that boy, grown older, is counting the alternations of light and darkness which penetrate the complexities with which the roots he has thrown off on all sides have encircled him.

Going out of the house was forbidden to us, in fact we had not even the freedom of all its parts. We perforce took our peeps at nature from behind the barriers. Beyond my reach there was this limitless thing called the Outside, of which flashes and sounds and scents used momentarily to come and touch me through its interstices. It seemed to want to play with me through the bars with so many gestures. But it was free and I was bound-there was no way of meeting. So the attraction was all the stronger. The chalk line has been wiped away to-day, but the confining ring is still there. The distant is just as distant, the outside is still beyond me; and I am reminded of the poem I wrote when I was older:

> The tame bird was in a cage, the free bird was in the forest,
> They met when the time came, it was a decree of fate.
> The free bird cries, "O my love, let us fly to wood."
> The cage bird whispers, "Come hither, let us both live in the cage."
> Says the free bird, "Among bars, where is there room to spread one's wings?"
> "Alas," cries the cage bird, "I should not know where to sit perched in the sky."

The parapets of our terraced roofs were higher than my head. When I had grown taller; when the tyranny of the servants had relaxed; when, with the coming of a newly married bride into the house, I had achieved some recognition as a companion of her leisure, then did I sometimes come up to the terrace in the middle of the day. By that time everybody in the house would have finished their meal; there would be an interval in the business of the household; over the inner apartments would rest the quiet of the midday siesta; the wet bathing clothes would be hanging over the parapets to dry; the crows would be picking at the leavings thrown on the refuse heap at the corner of the yard; in the solitude of that interval the caged bird would, through the gaps in the parapet, commune bill to bill with the free bird!

I would stand and gaze.... My glance first falls on the row of cocoanut trees on the further edge of our inner garden. Through these are seen the "Singhi's Garden" with its cluster of huts[6] and tank, and on the edge of the tank the dairy of our milkwoman, Tara; still further on, mixed up with the tree-tops, the various shapes and different heights of the terraced roofs of Calcutta, flashing back the blazing whiteness of the midday sun, stretch right away into the grayish blue of the eastern horizon. And some of these far distant dwellings from which stand forth their roofed stair-ways leading up to the terrace, look as if with uplifted finger and a wink they are hinting to me of the mysteries of their interiors. Like the beggar at the palace door who imagines impossible treasures to be held in the strong rooms closed to him, I can hardly tell of the wealth of play and freedom which these unknown dwellings seem to me crowded with. From the furthest depth of the sky full of burning sunshine overhead the thin shrill cry of a kite reaches my ear; and from the lane adjoining Singhi's Garden comes up, past the houses silent in their noonday slumber, the sing-song of the bangle-seller —*chai choori chai* ... and my whole being would fly away from the work-a-day world.

My father hardly ever stayed at home, he was constantly roaming about. His rooms on the third storey used to remain shut up. I would pass my hands through the venetian shutters, and thus opening the latch get the door open, and spend the afternoon lying motionless on his sofa at the south end. First of all it was a room always closed, and then there was the stolen entry, this gave it a deep flavour of mystery; further the broad empty expanse of terrace to the south, glowing in the rays of the sun would set me day-dreaming.

There was yet another attraction. The water-works had just been started in Calcutta, and in the first exuberance of its triumphant entry it did not stint even the Indian quarters of their supply. In that golden age of pipe water, it used to flow even up to my father's third storey rooms. And turning on the shower tap I would indulge to my heart's content in an untimely bath. Not so much for the comfort of it, as to give rein to my desire to do just as I fancied. The alternation of the joy of liberty, and the fear of being caught, made that shower of municipal water send arrows of delight thrilling into me.

It was perhaps because the possibility of contact with the outside was so remote that the joy of it came to me so much more readily. When material is in profusion, the mind gets lazy and leaves everything to it, forgetting that for a successful feast of joy its internal equipment counts for more than the external. This is the chief lesson which his infant state has to teach to man. There his possessions are few and trivial, yet he needs no more for his happiness. The world of play is spoilt for the unfortunate youngster who is burdened with an unlimited quantity of playthings.

To call our inner garden a garden is to say a deal too much. Its properties consisted of a citron tree, a couple of plum trees of different varieties, and a row of cocoanut trees. In the centre was a paved circle the cracks of which various grasses and weeds had invaded and planted in them their victorious standards. Only those flowering plants which refused to die of neglect continued uncomplainingly to perform their respective duties without casting any aspersions on the gardener. In the northern corner was a rice-husking shed, where the inmates of the inner apartments would occasionally foregather when household necessity demanded. This last vestige of rural life has since owned defeat and slunk away ashamed and unnoticed.

None the less I suspect that Adam's garden of Eden could hardly have been better adorned than this one of ours; for he and his paradise were alike naked; they needed not to be furnished with material things. It is only since his tasting of the fruit of the tree of knowledge, and till he can fully digest it, that man's need for external furniture and embellishment persistently grows. Our inner garden was my paradise; it was enough for me. I well remember how in the early autumn dawn I would run there as soon as I was awake. A scent of dewy grass and foliage would rush to meet me, and the morning with its cool fresh sunlight would peep out at me over the top of the Eastern garden wall from below the trembling tassels of the cocoanut palms.

There is another piece of vacant land to the north of the house which to this day we call the *golabari* (barn house). The name shows that in some remote past this must have been the place where the year's store of grain used to be kept in a barn. Then, as with brother and sister in infancy, the likeness between town and country was visible all over. Now the family resemblance can hardly be traced. This *golabari* would be my holiday haunt if I got the chance. It would hardly be correct to say that I went there to play-it was the place not play, which drew me. Why this was so, is difficult to tell. Perhaps its being a deserted bit of waste land lying in an out-of-the-way corner gave it its charm for me. It was entirely outside the living quarters and bore no stamp of usefulness; moreover it was as unadorned as it was useless, for no one had ever planted anything there; it was doubtless for these reasons that this desert spot offered no resistance to the free play of the boy's imagination. Whenever I got any loop-hole to evade the vigilance of my warders and could contrive to reach the *golabari* I felt I had a holiday indeed.

There was yet another place in our house which I have even yet not succeeded in finding out. A little girl playmate of my own age called this the "King's palace."[7] "I have just been there," she would sometimes tell me. But somehow the propitious moment never turned up when she could take me along with her. That was a wonderful place, and its playthings were as wonderful as the games that were played there. It seemed to me it must be somewhere very near-perhaps in the first or second storey; the only thing was one never seemed to be able to get there. How often have I asked my companion, "Only tell me, is it really inside the house or outside?" And she would always reply, "No, no, it's in this very house." I would sit and wonder: "Where then can it be? Don't I know all the rooms of the house?" Who the king might be I never cared to inquire; where his palace is still remains undiscovered; this much was clear-the king's palace was within our house.

Looking back on childhood's days the thing that recurs most often is the mystery which used to fill both life and world. Something undreamt of was lurking everywhere and the uppermost question every day was: when, Oh! when would we come across it? It was as if nature held something in her closed hands and was smilingly asking us: "What d'you think I have?" What was impossible for her to have was the thing we had no idea of.

Well do I remember the custard apple seed which I had planted and kept in a corner of the south verandah, and used to water every day. The thought that the seed might possibly grow into a tree kept me in a great state of fluttering wonder. Custard apple seeds still have the habit of sprouting, but no longer to the accompaniment of that feeling of wonder. The fault is not in the custard apple but in the mind. We had once stolen some rocks from an elder cousin's rockery and started a little rockery of our own. The plants which we sowed in its interstices were cared for so excessively that it was only because of their vegetable nature that they managed to put up with it till their untimely death. Words cannot recount the endless joy and wonder which this miniature mountain-top held for us. We had no doubt that this creation of ours would be a wonderful thing to our elders also. The day that we sought to put this to the proof, however, the hillock in the corner of our room, with all its rocks, and all its vegetation, vanished. The knowledge that the schoolroom floor was not a proper foundation for the erection of a mountain was imparted so rudely, and with such suddenness, that it gave us a considerable shock. The weight of stone of which the floor was relieved settled on our minds when we realised the gulf between our fancies and the will of our elders.

How intimately did the life of the world throb for us in those days! Earth, water, foliage and sky, they all spoke to us and would not be disregarded. How often were we struck by the poignant regret that we could only see the upper storey of the earth and knew nothing of its inner storey. All our planning was as to how we could pry beneath its dust-coloured cover. If, thought we, we could drive in bamboo after bamboo, one over the other, we might perhaps get into some sort of touch with its inmost depths.

During the *Magh* festival a series of wooden pillars used to be planted round the outer court-yard for supporting the chandeliers. Digging holes for these would begin on the first of *Magh*. The preparations for festivity are ever interesting to young folk. But this digging had a special attraction for me. Though I had watched it done year after year-and seen the hole grow bigger and bigger till the digger had completely disappeared inside, and yet nothing extraordinary, nothing worthy of the quest of prince or knight, had ever appeared-yet every time I had the feeling that the lid being lifted off a chest of mystery. I felt that a little bit more digging would do it. Year after year passed, but that bit never got done. There was a pull at the curtain but it was not drawn. The elders, thought I, can do whatever they please, why do they rest content with such shallow delving? If we young folk had the ordering of it, the inmost mystery of the earth would no longer be allowed to remain smothered in its dust covering.

And the thought that behind every part of the vault of blue reposed the mysteries of the sky would also spur our imaginings. When our Pundit, in illustration of some lesson in our Bengali science primer, told us that the blue sphere was not an enclosure, how thunderstruck we were! "Put ladder upon ladder," said he, "and go on mounting away, but you will never bump your head." He must be sparing of his ladders, I opined, and questioned with a rising inflection, "And what if we put more ladders, and more, and more?" When I realised that it was fruitless multiplying ladders I remained dumbfounded pondering over the matter. Surely, I concluded, such an astounding piece of news must be known only to those who are the world's schoolmasters!

**PART II**

# 4. SERVOCRACY

In the history of India the regime of the Slave Dynasty was not a happy one. In going back to the reign of the servants in my own life's history I can find nothing glorious or cheerful touching the period. There were frequent changes of king, but never a variation in the code of restraints and punishments with which we were afflicted. We, however, had no opportunity at the time for philosophising on the subject; our backs bore as best they could the blows which befell them: and we accepted as one of the laws of the universe that it is for the Big to hurt and for the Small to be hurt. It has taken me a long time to learn the opposite truth that it is the Big who suffer and the Small who cause suffering.

The quarry does not view virtue and vice from the standpoint of the hunter. That is why the alert bird, whose cry warns its fellows before the shot has sped, gets abused as vicious. We howled when we were beaten, which our chastisers did not consider good manners; it was in fact counted sedition against the servocracy. I cannot forget how, in order effectively to suppress such sedition, our heads used to be crammed into the huge water jars then in use; distasteful, doubtless, was this outcry to those who caused it; moreover, it was likely to have unpleasant consequences.

I now sometimes wonder why such cruel treatment was meted out to us by the servants. I cannot admit that there was on the whole anything in our behaviour or demeanour to have put us beyond the pale of human kindness. The real reason must have been that the whole of our burden was thrown on the servants, and the whole burden is a thing difficult to bear even for those who are nearest and dearest. If children are only allowed to be children, to run and play about and satisfy their curiosity, it becomes quite simple. Insoluble problems are only created if you try to confine them inside, keep them still or hamper their play. Then does the burden of the child, so lightly borne by its own childishness, fall heavily on the guardian-like that of the horse in the fable which was carried instead of being allowed to trot on its own legs: and though money procured bearers even for such a burden it could not prevent them taking it out of the unlucky beast at every step.

Of most of these tyrants of our childhood I remember only their cuffings and boxings, and nothing more. Only one personality stands out in my memory.

His name was Iswar. He had been a village schoolmaster before. He was a prim, proper and sedately dignified personage. The Earth seemed too earthy for him, with too little water to keep it sufficiently clean; so that he had to be in a constant state of warfare with its chronic soiled state. He would shoot his water-pot into the tank with a lightning movement so as to get his supply from an uncontaminated depth. It was he who, when bathing in the tank, would be continually thrusting away the surface impurities till he took a sudden plunge expecting, as it were, to catch the water unawares. When walking his right arm stood out at an angle from his body, as if, so it seemed to us, he could not trust the cleanliness even of his own garments. His whole bearing had the appearance of an effort to keep clear of the imperfections which, through unguarded avenues, find entrance into earth, water and air, and into the ways of men. Unfathomable was the depth of his gravity. With head slightly tilted he would mince his carefully selected words in a deep voice. His literary diction would give food for merriment to our elders behind his back, some of his high-flown phrases finding a permanent place in our family repertoire of witticisms. But I doubt whether the expressions he used would sound as remarkable to-day; showing how the literary and spoken languages, which used to be as sky from earth asunder, are now coming nearer each other.

This erstwhile schoolmaster had discovered a way of keeping us quiet in the evenings. Every evening he would gather us round the cracked castor-oil lamp and read out to us stories from the Ramayana and Mahabharata. Some of the other servants would also come and join the audience. The lamp would be throwing huge shadows right up to the beams of the roof, the little house lizards catching insects on the walls, the bats doing a mad dervish dance round and round the verandahs outside, and we listening in silent open-mouthed wonder.

I still remember, on the evening we came to the story of Kusha and Lava, and those two valiant lads were threatening to humble to the dust the renown of their father and uncles, how the tense silence of that dimly lighted room was bursting with eager anticipation. It was getting late, our prescribed period of wakefulness was drawing to a close, and yet the denouement was far off.

At this critical juncture my father's old follower Kishori came to the rescue, and finished the episode for us, at express speed, to the quickstep of Dasuraya's jingling verses. The impression of the soft slow chant of Krittivasa's[8] fourteen-syllabled measure was swept clean away and we were left overwhelmed by a flood of rhymes and alliterations.

On some occasions these readings would give rise to shastric discussions, which would at length be settled by the depth of Iswar's wise pronouncements. Though, as one of the children's servants, his rank in our domestic society was below that of many, yet, as with old Grandfather Bhisma in the Mahabharata, his supremacy would assert itself from his seat, below his juniors.

Our grave and reverend servitor had one weakness to which, for the sake of historical accuracy, I feel bound to allude. He used to take opium. This created a craving for rich food. So that when he brought us our morning goblets of milk the forces of attraction in his mind would be greater than those of repulsion. If we gave the least expression to our natural repugnance for this meal, no sense of responsibility for our health could prompt him to press it on us a second time.

Iswar also held somewhat narrow views as to our capacity for solid nourishment. We would sit down to our evening repast and a quantity of *luchis*[9] heaped on a thick round wooden tray would be placed before us. He would begin by gingerly dropping a few on each platter, from a sufficient height to safeguard himself from contamination[10] —like unwilling favours, wrested from the gods by dint of importunity, did they descend, so dexterously inhospitable was he. Next would come the inquiry whether he should give us any more. I knew the reply which would be most gratifying, and could not bring myself to deprive him by asking for another help.

Then again Iswar was entrusted with a daily allowance of money for procuring our afternoon light refreshment. He would ask us every morning what we should like to have. We knew that to mention the cheapest would be accounted best, so sometimes we ordered a light refection of puffed rice, and at others an indigestible one of boiled gram or roasted groundnuts. It was evident that Iswar was not as painstakingly punctilious in regard to our diet as with the shastric proprieties.

# 5. THE NORMAL SCHOOL

While at the Oriental Seminary I had discovered a way out of the degradation of being a mere pupil. I had started a class of my own in a corner of our verandah. The wooden bars of the railing were my pupils, and I would act the schoolmaster, cane in hand, seated on a chair in front of them. I had decided which were the good boys and which the bad-nay, further, I could distinguish clearly the quiet from the naughty, the clever from the stupid. The bad rails had suffered so much from my constant caning that they must have longed to give up the ghost had they been alive. And the more scarred they got with my strokes the worse they angered me, till I knew not how to punish them enough. None remain to bear witness to-day how tremendously I tyrannised over that poor dumb class of mine. My wooden pupils have since been replaced by cast-iron railings, nor have any of the new generation taken up their education in the same way-they could never have made the same impression.

I have since realised how much easier it is to acquire the manner than the matter. Without an effort had I assimilated all the impatience, the short temper, the partiality and the injustice displayed by my teachers to the exclusion of the rest of their teaching. My only consolation is that I had not the power of venting these barbarities on any sentient creature. Nevertheless the difference between my wooden pupils and those of the Seminary did not prevent my psychology from being identical with that of its schoolmasters.

I could not have been long at the Oriental Seminary, for I was still of tender age when I joined the Normal School. The only one of its features which I remember is that before the classes began all the boys had to sit in a row in the gallery and go through some kind of singing or chanting of verses-evidently an attempt at introducing an element of cheerfulness into the daily routine.

Unfortunately the words were English and the tune quite as foreign, so that we had not the faintest notion what sort of incantation we were practising; neither did the meaningless monotony of the performance tend to make us cheerful. This failed to disturb the serene self-satisfaction of the school authorities at having provided such a treat; they deemed it superfluous to inquire into the practical effect of their bounty; they would probably have counted it a crime for the boys not to be dutifully happy. Anyhow they rested content with taking the song as they found it, words and all, from the self-same English book which had furnished the theory.

The language into which this English resolved itself in our mouths cannot but be edifying to philologists. I can recall only one line:

Kallokee pullokee singill mellaling mellaling mellaling.

After much thought I have been able to guess at the original of a part of it. Of what words *kallokee* is the transformation still baffles me. The rest I think was:

...full of glee, singing merrily, merrily, merrily!

As my memories of the Normal School emerge from haziness and become clearer they are not the least sweet in any particular. Had I been able to associate with the other boys, the woes of learning might not have seemed so intolerable. But that turned out to be impossible-so nasty were most of the boys in their manners and habits. So, in the intervals of the classes, I would go up to the second storey and while away the time sitting near a window overlooking the street. I would count: one year-two years-three years —; wondering how many such would have to be got through like this.

Of the teachers I remember only one, whose language was so foul that, out of sheer contempt for him, I steadily refused to answer any one of his questions. Thus I sat silent throughout the year at the bottom of his class, and while the rest of the class was busy I would be left alone to attempt the solution of many an intricate problem.

One of these, I remember, on which I used to cogitate profoundly, was how to defeat an enemy without having arms. My preoccupation with this question, amidst the hum of the boys reciting their lessons, comes back to me even now. If I could properly train up a number of dogs, tigers and other ferocious beasts, and put a few lines of these on the field of battle, that, I thought, would serve very well as an inspiriting prelude. With our personal prowess let loose thereafter, victory should by no means be out of reach. And, as the picture of this wonderfully simple strategy waxed vivid in my imagination, the victory of my side became assured beyond doubt.

While work had not yet come into my life I always found it easy to devise short cuts to achievement; since I have been working I find that what is hard is hard indeed, and what is difficult remains difficult. This, of course, is less comforting; but nowhere near so bad as the discomfort of trying to take shortcuts.

When at length a year of that class had passed, we were examined in Bengali by Pandit Madhusudan Vachaspati. I got the largest number of marks of all the boys. The teacher complained to the school authorities that there had been favouritism in my case. So I was examined a second time, with the superintendent of the school seated beside the examiner. This time, also, I got a top place.

## 6. VERSIFICATION

I could not have been more than eight years old at the time. Jyoti, a son of a niece of my father's, was considerably older than I. He had just gained an entrance into English literature, and would recite Hamlet's soliloquy with great gusto. Why he should have taken it into his head to get a child, as I was, to write poetry I cannot tell. One afternoon he sent for me to his room, and asked me to try and make up a verse; after which he explained to me the construction of the *payar* metre of fourteen syllables.

I had up to then only seen poems in printed books-no mistakes penned through, no sign to the eye of doubt or trouble or any human weakness. I could not have dared even to imagine that any effort of mine could produce such poetry.

One day a thief had been caught in our house. Overpowered by curiosity, yet in fear and trembling, I ventured to the spot to take a peep at him. I found he was just an ordinary man! And when he was somewhat roughly handled by our door-keeper I felt a great pity. I had a similar experience with poetry.

When, after stringing together a few words at my own sweet will, I found them turned into a *payar* verse I felt I had no illusions left about the glories of poetising. So when poor Poetry is mishandled, even now I feel as unhappy as I did about the thief. Many a time have I been moved to pity and yet been unable to restrain impatient hands itching for the assault. Thieves have scarcely suffered so much, and from so many.

The first feeling of awe once overcome there was no holding me back. I managed to get hold of a blue-paper manuscript book by the favour of one of the officers of our estate. With my own hands I ruled it with pencil lines, at not very regular intervals, and thereon I began to write verses in a large childish scrawl.

Like a young deer which butts here, there and everywhere with its newly sprouting horns, I made myself a nuisance with my budding poetry. More so my elder[11] brother, whose pride in my performance impelled him to hunt about the house for an audience.

I recollect how, as the pair of us, one day, were coming out of the estate offices on the ground floor, after a conquering expedition against the officers, we came across the editor of "The National Paper," Nabagopal Mitter, who had just stepped into the house. My brother tackled him without further ado: "Look here, Nabagopal Babu! won't you listen to a poem which Rabi has written?" The reading forthwith followed.

My works had not as yet become voluminous. The poet could carry all his effusions about in his pockets. I was writer, printer and publisher, all in one; my brother, as advertiser, being my only colleague. I had composed some verses on The Lotus which I recited to Nabagopal Babu then and there, at the foot of the stairs, in a voice pitched as high as my enthusiasm. "Well done!" said he with a smile. "But what is a *dwirepha*?"[12]

How I had got hold of this word I do not remember. The ordinary name would have fitted the metre quite as well. But this was the one word in the whole poem on which I had pinned my hopes. It had doubtless duly impressed our officers. But curiously enough Nabagopal Babu did not succumb to it-on the contrary he smiled! He could not be an understanding man, I felt sure. I never read poetry to him again. I have since added many years to my age but have not been able to improve upon my test of what does or does not constitute understanding in my hearer. However Nabagopal Babu might smile, the word *dwirepha*, like a bee drunk with honey, stuck to its place, unmoved.

## 7. VARIOUS LEARNING

One of the teachers of the Normal School also gave us private lessons at home. His body was lean, his features dry, his voice sharp. He looked like a cane incarnate. His hours were from six to half-past-nine in the morning. With him our reading ranged from popular literary and science readers in Bengali to the epic of Meghnadvadha.

My third brother was very keen on imparting to us a variety of knowledge. So at home we had to go through much more than what was required by the school course. We had to get up before dawn and, clad in loin-cloths, begin with a bout or two with a blind wrestler. Without a pause we donned our tunics on our dusty bodies, and started on our courses of literature, mathematics, geography and history. On our return from school our drawing and gymnastic masters would be ready for us. In the evening Aghore Babu came for our English lessons. It was only after nine that we were free.

On Sunday morning we had singing lessons with Vishnu. Then, almost every Sunday, came Sitanath Dutta to give us demonstrations in physical science. The last were of great interest to me. I remember distinctly the feeling of wonder which filled me when he put some water, with sawdust in it, on the fire in a glass vessel, and showed us how the lightened hot water came up, and the cold water went down and how finally the water began to boil. I also felt a great elation the day I learnt that water is a separable part of milk, and that milk thickens when boiled because the water frees itself as vapour from the connexion. Sunday did not feel Sunday-like unless Sitanath Babu turned up.

There was also an hour when we would be told all about human bones by a pupil of the Campbell Medical School, for which purpose a skeleton, with the bones fastened together by wires was hung up in our schoolroom. And finally, time was also found for Pandit Heramba Tatwaratna to come and get us to learn by rote rules of Sanscrit grammar. I am not sure which of them, the names of the bones or the *sutras* of the grammarian, were the more jaw-breaking. I think the latter took the palm.

We began to learn English after we had made considerable progress in learning through the medium of Bengali. Aghore Babu, our English tutor, was attending the Medical College, so he came to teach us in the evening.

Books tell us that the discovery of fire was one of the biggest discoveries of man. I do not wish to dispute this. But I cannot help feeling how fortunate the little birds are that their parents cannot light lamps of an evening. They have their language lessons early in the morning and you must have noticed how gleefully they learn them. Of course we must not forget that they do not have to learn the English language!

The health of this medical-student tutor of ours was so good that even the fervent and united wishes of his three pupils were not enough to cause his absence even for a day. Only once was he laid up with a broken head when, on the occasion of a fight between the Indian and Eurasian students of the Medical College, a chair was thrown at him. It was a regrettable occurrence; nevertheless we were not able to take it as a personal sorrow, and his recovery somehow seemed to us needlessly swift.

It is evening. The rain is pouring in lance-like showers. Our lane is under knee-deep water. The tank has overflown into the garden, and the bushy tops of the Bael trees are seen standing out over the waters. Our whole being, on this delightful rainy evening, is radiating rapture like the *Kadamba* flower its fragrant spikes. The time for the arrival of our tutor is over by just a few minutes. Yet there is no certainty...! We are sitting on the verandah overlooking the lane[13] watching and watching with a piteous gaze. All of a sudden, with a great big thump, our hearts seem to fall in a swoon. The familiar black umbrella has turned the corner undefeated even by such weather! Could it not be somebody else? It certainly could not! In the wide wide world there might be found another, his equal in pertinacity, but never in this little lane of ours.

Looking back on his period as a whole, I cannot say that Aghore Babu was a hard man. He did not rule us with a rod. Even his rebukes did not amount to scoldings. But whatever may have been his personal merits, his time was *evening*, and his subject *English*! I am certain that even an angel would have seemed a veritable messenger of Yama[14] to any Bengali boy if he came to him at the end of his miserable day at school, and lighted a dismally dim lamp to teach him English.

How well do I remember the day our tutor tried to impress on us the attractiveness of the English language. With this object he recited to us with great unction some lines-prose or poetry we could not tell-out of an English book. It had a most unlooked for effect on us. We laughed so immoderately that he had to dismiss us for that evening. He must have realised that he held no easy brief-that to get us to pronounce in his favour would entail a contest ranging over years.

Aghore Babu would sometimes try to bring the zephyr of outside knowledge to play on the arid routine of our schoolroom. One day he brought a paper parcel out of his pocket and said: "I'll show you to-day a wonderful piece of work of the Creator." With this he untied the paper wrapping and, producing a portion of the vocal organs of a human being, proceeded to expound the marvels of its mechanism.

I can still call to mind the shock this gave me at the time. I had always thought the whole man spoke-had never even imagined that the act of speech could be viewed in this detached way. However wonderful the mechanism of a part may be, it is certainly less so than the whole man. Not that I put it to myself in so many words, but that was the cause of my dismay. It was perhaps because the tutor had lost sight of this truth that the pupil could not respond to the enthusiasm with which he was discoursing on the subject.

Another day he took us to the dissecting room of the Medical College. The body of an old woman was stretched on the table. This did not disturb me so much. But an amputated leg which was lying on the floor upset me altogether. To view man in this fragmentary way seemed to me so horrid, so absurd that I could not get rid of the impression of that dark, unmeaning leg for many a day.

After getting through Peary Sarkar's first and second English readers we entered upon McCulloch's Course of Reading. Our bodies were weary at the end of the day, our minds yearning for the inner apartments, the book was black and thick with difficult words, and the subject-matter could hardly have been more inviting, for in those days, Mother Saraswati's[15] maternal tenderness was not in evidence. Children's books were not full of pictures then as they are now. Moreover, at the gateway of every reading lesson stood sentinel an array of words, with separated syllables, and forbidding accent marks like fixed bayonets, barring the way to the infant mind. I had repeatedly attacked their serried ranks in vain.

Our tutor would try to shame us by recounting the exploits of some other brilliant pupil of his. We felt duly ashamed, and also not well-disposed towards that other pupil, but this did not help to dispel the darkness which clung to that black volume.

Providence, out of pity for mankind, has instilled a soporific charm into all tedious things. No sooner did our English lessons begin than our heads began to nod. Sprinkling water into our eyes, or taking a run round the verandahs, were palliatives which had no lasting effect. If by any chance my eldest brother happened to be passing that way, and caught a glimpse of our sleep-tormented condition, we would get let off for the rest of the evening. It did not take our drowsiness another moment to get completely cured.

## 8. MY FIRST OUTING

Once, when the dengue fever was raging in Calcutta, some portion of our extensive family had to take shelter in Chhatu Babu's river-side villa. We were among them.

This was my first outing. The bank of the Ganges welcomed me into its lap like a friend of a former birth. There, in front of the servants' quarters, was a grove of guava trees; and, sitting in the verandah under the shade of these, gazing at the flowing current through the gaps between their trunks, my days would pass. Every morning, as I awoke, I somehow felt the day coming to me like a new gilt-edged letter, with some unheard-of news awaiting me on the opening of the envelope. And, lest I should lose any fragment of it, I would hurry through my toilet to my chair outside. Every day there was the ebb and flow of the tide on the Ganges; the various gait of so many different boats; the shifting of the shadows of the trees from west to east; and, over the fringe of shade-patches of the woods on the opposite bank, the gush of golden life-blood through the pierced breast of the evening sky. Some days would be cloudy from early morning; the opposite woods black; black shadows moving over the river. Then with a rush would come the vociferous rain, blotting out the horizon; the dim line of the other bank taking its leave in tears: the river swelling with suppressed heavings; and the moist wind making free with the foliage of the trees overhead.

I felt that out of the bowels of wall, beam and rafter, I had a new birth into the outside. In making fresh acquaintance with things, the dingy covering of petty habits seemed to drop off the world. I am sure that the sugar-cane molasses, which I had with cold *luchis* for my breakfast, could not have tasted different from the ambrosia which *Indra*[16] quaffs in his heaven; for, the immortality is not in the nectar but in the taster, and thus is missed by those who seek it.

Behind the house was a walled-in enclosure with a tank and a flight of steps leading into the water from a bathing platform. On one side of the platform was an immense Jambolan tree, and all round were various fruit trees, growing in thick clusters, in the shade of which the tank nestled in its privacy. The veiled beauty of this retired little inner garden had a wonderful charm for me, so different from the broad expanse of the river-bank in front. It was like the bride of the house, in the seclusion of her midday siesta, resting on a many-coloured quilt of her own embroidering, murmuring low the secrets of her heart. Many a midday hour did I spend alone under that Jambolan tree dreaming of the fearsome kingdom of the Yakshas[17] within the depths of the tank.

I had a great curiosity to see a Bengal village. Its clusters of cottages, its thatched pavilions, its lanes and bathing places, its games and gatherings, its fields and markets, its life as a whole as I saw it in imagination, greatly attracted me. Just such a village was right on the other side of our garden wall, but it was forbidden to us. We had come out, but not into freedom. We had been in a cage, and were now on a perch, but the chain was still there.

One morning two of our elders went out for a stroll into the village. I could not restrain my eagerness any longer, and, slipping out unperceived, followed them for some distance. As I went along the deeply shaded lane, with its close thorny *seora* hedges, by the side of the tank covered with green water weeds, I rapturously took in picture after picture. I still remember the man with bare body, engaged in a belated toilet on the edge of the tank, cleaning his teeth with the chewed end of a twig. Suddenly my elders became aware of my presence behind them. "Get away, get away, go back at once!" they scolded. They were scandalised. My feet were bare, I had no scarf or upper-robe over my tunic, I was not dressed fit to come out; as if it was my fault! I never owned any socks or superfluous apparel, so not only went back disappointed for that morning, but had no chance of repairing my shortcomings and being allowed to come out any other day. However though the Beyond was thus shut out from behind, in front the Ganges freed me from all bondage, and my mind, whenever it listed, could embark on the boats gaily sailing along, and hie away to lands not named in any geography.

This was forty years ago. Since then I have never set foot again in that *champak*-shaded villa garden. The same old house and the same old trees must still be there, but I know it cannot any longer be the same-for where am I now to get that fresh feeling of wonder which made it what it was?

We returned to our Jorasanko house in town. And my days were as so many mouthfuls offered up to be gulped down into the yawning interior of the Normal School.

## 9. PRACTISING POETRY

That blue manuscript book was soon filled, like the hive of some insect, with a network of variously slanting lines and the thick and thin strokes of letters. The eager pressure of the boy writer soon crumpled its leaves; and then the edges got frayed, and twisted up claw-like as if to hold fast the writing within, till at last, down what river *Baitarani*[18] I know not, its pages were swept away by merciful oblivion. Anyhow they escaped the pangs of a passage through the printing press and need fear no birth into this vale of woe.

I cannot claim to have been a passive witness of the spread of my reputation as a poet. Though Satkari Babu was not a teacher of our class he was very fond of me. He had written a book on Natural History-wherein I hope no unkind humorist will try to find a reason for such fondness. He sent for me one day and asked: "So you write poetry, do you?" I did not conceal the fact. From that time on, he would now and then ask me to complete a quatrain by adding a couplet of my own to one given by him.

Gobinda Babu of our school was very dark, and short and fat. He was the Superintendent. He sat, in his black suit, with his account books, in an office room on the second storey. We were all afraid of him, for he was the rod-bearing judge. On one occasion I had escaped from the attentions of some bullies into his room. The persecutors were five or six older boys. I had no one to bear witness on my side-except my tears. I won my case and since then Govinda Babu had a soft corner in his heart for me.

One day he called me into his room during the recess. I went in fear and trembling but had no sooner stepped before him than he also accosted me with the question: "So you write poetry?" I did not hesitate to make the admission. He commissioned me to write a poem on some high moral precept which I do not remember. The amount of condescension and affability which such a request coming from him implied can only be appreciated by those who were his pupils. When I finished and handed him the verses next day, he took me to the highest class and made me stand before the boys. "Recite," he commanded. And I recited loudly.

The only praiseworthy thing about this moral poem was that it soon got lost. Its moral effect on that class was far from encouraging-the sentiment it aroused being not one of regard for its author. Most of them were certain that it was not my own composition. One said he could produce the book from which it was copied, but was not pressed to do so; the process of proving is such a nuisance to those who want to believe. Finally the number of seekers after poetic fame began to increase alarmingly; moreover their methods were not those which are recognised as roads to moral improvement.

Nowadays there is nothing strange in a youngster writing verses. The glamour of poesy is gone. I remember how the few women who wrote poetry in those days were looked upon as miraculous creations of the Deity. If one hears to-day that some young lady does not write poems one feels sceptical. Poetry now sprouts long before the highest Bengali class is reached; so that no modern Gobinda Babu would have taken any notice of the poetic exploit I have recounted.

**PART III**

## 10. SRIKANTHA BABU

At this time I was blessed with a hearer the like of whom I shall never get again. He had so inordinate a capacity for being pleased as to have utterly disqualified him for the post of critic in any of our monthly Reviews. The old man was like a perfectly ripe Alfonso mango-not a trace of acid or coarse fibre in his composition. His tender clean-shaven face was rounded off by an all-pervading baldness; there was not the vestige of a tooth to worry the inside of his mouth; and his big smiling eyes gleamed with a constant delight. When he spoke in his soft deep voice, his mouth and eyes and hands all spoke likewise. He was of the old school of Persian culture and knew not a word of English. His inseparable companions were a hubble-bubble at his left, and a *sitar* on his lap; and from his throat flowed song unceasing.

Srikantha Babu had no need to wait for a formal introduction, for none could resist the natural claims of his genial heart. Once he took us to be photographed with him in some big English photographic studio. There he so captivated the proprietor with his artless story, in a jumble of Hindusthani and Bengali, of how he was a poor man, but badly wanted this particular photograph taken, that the man smilingly allowed him a reduced rate. Nor did such bargaining sound at all incongruous in that unbending English establishment, so naïve was Srikantha Babu, so unconscious of any possibility of giving offence. He would sometimes take me along to a European missionary's house. There, also, with his playing and singing, his caresses of the missionary's little girl and his unstinted admiration of the little booted feet of the missionary's lady, he would enliven the gathering as no one else could have done. Another behaving so absurdly would have been deemed a bore, but his transparent simplicity pleased all and drew them to join in his gaiety.

Srikantha Babu was impervious to rudeness or insolence. There was at the time a singer of some repute retained in our establishment. When the latter was the worse for liquor he would rail at poor Srikantha Babu's singing in no very choice terms. This he would bear unflinchingly, with no attempt at retort. When at last the man's incorrigible rudeness brought about his dismissal Srikantha Babu anxiously interceded for him. "It was not he, it was the liquor," he insisted.

He could not bear to see anyone sorrowing or even to hear of it. So when any one of the boys wanted to torment him they had only to read out passages from Vidyasagar's "Banishment of Sita"; whereat he would be greatly exercised, thrusting out his hands in protest and begging and praying of them to stop.

This old man was the friend alike of my father, my elder brothers and ourselves. He was of an age with each and every one of us. As any piece of stone is good enough for the freshet to dance round and gambol with, so the least provocation would suffice to make him beside himself with joy. Once I had composed a hymn, and had not failed to make due allusion to the trials and tribulations of this world. Srikantha Babu was convinced that my father would be overjoyed at such a perfect gem of a devotional poem. With unbounded enthusiasm he volunteered personally to acquaint him with it. By a piece of good fortune I was not there at the time but heard afterwards that my father was hugely amused that the sorrows of the world should have so early moved his youngest son to the point of versification. I am sure Gobinda Babu, the superintendent, would have shown more respect for my effort on so serious a subject.

In singing I was Srikantha Babu's favorite pupil. He had taught me a song: "No more of Vraja[19] for me," and would drag me about to everyone's rooms and get me to sing it to them. I would sing and he would thrum an accompaniment on his *sitar* and when we came to the chorus he would join in, and repeat it over and over again, smiling and nodding his head at each one in turn, as if nudging them on to a more enthusiastic appreciation.

He was a devoted admirer of my father. A hymn had been set to one of his tunes, "For He is the heart of our hearts." When he sang this to my father Srikantha Babu got so excited that he jumped up from his seat and in alternation violently twanged his *sitar* as he sang: "For He is the heart of our hearts" and then waved his hand about my father's face as he changed the words to "For *you* are the heart of our hearts."

When the old man paid his last visit to my father, the latter, himself bed-ridden, was at a river-side villa in Chinsurah. Srikantha Babu, stricken with his last illness, could not rise unaided and had to push open his eyelids to see. In this state, tended by his daughter, he journeyed to Chinsurah from his place in Birbhoom. With a great effort he managed to take the dust of my father's feet and then return to his lodgings in Chinsurah where he breathed his last a few days later. I heard afterwards from his daughter that he went to his eternal youth with the song "How sweet is thy mercy, Lord!" on his lips.

## 11. OUR BENGALI COURSE ENDS

At School we were then in the class below the highest one. At home we had advanced in Bengali much further than the subjects taught in the class. We had been through Akshay Datta's book on Popular Physics, and had also finished the epic of Meghnadvadha. We read our physics without any reference to physical objects and so our knowledge of the subject was correspondingly bookish. In fact the time spent on it had been thoroughly wasted; much more so to my mind than if it had been wasted in doing nothing. The Meghnadvadha, also, was not a thing of joy to us. The tastiest tit-bit may not be relished when thrown at one's head. To employ an epic to teach language is like using a sword to shave with-sad for the sword, bad for the chin. A poem should be taught from the emotional standpoint; inveigling it into service as grammar-cum-dictionary is not calculated to propitiate the divine Saraswati.

All of a sudden our Normal School career came to an end; and thereby hangs a tale. One of our school teachers wanted to borrow a copy of my grandfather's life by Mitra from our library. My nephew and classmate Satya managed to screw up courage enough to volunteer to mention this to my father. He came to the conclusion that everyday Bengali would hardly do to approach him with. So he concocted and delivered himself of an archaic phrase with such meticulous precision that my father must have felt our study of the Bengali language had gone a bit too far and was in danger of over-reaching itself. So the next morning, when according to our wont our table had been placed in the south verandah, the blackboard hung up on a nail in the wall, and everything was in readiness for our lessons with Nilkamal Babu, we three were sent for by my father to his room upstairs. "You need not do any more Bengali lessons," he said. Our minds danced for very joy.

Nilkamal Babu was waiting downstairs, our books were lying open on the table, and the idea of getting us once more to go through the Meghnadvadha doubtless still occupied his mind. But as on one's death-bed the various routine of daily life seems unreal, so, in a moment, did everything, from the Pandit down to the nail on which the blackboard was hung, become for us as empty as a mirage. Our sole trouble was how to give this news to Nilkamal Babu with due decorum. We did it at last with considerable restraint, while the geometrical figures on the blackboard stared at us in wonder and the blank verse of the Meghnadvadha looked blankly on.

Our Pandit's parting words were: "At the call of duty I may have been sometimes harsh with you-do not keep that in remembrance. You will learn the value of what I have taught you later on."

Indeed I have learnt that value. It was because we were taught in our own language that our minds quickened. Learning should as far as possible follow the process of eating. When the taste begins from the first bite, the stomach is awakened to its function before it is loaded, so that its digestive juices get full play. Nothing like this happens, however, when the Bengali boy is taught in English. The first bite bids fair to wrench loose both rows of teeth-like a veritable earthquake in the mouth! And by the time he discovers that the morsel is not of the genus stone, but a digestible bonbon, half his allotted span of life is over. While one is choking and spluttering over the spelling and grammar, the inside remains starved, and when at length the taste is felt, the appetite has vanished. If the whole mind does not work from the beginning its full powers remain undeveloped to the end. While all around was the cry for English teaching, my third brother was brave enough to keep us to our Bengali course. To him in heaven my grateful reverence.

## 12. THE PROFESSOR

On leaving the Normal School we were sent to the Bengal Academy, a Eurasian institution. We felt we had gained an access of dignity, that we had grown up-at least into the first storey of freedom. In point of fact the only progress we made in that academy was towards freedom. What we were taught there we never understood, nor did we make any attempt to learn, nor did it seem to make any difference to anybody that we did not. The boys here were annoying but not disgusting-which was a great comfort. They wrote ass on their palms and slapped it on to our backs with a cordial "hello!" They gave us a dig in the ribs from behind and looked innocently another way. They dabbed banana pulp on our heads and made away unperceived. Nevertheless it was like coming out of slime on to rock-we were worried but not soiled.

This school had one great advantage for me. No one there cherished the forlorn hope that boys of our sort could make any advance in learning. It was a petty institution with an insufficient income, so that we had one supreme merit in the eyes of its authorities-we paid our fees regularly. This prevented even the Latin Grammar from proving a stumbling block, and the most egregious of blunders left our backs unscathed. Pity for us had nothing to do with it-the school authorities had spoken to the teachers!

Still, harmless though it was, after all it was a school. The rooms were cruelly dismal with their walls on guard like policemen. The house was more like a pigeon-holed box than a human habitation. No decoration, no pictures, not a touch of colour, not an attempt to attract the boyish heart. The fact that likes and dislikes form a large part of the child mind was completely ignored. Naturally our whole being was depressed as we stepped through its doorway into the narrow quadrangle-and playing truant became chronic with us.

In this we found an accomplice. My elder brothers had a Persian tutor. We used to call him Munshi. He was of middle age and all skin and bone, as though dark parchment had been stretched over his skeleton without any filling of flesh and blood. He probably knew Persian well, his knowledge of English was quite fair, but in neither of these directions lay his ambition. His belief was that his proficiency in singlestick was matched only by his skill in song. He would stand in the sun in the middle of our courtyard and go through a wonderful series of antics with a staff-his own shadow being his antagonist. I need hardly add that his shadow never got the better of him and when at the end he gave a great big shout and whacked it on the head with a victorious smile, it lay submissively prone at his feet. His singing, nasal and out of tune, sounded like a gruesome mixture of groaning and moaning coming from some ghost-world. Our singing master Vishnu would sometimes chaff him: "Look here, Munshi, you'll be taking the bread out of our mouths at this rate!" To which his only reply would be a disdainful smile.

This shows that the Munshi was amenable to soft words; and in fact, whenever we wanted we could persuade him to write to the school authorities to excuse us from attendance. The school authorities took no pains to scrutinise these letters, they knew it would be all the same whether we attended or not, so far as educational results were concerned.

I have now a school of my own in which the boys are up to all kinds of mischief, for boys will be mischievous-and schoolmasters unforgiving. When any of us are beset with undue uneasiness at their conduct and are stirred into a resolution to deal out condign punishment, the misdeeds of my own schooldays confront me in a row and smile at me.

I now clearly see that the mistake is to judge boys by the standard of grown-ups, to forget that a child is quick and mobile like a running stream; and that, in the case of such, any touch of imperfection need cause no great alarm, for the speed of the flow is itself the best corrective. When stagnation sets in then comes the danger. So it is for the teacher, more than the pupil, to beware of wrongdoing.

There was a separate refreshment room for Bengali boys for meeting their caste requirements. This was where we struck up a friendship with some of the others. They were all older than we. One of these will bear to be dilated upon.

His specialty was the art of Magic, so much so that he had actually written and published a little booklet on it, the front page of which bore his name with the title of Professor. I had never before come across a schoolboy whose name had appeared in print, so that my reverence for him-as a professor of magic I mean-was profound. How could I have brought myself to believe that anything questionable could possibly find place in the straight and upright ranks of printed letters? To be able to record one's own words in indelible ink-was that a slight thing? To stand unscreened yet unabashed, self-confessed before the world, —how could one withhold belief in the face of such supreme self-confidence? I remember how once I got the types for the letters of my name from some printing press, and what a memorable thing it seemed when I inked and pressed them on paper and found my name imprinted.

We used to give a lift in our carriage to this schoolfellow and author-friend of ours. This led to visiting terms. He was also great at theatricals. With his help we erected a stage on our wrestling ground with painted paper stretched over a split bamboo framework. But a peremptory negative from upstairs prevented any play from being acted thereon.

A comedy of errors was however played later on without any stage at all. The author of this has already been introduced to the reader in these pages. He was none other than my nephew Satya. Those who behold his present calm and sedate demeanour would be shocked to learn of the tricks of which he was the originator.

The event of which I am writing happened sometime afterwards when I was twelve or thirteen. Our magician friend had told of so many strange properties of things that I was consumed with curiosity to see them for myself. But the materials of which he spoke were invariably so rare or distant that one could hardly hope to get hold of them without the help of Sindbad the sailor. Once, as it happened, the Professor forgot himself so far as to mention accessible things. Who could ever believe that a seed dipped and dried twenty-one times in the juice of a species of cactus would sprout and flower and fruit all in the space of an hour? I was determined to test this, not daring withal to doubt the assurance of a Professor whose name appeared in a printed book.

I got our gardener to furnish me with a plentiful supply of the milky juice, and betook myself, on a Sunday afternoon, to our mystic nook in a corner of the roof terrace, to experiment with the stone of a mango. I was wrapt in my task of dipping and drying-but the grown-up reader will probably not wait to ask me the result. In the meantime, I little knew that Satya, in another corner, had, in the space of an hour, caused to root and sprout a mystical plant of his own creation. This was to bear curious fruit later on.

After the day of this experiment the Professor rather avoided me, as I gradually came to perceive. He would not sit on the same side in the carriage, and altogether seemed to fight shy of me.

One day, all of a sudden, he proposed that each one in turn should jump off the bench in our schoolroom. He wanted to observe the differences in style, he said. Such scientific curiosity did not appear queer in a professor of magic. Everyone jumped, so did I. He shook his head with a subdued "h'm." No amount of persuasion could draw anything further out of him.

Another day he informed us that some good friends of his wanted to make our acquaintance and asked us to accompany him to their house. Our guardians had no objection, so off we went. The crowd in the room seemed full of curiosity. They expressed their eagerness to hear me sing. I sang a song or two. Mere child as I was I could hardly have bellowed like a bull. "Quite a sweet voice," they all agreed.

When refreshments were put before us they sat round and watched us eat. I was bashful by nature and not used to strange company; moreover the habit I acquired during the attendance of our servant Iswar left me a poor eater for good. They all seemed impressed with the delicacy of my appetite.

In the fifth act I got some curiously warm letters from our Professor which revealed the whole situation. And here let the curtain fall.

I subsequently learnt from Satya that while I had been practising magic on the mango seed, he had successfully convinced the Professor that I was dressed as a boy by our guardians merely for getting me a better schooling, but that really this was only a disguise. To those who are curious in regard to imaginary science I should explain that a girl is supposed to jump with her left foot forward, and this is what I had done on the occasion of the Professor's trial. I little realised at the time what a tremendously false step mine had been!

## 13. MY FATHER

Shortly after my birth my father took to constantly travelling about. So it is no exaggeration to say that in my early childhood I hardly knew him. He would now and then come back home all of a sudden, and with him came foreign servants with whom I felt extremely eager to make friends. Once there came in this way a young Panjabi servant named Lenu. The cordiality of the reception he got from us would have been worthy of Ranjit Singh himself. Not only was he a foreigner, but a Panjabi to boot, —what wonder he stole our hearts away?

We had the same reverence for the whole Panjabi nation as for Bhima and Arjuna of the Mahabharata. They were warriors; and if they had sometimes fought and lost, that was clearly the enemy's fault. It was glorious to have Lenu, of the Panjab, in our very home.

My sister-in-law had a model war-ship under a glass case, which, when wound up, rocked on blue-painted silken waves to the tinkling of a musical box. I would beg hard for the loan of this to display its marvels to the admiring Lenu.

Caged in the house as we were, anything savouring of foreign parts had a peculiar charm for me. This was one of the reasons why I made so much of Lenu. This was also the reason why Gabriel, the Jew, with his embroidered gaberdine, who came to sell *attars* and scented oils, stirred me so; and the huge Kabulis, with their dusty, baggy trousers and knapsacks and bundles, wrought on my young mind a fearful fascination.

Anyhow, when my father came, we would be content with wandering round about his entourage and in the company of his servants. We did not reach his immediate presence.

Once while my father was away in the Himalayas, that old bogey of the British Government, the Russian invasion, came to be a subject of agitated conversation among the people. Some well-meaning lady friend had enlarged on the impending danger to my mother with all the circumstance of a prolific imagination. How could a body tell from which of the Tibetan passes the Russian host might suddenly flash forth like a baleful comet?

My mother was seriously alarmed. Possibly the other members of the family did not share her misgivings; so, despairing of grown-up sympathy, she sought my boyish support. "Won't you write to your father about the Russians?" she asked.

That letter, carrying the tidings of my mother's anxieties, was my first one to my father. I did not know how to begin or end a letter, or anything at all about it. I went to Mahananda, the estate munshi.[20] The resulting style of address was doubtless correct enough, but the sentiments could not have escaped the musty flavour inseparable from literature emanating from an estate office.

I got a reply to my letter. My father asked me not to be afraid; if the Russians came he would drive them away himself. This confident assurance did not seem to have the effect of relieving my mother's fears, but it served to free me from all timidity as regards my father. After that I wanted to write to him every day and pestered Mahananda accordingly. Unable to withstand my importunity he would make out drafts for me to copy. But I did not know that there was the postage to be paid for. I had an idea that letters placed in Mahananda's hands got to their destination without any need for further worry. It is hardly necessary to mention that, Mahananda being considerably older than myself, these letters never reached the Himalayan hill-tops.

When, after his long absences, my father came home even for a few days, the whole house seemed filled with the weight of his presence. We would see our elders at certain hours, formally robed in their *chogas*, passing to his rooms with restrained gait and sobered mien, casting away any *pan*[21] they might have been chewing. Everyone seemed on the alert. To make sure of nothing going wrong, my mother would superintend the cooking herself. The old mace-bearer, Kinu, with his white livery and crested turban, on guard at my father's door, would warn us not to be boisterous in the verandah in front of his rooms during his midday siesta. We had to walk past quietly, talking in whispers, and dared not even take a peep inside.

236

On one occasion my father came home to invest the three of us with the sacred thread. With the help of Pandit Vedantavagish he had collected the old Vedic rites for the purpose. For days together we were taught to chant in correct accents the selections from the Upanishads, arranged by my father under the name of "Brahma Dharma," seated in the prayer hall with Becharam Babu. Finally, with shaven heads and gold rings in our ears, we three budding Brahmins went into a three-days' retreat in a portion of the third storey.

It was great fun. The earrings gave us a good handle to pull each other's ears with. We found a little drum lying in one of the rooms; taking this we would stand out in the verandah, and, when we caught sight of any servant passing alone in the storey below, we would rap a tattoo on it. This would make the man look up, only to beat a hasty retreat the next moment with averted eyes.[22] In short we cannot claim that these days of our retirement were passed in ascetic meditation.

I am however persuaded that boys like ourselves could not have been rare in the hermitages of old. And if some ancient document has it that the ten or twelve-year old Saradwata or Sarngarava[23] is spending the whole of the days of his boyhood offering oblations and chanting *mantras*, we are not compelled to put unquestioning faith in the statement; because the book of Boy Nature is even older and also more authentic.

After we had attained full brahminhood I became very keen on repeating the *gayatri*.[24] I would meditate on it with great concentration. It is hardly a text the full meaning of which I could have grasped at that age. I well remember what efforts I made to extend the range of my consciousness with the help of the initial invocation of "Earth, firmament and heaven." How I felt or thought it is difficult to express clearly, but this much is certain that to be clear about the meaning of words is not the most important function of the human understanding.

The main object of teaching is not to explain meanings, but to knock at the door of the mind. If any boy is asked to give an account of what is awakened in him at such knocking, he will probably say something very silly. For what happens within is much bigger than what he can express in words. Those who pin their faith on University examinations as a test of all educational results take no account of this fact.

I can recollect many things which I did not understand, but which stirred me deeply. Once, on the roof terrace of our river-side villa, my eldest brother, at the sudden gathering of clouds, repeated aloud some stanzas from Kalidas's "Cloud Messenger." I could not, nor had I the need to, understand a word of the Sanskrit. His ecstatic declamation of the sonorous rhythm was enough for me.

Then, again, before I could properly understand English, a profusely illustrated edition of "The Old Curiosity Shop" fell into my hands. I went through the whole of it, though at least nine-tenths of the words were unknown to me. Yet, with the vague ideas I conjured up from the rest, I spun out a variously coloured thread on which to string the illustrations. Any university examiner would have given me a great big zero, but the reading of the book had not proved for me quite so empty as all that.

Another time I had accompanied my father on a trip on the Ganges in his houseboat. Among the books he had with him was an old Fort William edition of Jayadeva's *Gita Govinda*. It was in the Bengali character. The verses were not printed in separate lines, but ran on like prose. I did not then know anything of Sanskrit, yet because of my knowledge of Bengali many of the words were familiar. I cannot tell how often I read that *Gita Govinda*. I can well remember this line:

The night that was passed in the lonely forest cottage.

It spread an atmosphere of vague beauty over my mind. That one Sanskrit word, Nibhrita-nikunja-griham, meaning "the lonely forest cottage" was quite enough for me.

I had to discover for myself the intricate metre of Jayadeva, because its divisions were lost in the clumsy prose form of the book. And this discovery gave me very great delight. Of course I did not fully comprehend Jayadeva's meaning. It would hardly be correct to aver that I had got

237

it even partly. But the sound of the words and the lilt of the metre filled my mind with pictures of wonderful beauty, which impelled me to copy out the whole of the book for my own use.

The same thing happened, when I was a little older, with a verse from Kalidas's "Birth of the War God." The verse moved me greatly, though the only words of which I gathered the sense, were "the breeze carrying the spray-mist of the falling waters of the sacred Mandakini and shaking the deodar leaves." These left me pining to taste the beauties of the whole. When, later, a Pandit explained to me that in the next two lines the breeze went on "splitting the feathers of the peacock plume on the head of the eager deer-hunter," the thinness of this last conceit disappointed me. I was much better off when I had relied only upon my imagination to complete the verse.

Whoever goes back to his early childhood will agree that his greatest gains were not in proportion to the completeness of his understanding. Our Kathakas[25] I know this truth well. So their narratives always have a good proportion of ear-filling Sanskrit words and abstruse remarks not calculated to be fully understood by their simple hearers, but only to be suggestive.

The value of such suggestion is by no means to be despised by those who measure education in terms of material gains and losses. These insist on trying to sum up the account and find out exactly how much of the lesson imparted can be rendered up. But children, and those who are not over-educated, dwell in that primal paradise where men can come to know without fully comprehending each step. And only when that paradise is lost comes the evil day when everything needs must be understood. The road which leads to knowledge, without going through the dreary process of understanding, that is the royal road. If that be barred, though the world's marketing may yet go on as usual, the open sea and the mountain top cease to be possible of access.

So, as I was saying, though at that age I could not realise the full meaning of the *Gayatri*, there was something in me which could do without a complete understanding. I am reminded of a day when, as I was seated on the cement floor in a corner of our schoolroom meditating on the text, my eyes overflowed with tears. Why those tears came I knew not; and to a strict cross-questioner I would probably have given some explanation having nothing to do with the *Gayatri*. The fact of the matter is that what is going on in the inner recesses of consciousness is not always known to the dweller on the surface.

## 14. A JOURNEY WITH MY FATHER

My shaven head after the sacred thread ceremony caused me one great anxiety. However partial Eurasian lads may be to things appertaining to the Cow, their reverence for the Brahmin[26] is notoriously lacking. So that, apart from other missiles, our shaven heads were sure to be pelted with jeers. While I was worrying over this possibility I was one day summoned upstairs to my father. How would I like to go with him to the Himalayas, I was asked. Away from the Bengal Academy and off to the Himalayas! Would I like it? O that I could have rent the skies with a shout, that might have given some idea of the How!

On the day of our leaving home my father, as was his habit, assembled the whole family in the prayer hall for divine service. After I had taken the dust of the feet of my elders I got into the carriage with my father. This was the first time in my life that I had a full suit of clothes made for me. My father himself had selected the pattern and colour. A gold embroidered velvet cap completed my costume. This I carried in my hand, being assailed with misgivings as to its effect in juxtaposition to my hairless head. As I got into the carriage my father insisted on my wearing it, so I had to put it on. Every time he looked another way I took it off. Every time I caught his eye it had to resume its proper place.

My father was very particular in all his arrangements and orderings. He disliked leaving things vague or undetermined and never allowed slovenliness or makeshifts. He had a well-defined code to regulate his relations with others and theirs with him. In this he was different from the generality of his countrymen. With the rest of us a little carelessness this way or that did not signify; so in our dealings with him we had to be anxiously careful. It was not so much the little less or more that he objected to as the failure to be up to the standard.

My father had also a way of picturing to himself every detail of what he wanted done. On the occasion of any ceremonial gathering, at which he could not be present, he would think out and assign the place for each thing, the duty for each member of the family, the seat for each guest; nothing would escape him. After it was all over he would ask each one for a separate account and thus gain a complete impression of the whole for himself. So, while I was with him on his travels, though nothing would induce him to put obstacles in the way of my amusing myself as I pleased, he left no loophole in the strict rules of conduct which he prescribed for me in other respects.

Our first halt was to be for a few days at Bolpur. Satya had been there a short time before with his parents. No self-respecting nineteenth century infant would have credited the account of his travels which he gave us on his return. But we were different, and had had no opportunity of learning to determine the line between the possible and the impossible. Our Mahabharata and Ramayana gave us no clue to it. Nor had we then any children's illustrated books to guide us in the way a child should go. All the hard and fast laws which govern the world we learnt by knocking up against them.

Satya had told us that, unless one was very very expert, getting into a railway carriage was a terribly dangerous affair-the least slip, and it was all up. Then, again, a fellow had to hold on to his seat with all his might, otherwise the jolt at starting was so tremendous there was no telling where one would get thrown off to. So when we got to the railway station I was all a-quiver. So easily did we get into our compartment, however, that I felt sure the worst was yet to come. And when, at length, we made an absurdly smooth start, without any semblance of adventure, I felt woefully disappointed.

The train sped on; the broad fields with their blue-green border trees, and the villages nestling in their shade flew past in a stream of pictures which melted away like a flood of mirages. It was evening when we reached Bolpur. As I got into the palanquin I closed my eyes. I wanted to preserve the whole of the wonderful vision to be unfolded before my waking eyes in the morning light. The freshness of the experience would be spoilt, I feared, by incomplete glimpses caught in the vagueness of the dusk.

When I woke at dawn my heart was thrilling tremulously as I stepped outside. My predecessor had told me that Bolpur had one feature which was to be found nowhere else in the world. This was the path leading from the main buildings to the servants' quarters which, though not covered over in any way, did not allow a ray of the sun or a drop of rain to touch anybody passing along it. I started to hunt for this wonderful path, but the reader will perhaps not wonder at my failure to find it to this day.

Town bred as I was, I had never seen a rice-field, and I had a charming portrait of the cowherd boy, of whom we had read, pictured on the canvas of my imagination. I had heard from Satya that the Bolpur house was surrounded by fields of ripening rice, and that playing in these with cowherd boys was an everyday affair, of which the plucking, cooking and eating of the rice was the crowning feature. I eagerly looked about me. But where, oh, where was the rice-field on all that barren heath? Cowherd boys there might have been somewhere about, yet how to distinguish them from any other boys, that was the question!

However it did not take me long to get over what I could not see, —what I did see was quite enough. There was no servant rule here, and the only ring which encircled me was the blue of the horizon which the presiding goddess of these solitudes had drawn round them. Within this I was free to move about as I chose.

Though I was yet a mere child my father did not place any restriction on my wanderings. In the hollows of the sandy soil the rainwater had ploughed deep furrows, carving out miniature mountain ranges full of red gravel and pebbles of various shapes through which ran tiny streams, revealing the geography of Lilliput. From this region I would gather in the lap of my tunic many curious pieces of stone and take the collection to my father. He never made light of my labours. On the contrary he waxed enthusiastic.

"How wonderful!" he exclaimed. "Wherever did you get all these?"

"There are many many more, thousands and thousands!" I burst out. "I could bring as many every day."

"That *would* be nice!" he replied. "Why not decorate my little hill with them?"

An attempt had been made to dig a tank in the garden, but the subsoil water proving too low, it had been abandoned, unfinished, with the excavated earth left piled up into a hillock. On the top of this height my father used to sit for his morning prayer, and as he sat the sun would rise at the edge of the undulating expanse which stretched away to the eastern horizon in front of him. This was the hill he asked me to decorate.

I was very troubled, on leaving Bolpur, that I could not carry away with me my store of stones. It is still difficult for me to realise that I have no absolute claim to keep up a close relationship with things, merely because I have gathered them together. If my fate had granted me the prayer, which I had pressed with such insistence, and undertaken that I should carry this load of stones about with me for ever, then I should scarcely have had the hardihood to laugh at it to-day.

In one of the ravines I came upon a hollow full of spring water which overflowed as a little rivulet, where sported tiny fish battling their way up the current.

"I've found such a lovely spring," I told my father. "Couldn't we get our bathing and drinking water from there?"

"The very thing," he agreed, sharing my rapture, and gave orders for our water supply to be drawn from that spring.

I was never tired of roaming about among those miniature hills and dales in hopes of lighting on something never known before. I was the Livingstone of this undiscovered land which looked as if seen through the wrong end of a telescope. Everything there, the dwarf date palms, the scrubby wild plums and the stunted jambolans, was in keeping with the miniature mountain ranges, the little rivulet and the tiny fish I had discovered.

Probably in order to teach me to be careful my father placed a little small change in my charge and required me to keep an account of it. He also entrusted me with the duty of winding his valuable gold watch for him. He overlooked the risk of damage in his desire to train me to a sense of responsibility. When we went out together for our morning walk he would ask me to give alms to any beggars we came across. But I never could render him a proper account at the end of it. One day my balance was larger than the account warranted.

"I really must make you my cashier," observed my father. "Money seems to have a way of growing in your hands!"

That watch of his I wound up with such indefatigable zeal that it had very soon to be sent to the watchmaker's in Calcutta.

I am reminded of the time when, later in life, I was appointed to manage the estate and had to lay before my father, owing to his failing eye-sight, a statement of accounts on the second or third of every month. I had first to read out the totals under each head, and if he had any doubts on any point he would ask for the details. If I made any attempt to slur over or keep out of sight any item which I feared he would not like, it was sure to come out. So these first few days of the month were very anxious ones for me.

As I have said, my father had the habit of keeping everything clearly before his mind, — whether figures of accounts, or ceremonial arrangements, or additions or alterations to property. He had never seen the new prayer hall built at Bolpur, and yet he was familiar with every detail of it from questioning those who came to see him after a visit to Bolpur. He had an extraordinary memory, and when once he got hold of a fact it never escaped him.

My father had marked his favourite verses in his copy of the *Bhagavadgita*. He asked me to copy these out, with their translation, for him. At home, I had been a boy of no account, but here, when these important functions were entrusted to me, I felt the glory of the situation.

By this time I was rid of my blue manuscript book and had got hold of a bound volume of one of Lett's diaries. I now saw to it that my poetising should not lack any of the dignity of outward circumstance. It was not only a case of writing poems, but of holding myself forth as a poet before my own imagination. So when I wrote poetry at Bolpur I loved to do it sprawling under a young coconut palm. This seemed to me the true poetic way. Resting thus on the hard unturfed gravel in the burning heat of the day I composed a martial ballad on the "Defeat of King Prithwi." In spite of the superabundance of its martial spirit, it could not escape an early death. That bound volume of Lett's diary has now followed the way of its elder sister, the blue manuscript book, leaving no address behind.

We left Bolpur and making short halts on the way at Sahebganj, Dinapore, Allahabad and Cawnpore we stopped at last at Amritsar.

An incident on the way remains engraved on my memory. The train had stopped at some big station. The ticket examiner came and punched our tickets. He looked at me curiously as if he had some doubt which he did not care to express. He went off and came back with a companion. Both of them fidgetted about for a time near the door of our compartment and then again retired. At last came the station master himself. He looked at my half-ticket and then asked:

"Is not the boy over twelve?"

"No," said my father.

I was then only eleven, but looked older than my age.

"You must pay the full fare for him," said the station master.

My father's eyes flashed as, without a word, he took out a currency note from his box and handed it to the station master. When they brought my father his change he flung it disdainfully back at them, while the station master stood abashed at this exposure of the meanness of his implied doubt.

The golden temple of Amritsar comes back to me like a dream. Many a morning have I accompanied my father to this *Gurudarbar* of the Sikhs in the middle of the lake. There the sacred chanting resounds continually. My father, seated amidst the throng of worshippers, would sometimes add his voice to the hymn of praise, and finding a stranger joining in their devotions they would wax enthusiastically cordial, and we would return loaded with the sanctified offerings of sugar crystals and other sweets.

One day my father invited one of the chanting choir to our place and got him to sing us some of their sacred songs. The man went away probably more than satisfied with the reward he received. The result was that we had to take stern measures of self-defence, —such an insistent army of singers invaded us. When they found our house impregnable, the musicians began to waylay us in the streets. And as we went out for our walk in the morning, every now and then would appear a *Tambura*,[27] slung over a shoulder, at which we felt like game birds at the sight of the muzzle of the hunter's gun. Indeed, so wary did we become that the twang of the *Tambura*, from a distance, scared us away and utterly failed to bag us.

When evening fell, my father would sit out in the verandah facing the garden. I would then be summoned to sing to him. The moon has risen; its beams, passing though the trees, have fallen on the verandah floor; I am singing in the *Behaga* mode:

O Companion in the darkest passage of life....

My father with bowed head and clasped hands is intently listening. I can recall this evening scene even now.

I have told of my father's amusement on hearing from Srikantha Babu of my maiden attempt at a devotional poem. I am reminded how, later, I had my recompense. On the occasion of one of our *Magh* festivals several of the hymns were of my composition. One of them was

"The eye sees thee not, who art the pupil of every eye...."

My father was then bed-ridden at Chinsurah. He sent for me and my brother Jyoti. He asked my brother to accompany me on the harmonium and got me to sing all my hymns one after the other, —some of them I had to sing twice over. When I had finished he said:

"If the king of the country had known the language and could appreciate its literature, he would doubtless have rewarded the poet. Since that is not so, I suppose I must do it." With which he handed me a cheque.

My father had brought with him some volumes of the Peter Parley series from which to teach me. He selected the life of Benjamin Franklin to begin with. He thought it would read like a story book and be both entertaining and instructive. But he found out his mistake soon after we began it. Benjamin Franklin was much too business-like a person. The narrowness of his calculated morality disgusted my father. In some cases he would get so impatient at the worldly prudence of Franklin that he could not help using strong words of denunciation. Before this I had nothing to do with Sanskrit beyond getting some rules of grammar by rote. My father started me on the second Sanskrit reader at one bound, leaving me to learn the declensions as we went on. The advance I had made in Bengali[28] stood me in good stead. My father also encouraged me to try Sanskrit composition from the very outset. With the vocabulary acquired from my Sanskrit reader I built up grandiose compound words with a profuse sprinkling of sonorous 'm's and 'n's making altogether a most diabolical medley of the language of the gods. But my father never scoffed at my temerity.

Then there were the readings from Proctor's Popular Astronomy which my father explained to me in easy language and which I then rendered into Bengali.

Among the books which my father had brought for his own use, my attention would be mostly attracted by a ten or twelve volume edition of Gibbon's Rome. They looked remarkably dry. "Being a boy," I thought, "I am helpless and read many books because I have to. But why should a grown up person, who need not read unless he pleases, bother himself so?"

## 15. AT THE HIMALAYAS

We stayed about a month in Amritsar, and, towards the middle of April, started for the Dalhousie Hills. The last few days at Amritsar seemed as if they would never pass, the call of the Himalayas was so strong upon me.

The terraced hill sides, as we went up in a *jhampan*, were all aflame with the beauty of the flowering spring crops. Every morning we would make a start after our bread and milk, and before sunset take shelter for the night in the next staging bungalow. My eyes had no rest the livelong day, so great was my fear lest anything should escape them. Wherever, at a turn of the road into a gorge, the great forest trees were found clustering closer, and from underneath their shade a little waterfall trickling out, like a little daughter of the hermitage playing at the feet of hoary sages wrapt in meditation, babbling its way over the black moss-covered rocks, there the *jhampan* bearers would put down their burden, and take a rest. Why, oh why, had we to leave such spots behind, cried my thirsting heart, why could we not stay on there for ever?

This is the great advantage of the first vision: the mind is not then aware that there are many more such to come. When this comes to be known to that calculating organ it promptly tries to make a saving in its expenditure of attention. It is only when it believes something to be rare that the mind ceases to be miserly in assigning values. So in the streets of Calcutta I sometimes imagine myself a foreigner, and only then do I discover how much is to be seen, which is lost so long as its full value in attention is not paid. It is the hunger to really see which drives people to travel to strange places.

My father left his little cash-box in my charge. He had no reason to imagine that I was the fittest custodian of the considerable sums he kept in it for use on the way. He would certainly have felt safer with it in the hands of Kishori, his attendant. So I can only suppose he wanted to train me to the responsibility. One day as we reached the staging bungalow, I forgot to make it over to him and left it lying on a table. This earned me a reprimand.

Every time we got down at the end of a stage, my father had chairs placed for us outside the bungalow and there we sat. As dusk came on the stars blazed out wonderfully through the clear mountain atmosphere, and my father showed me the constellations or treated me to an astronomical discourse.

The house we had taken at Bakrota was on the highest hill-top. Though it was nearing May it was still bitterly cold there, so much so that on the shady side of the hill the winter frosts had not yet melted.

My father was not at all nervous about allowing me to wander about freely even here. Some way below our house there stretched a spur thickly wooded with Deodars. Into this wilderness I would venture alone with my iron-spiked staff. These lordly forest trees, with their huge shadows, towering there like so many giants-what immense lives had they lived through the centuries! And yet this boy of only the other day was crawling round about their trunks unchallenged. I seemed to feel a presence, the moment I stepped into their shade, as of the solid coolness of some old-world saurian, and the checkered light and shade on the leafy mould seemed like its scales.

My room was at one end of the house. Lying on my bed I could see, through the uncurtained windows, the distant snowy peaks shimmering dimly in the starlight. Sometimes, at what hour I could not make out, I, half awakened, would see my father, wrapped in a red shawl, with a lighted lamp in his hand, softly passing by to the glazed verandah where he sat at his devotions. After one more sleep I would find him at my bedside, rousing me with a push, before yet the darkness of night had passed. This was my appointed hour for memorising Sanscrit declensions. What an excruciatingly wintry awakening from the caressing warmth of my blankets!

By the time the sun rose, my father, after his prayers, finished with me our morning milk, and then, I standing at his side, he would once more hold communion with God, chanting the Upanishads.

Then we would go out for a walk. But how should I keep pace with him? Many an older person could not! So, after a while, I would give it up and scramble back home through some short cut up the mountain side.

After my father's return I had an hour of English lessons. After ten o'clock came the bath in icy-cold water; it was no use asking the servants to temper it with even a jugful of hot water without my father's permission. To give me courage my father would tell of the unbearably freezing baths he had himself been through in his younger days.

Another penance was the drinking of milk. My father was very fond of milk and could take quantities of it. But whether it was a failure to inherit this capacity, or that the unfavourable environment of which I have told proved the stronger, my appetite for milk was grievously wanting. Unfortunately we used to have our milk together. So I had to throw myself on the mercy of the servants; and to their human kindness (or frailty) I was indebted for my goblet being thenceforth more than half full of foam.

After our midday meal lessons began again. But this was more than flesh and blood could stand. My outraged morning sleep *would* have its revenge and I would be toppling over with uncontrollable drowsiness. Nevertheless, no sooner did my father take pity on my plight and let me off, than my sleepiness was off likewise. Then ho! for the mountains.

Staff in hand I would often wander away from one peak to another, but my father did not object. To the end of his life, I have observed, he never stood in the way of our independence. Many a time have I said or done things repugnant alike to his taste and his judgment; with a word he could have stopped me; but he preferred to wait till the prompting to refrain came from within. A passive acceptance by us of the correct and the proper did not satisfy him; he wanted us to love truth with our whole hearts; he knew that mere acquiescence without love is empty. He also knew that truth, if strayed from, can be found again, but a forced or blind acceptance of it from the outside effectually bars the way in.

In my early youth I had conceived a fancy to journey along the Grand Trunk Road, right up to Peshawar, in a bullock cart. No one else supported the scheme, and doubtless there was much to be urged against it as a practical proposition. But when I discoursed on it to my father he was sure it was a splendid idea-travelling by railroad was not worth the name! With which observation he proceeded to recount to me his own adventurous wanderings on foot and horseback. Of any chance of discomfort or peril he had not a word to say.

Another time, when I had just been appointed Secretary of the Adi Brahma Samaj, I went over to my father, at his Park Street residence, and informed him that I did not approve of the practice of only Brahmins conducting divine service to the exclusion of other castes. He unhesitatingly gave me permission to correct this if I could. When I got the authority I found I lacked the power. I was able to discover imperfections but could not create perfection! Where were the men? Where was the strength in me to attract the right man? Had I the means to build in the place of what I might break? Till the right man comes any form is better than none-this, I felt, must have been my father's view of the existing order. But he did not for a moment try to discourage me by pointing out the difficulties.

As he allowed me to wander about the mountains at my will, so in the quest for truth he left me free to select my path. He was not deterred by the danger of my making mistakes, he was not alarmed at the prospect of my encountering sorrow. He held up a standard, not a disciplinary rod.

I would often talk to my father of home. Whenever I got a letter from anyone at home I hastened to show it to him. I verily believe I was thus the means of giving him many a picture he could have got from none else. My father also let me read letters to him from my elder brothers. This was his way of teaching me how I ought to write to him; for he by no means underrated the importance of outward forms and ceremonial.

I am reminded of how in one of my second brother's letters he was complaining in somewhat sanscritised phraseology of being worked to death tied by the neck to his post of duty. My father asked me to explain the sentiment. I did it in my way, but he thought a different explanation would fit better. My overweening conceit made me stick to my guns and argue the point with him at length. Another would have shut me up with a snub, but my father patiently heard me out and took pains to justify his view to me.

My father would sometimes tell me funny stories. He had many an anecdote of the gilded youth of his time. There were some exquisites for whose delicate skins the embroidered borders of even Dacca muslins were too coarse, so that to wear muslins with the border torn off became, for a time, the tip-top thing to do.

I was also highly amused to hear from my father for the first time the story of the milkman who was suspected of watering his milk, and the more men one of his customers detailed to look after his milking the bluer the fluid became, till, at last, when the customer himself interviewed him and asked for an explanation, the milkman avowed that if more superintendents had to be satisfied it would only make the milk fit to breed fish!

After I had thus spent a few months with him my father sent me back home with his attendant Kishori.

**PART IV**

## 16. MY RETURN

The chains of the rigorous regime which had bound me snapped for good when I set out from home. On my return I gained an accession of rights. In my case my very nearness had so long kept me out of mind; now that I had been out of sight I came back into view.

I got a foretaste of appreciation while still on the return journey. Travelling alone as I was, with an attendant, brimming with health and spirits, and conspicuous with my gold-worked cap, all the English people I came across in the train made much of me.

When I arrived it was not merely a home-coming from travel, it was also a return from my exile in the servants' quarters to my proper place in the inner apartments. Whenever the inner household assembled in my mother's room I now occupied a seat of honour. And she who was then the youngest bride of our house lavished on me a wealth of affection and regard.

In infancy the loving care of woman is to be had without the asking, and, being as much a necessity as light and air, is as simply accepted without any conscious response; rather does the growing child often display an eagerness to free itself from the encircling web of woman's solicitude. But the unfortunate creature who is deprived of this in its proper season is beggared indeed. This had been my plight. So after being brought up in the servants' quarters when I suddenly came in for a profusion of womanly affection, I could hardly remain unconscious of it.

In the days when the inner apartments were as yet far away from me, they were the elysium of my imagination. The zenana, which from an outside view is a place of confinement, for me was the abode of all freedom. Neither school nor Pandit were there; nor, it seemed to me, did anybody have to do what they did not want to. Its secluded leisure had something mysterious about it; one played about, or did as one liked and had not to render an account of one's doings. Specially so with my youngest sister, to whom, though she attended Nilkamal Pandit's class with us, it seemed to make no difference in his behaviour whether she did her lessons well or ill. Then again, while, by ten o'clock, we had to hurry through our breakfast and be ready for school, she, with her queue dangling behind, walked unconcernedly away, withinwards, tantalising us to distraction.

And when the new bride, adorned with her necklace of gold, came into our house, the mystery of the inner apartments deepened. She, who came from outside and yet became one of us, who was unknown and yet our own, attracted me strangely-with her I burned to make friends. But if by much contriving I managed to draw near, my youngest sister would hustle me off with: "What d'you boys want here-get away outside." The insult added to the disappointment cut me to the quick. Through the glass doors of their cabinets one could catch glimpses of all manner of curious playthings-creations of porcelain and glass-gorgeous in colouring and ornamentation. We were not deemed worthy even to touch them, much less could we muster up courage to ask for any to play with. Nevertheless these rare and wonderful objects, as they were to us boys, served to tinge with an additional attraction the lure of the inner apartments.

Thus had I been kept at arm's length with repeated rebuffs. As the outer world, so, for me, the interior, was unattainable. Wherefore the impressions of it that I did get appeared to me like pictures.

After nine in the evening, my lessons with Aghore Babu over, I am retiring within for the night. A murky flickering lantern is hanging in the long venetian-screened corridor leading from the outer to the inner apartments. At its end this passage turns into a flight of four or five steps, to which the light does not reach, and down which I pass into the galleries running round the first inner quadrangle. A shaft of moonlight slants from the eastern sky into the western angle of these verandahs, leaving the rest in darkness. In this patch of light the maids have gathered and are squatting close together, with legs outstretched, rolling cotton waste into lamp-wicks, and chatting in undertones of their village homes. Many such pictures are indelibly printed on my memory.

Then after our supper, the washing of our hands and feet on the verandah before stretching ourselves on the ample expanse of our bed; whereupon one of the nurses Tinkari or Sankari comes and sits by our heads and softly croons to us the story of the prince travelling on and on over the lonely moor, and, as it comes to an end, silence falls on the room. With my face to the wall I gaze at the black and white patches, made by the plaster of the walls fallen off here and there, showing faintly in the dim light; and out of these I conjure up many a fantastic image as I drop off to sleep. And sometimes, in the middle of the night, I hear through my half-broken sleep the shouts of old Swarup, the watchman, going his rounds from verandah to verandah.

Then came the new order, when I got in profusion from this inner unknown dreamland of my fancies the recognition for which I had all along been pining; when that which naturally should have come day by day was suddenly made good to me with accumulated arrears. I cannot say that my head was not turned.

The little traveller was full of the story of his travels, and, with the strain of each repetition, the narrative got looser and looser till it utterly refused to fit into the facts. Like everything else, alas, a story also gets stale and the glory of the teller suffers likewise; that is why he has to add fresh colouring every time to keep up its freshness.

After my return from the hills I was the principal speaker at my mother's open air gatherings on the roof terrace in the evenings. The temptation to become famous in the eyes of one's mother is as difficult to resist as such fame is easy to earn. While I was at the Normal School, when I first came across the information in some reader that the Sun was hundreds and thousands of times as big as the Earth, I at once disclosed it to my mother. It served to prove that he who was small to look at might yet have a considerable amount of bigness about him. I used also to recite to her the scraps of poetry used as illustrations in the chapter on prosody or rhetoric of our Bengali grammar. Now I retailed at her evening gatherings the astronomical tit-bits I had gleaned from Proctor.

My father's follower Kishori belonged at one time to a band of reciters of Dasarathi's jingling versions of the Epics. While we were together in the hills he often said to me: "Oh, my little brother,[29] if I only had had you in our troupe we could have got up a splendid performance." This would open up to me a tempting picture of wandering as a minstrel boy from place to place, reciting and singing. I learnt from him many of the songs in his repertoire and these were in even greater request than my talks about the photosphere of the Sun or the many moons of Saturn.

But the achievement of mine which appealed most to my mother was that while the rest of the inmates of the inner apartments had to be content with Krittivasa's Bengali rendering of the Ramayana, I had been reading with my father the original of Maharshi Valmiki himself, Sanscrit metre and all. "Read me some of that Ramayana, *do!*" she said, overjoyed at this news which I had given her.

Alas, my reading of Valmiki had been limited to the short extract from his Ramayana given in my Sanskrit reader, and even that I had not fully mastered. Moreover, on looking over it now, I found that my memory had played me false and much of what I thought I knew had become hazy. But I lacked the courage to plead "I have forgotten" to the eager mother awaiting the display of her son's marvellous talents; so that, in the reading I gave, a large divergence occurred between Valmiki's intention and my explanation. That tender-hearted sage, from his seat in heaven, must have forgiven the temerity of the boy seeking the glory of his mother's approbation, but not so Madhusudan,[30] the taker down of Pride.

My mother, unable to contain her feelings at my extraordinary exploit, wanted all to share her admiration. "You must read this to Dwijendra," (my eldest brother), she said.

"In for it!" thought I, as I put forth all the excuses I could think of, but my mother would have none of them. She sent for my brother Dwijendra, and, as soon as he arrived, greeted him, with: "Just hear Rabi read Valmiki's Ramayan, how splendidly he does it."

It had to be done! But Madhusudan relented and let me off with just a taste of his pride-reducing power. My brother must have been called away while busy with some literary work of his own. He showed no anxiety to hear me render the Sanscrit into Bengali, and as soon as I had read out a few verses he simply remarked "Very good" and walked away.

After my promotion to the inner apartments I felt it all the more difficult to resume my school life. I resorted to all manner of subterfuges to escape the Bengal Academy. Then they tried putting me at St. Xavier's. But the result was no better.

My elder brothers, after a few spasmodic efforts, gave up all hopes of me-they even ceased to scold me. One day my eldest sister said: "We had all hoped Rabi would grow up to be a man, but he has disappointed us the worst." I felt that my value in the social world was distinctly depreciating; nevertheless I could not make up my mind to be tied to the eternal grind of the school mill which, divorced as it was from all life and beauty, seemed such a hideously cruel combination of hospital and gaol.

One precious memory of St. Xavier's I still hold fresh and pure-the memory of its teachers. Not that they were all of the same excellence. In particular, in those who taught in our class I could discern no reverential resignation of spirit. They were in nowise above the teaching-machine variety of school masters. As it is, the educational engine is remorselessly powerful; when to it is coupled the stone mill of the outward forms of religion the heart of youth is crushed dry indeed. This power-propelled grindstone type we had at St. Xavier's. Yet, as I say, I possess a memory which elevates my impression of the teachers there to an ideal plane.

This is the memory of Father DePeneranda. He had very little to do with us-if I remember right he had only for a while taken the place of one of the masters of our class. He was a Spaniard and seemed to have an impediment in speaking English. It was perhaps for this reason that the boys paid but little heed to what he was saying. It seemed to me that this inattentiveness of his pupils hurt him, but he bore it meekly day after day. I know not why, but my heart went out to him in sympathy. His features were not handsome, but his countenance had for me a strange attraction. Whenever I looked on him his spirit seemed to be in prayer, a deep peace to pervade him within and without.

We had half-an-hour for writing our copybooks; that was a time when, pen in hand, I used to become absent-minded and my thoughts wandered hither and thither. One day Father De-Peneranda was in charge of this class. He was pacing up and down behind our benches. He must have noticed more than once that my pen was not moving. All of a sudden he stopped behind my seat. Bending over me he gently laid his hand on my shoulder and tenderly inquired: "Are you not well, Tagore?" It was only a simple question, but one I have never been able to forget.

I cannot speak for the other boys but I felt in him the presence of a great soul, and even to-day the recollection of it seems to give me a passport into the silent seclusion of the temple of God.

There was another old Father whom all the boys loved. This was Father Henry. He taught in the higher classes; so I did not know him well. But one thing about him I remember. He knew Bengali. He once asked Nirada, a boy in his class, the derivation of his name. Poor Nirada[31] had so long been supremely easy in mind about himself-the derivation of his name, in particular, had not troubled him in the least; so that he was utterly unprepared to answer this question. And yet, with so many abstruse and unknown words in the dictionary, to be worsted by one's own name would have been as ridiculous a mishap as getting run over by one's own carriage, so Nirada unblushingly replied: "*Ni* —privative, *rode* —sun-rays; thence Nirode-that which causes an absence of the sun's rays!"

## 17. HOME STUDIES

Gyan Babu, son of Pandit Vedantavagish, was now our tutor at home. When he found he could not secure my attention for the school course, he gave up the attempt as hopeless and went on a different tack. He took me through Kalidas's "Birth of the War-god," translating it to me as we went on. He also read Macbeth to me, first explaining the text in Bengali, and then confining me to the school room till I had rendered the day's reading into Bengali verse. In this way he got me to translate the whole play. I was fortunate enough to lose this translation and so am relieved to that extent of the burden of my *karma*.

It was Pandit Ramsarvaswa's duty to see to the progress of our Sanskrit. He likewise gave up the fruitless task of teaching grammar to his unwilling pupil, and read Sakuntala with me instead. One day he took it into his head to show my translation of Macbeth to Pandit Vidyasagar and took me over to his house.

Rajkrishna Mukherji had called at the time and was seated with him. My heart went pit-a-pat as I entered the great Pandit's study, packed full of books; nor did his austere visage assist in reviving my courage. Nevertheless, as this was the first time I had had such a distinguished audience, my desire to win renown was strong within me. I returned home, I believe, with some reason for an access of enthusiasm. As for Rajkrishna Babu, he contented himself with admonishing me to be careful to keep the language and metre of the Witches' parts different from that of the human characters.

During my boyhood Bengali literature was meagre in body, and I think I must have finished all the readable and unreadable books that there were at the time. Juvenile literature in those days had not evolved a distinct type of its own-but that I am sure did me no harm. The watery stuff into which literary nectar is now diluted for being served up to the young takes full account of their childishness, but none of them as growing human beings. Children's books should be such as can partly be understood by them and partly not. In our childhood we read every available book from one end to the other; and both what we understood, and what we did not, went on working within us. That is how the world itself reacts on the child consciousness. The child makes its own what it understands, while that which is beyond leads it on a step forward.

When Dinabandhu Mitra's satires came out I was not of an age for which they were suitable. A kinswoman of ours was reading a copy, but no entreaties of mine could induce her to lend it to me. She used to keep it under lock and key. Its inaccessibility made me want it all the more and I threw out the challenge that read the book I must and would.

One afternoon she was playing cards, and her keys, tied to a corner of her *sari*, hung over her shoulder. I had never paid any attention to cards, in fact I could not stand card games. But my behaviour that day would hardly have borne this out, so engrossed was I in their playing. At last, in the excitement of one side being about to make a score, I seized my opportunity and set about untying the knot which held the keys. I was not skilful, and moreover excited and hasty and so got caught. The owner of the *sari* and of the keys took the fold off her shoulder with a smile, and laid the keys on her lap as she went on with the game.

Then I hit on a stratagem. My kinswoman was fond of *pan*,[32] and I hastened to place some before her. This entailed her rising later on to get rid of the chewed *pan*, and, as she did so, her keys fell off her lap and were replaced over her shoulder. This time they got stolen, the culprit got off, and the book got read! Its owner tried to scold me, but the attempt was not a success, we both laughed so.

Dr. Rajendralal Mitra used to edit an illustrated monthly miscellany. My third brother had a bound annual volume of it in his bookcase. This I managed to secure and the delight of reading it through, over and over again, still comes back to me. Many a holiday noontide has passed with me stretched on my back on my bed, that square volume on my breast, reading about the Narwhal whale, or the curiosities of justice as administered by the Kazis of old, or the romantic story of Krishna-kumari.

Why do we not have such magazines now-a-days? We have philosophical and scientific articles on the one hand, and insipid stories and travels on the other, but no such unpretentious miscellanies which the ordinary person can read in comfort-such as Chambers's or Cassell's or the Strand in England-which supply the general reader with a simple, but satisfying fare and are of the greatest use to the greatest number.

I came across another little periodical in my young days called the *Abodhabandhu* (ignorant man's friend). I found a collection of its monthly numbers in my eldest brother's library and devoured them day after day, seated on the doorsill of his study, facing a bit of terrace to the South. It was in the pages of this magazine that I made my first acquaintance with the poetry of Viharilal Chakravarti. His poems appealed to me the most of all that I read at the time. The artless flute-strains of his lyrics awoke within me the music of fields and forest-glades.

Into these same pages I have wept many a tear over a pathetic translation of Paul and Virginie. That wonderful sea, the breeze-stirred cocoanut forests on its shore, and the slopes beyond lively with the gambols of mountain goats, —a delightfully refreshing mirage they conjured up on that terraced roof in Calcutta. And oh! the romantic courting that went on in the forest paths of that secluded island, between the Bengali boy reader and little Virginie with the many-coloured kerchief round her head!

Then came Bankim's *Bangadarsan*, taking the Bengali heart by storm. It was bad enough to have to wait till the next monthly number was out, but to be kept waiting further till my elders had done with it was simply intolerable! Now he who will may swallow at a mouthful the whole of *Chandrashekhar* or *Bishabriksha* but the process of longing and anticipating, month after month; of spreading over the long intervals the concentrated joy of each short reading, revolving every instalment over and over in the mind while watching and waiting for the next; the combination of satisfaction with unsatisfied craving, of burning curiosity with its appeasement; these long drawn out delights of going through the original serial none will ever taste again.

The compilations from the old poets by Sarada Mitter and Akshay Sarkar were also of great interest to me. Our elders were subscribers, but not very regular readers, of these series, so that it was not difficult for me to get at them. Vidyapati's quaint and corrupt Maithili language attracted me all the more because of its unintelligibility. I tried to make out his sense without the help of the compiler's notes, jotting down in my own note book all the more obscure words with their context as many times as they occurred. I also noted grammatical peculiarities according to my lights.

## 18. MY HOME ENVIRONMENT

One great advantage which I enjoyed in my younger days was the literary and artistic atmosphere which pervaded our house. I remember how, when I was quite a child, I would be leaning against the verandah railings which overlooked the detached building comprising the reception rooms. These rooms would be lighted up every evening. Splendid carriages would draw up under the portico, and visitors would be constantly coming and going. What was happening I could not very well make out, but would keep staring at the rows of lighted casements from my place in the darkness. The intervening space was not great but the gulf between my infant world and these lights was immense.

My elder cousin Ganendra had just got a drama written by Pandit Tarkaratna and was having it staged in the house. His enthusiasm for literature and the fine arts knew no bounds. He was the centre of the group who seem to have been almost consciously striving to bring about from every side the renascence which we see to-day. A pronounced nationalism in dress, literature, music, art and the drama had awakened in and around him. He was a keen student of the history of different countries and had begun but could not complete a historical work in Bengali. He had translated and published the Sanskrit drama, Vikramorvasi, and many a well-known hymn is his composition. He may be said to have given us the lead in writing patriotic poems and songs. This was in the days when the Hindu Mela was an annual institution and there his song "Ashamed am I to sing of India's glories" used to be sung.

I was still a child when my cousin Ganendra died in the prime of his youth, but for those who have once beheld him it is impossible to forget his handsome, tall and stately figure. He had an irresistible social influence. He could draw men round him and keep them bound to him; while his powerful attraction was there, disruption was out of the question. He was one of those —a type peculiar to our country-who, by their personal magnetism, easily establish themselves in the centre of their family or village. In any other country, where large political, social or commercial groups are being formed, such would as naturally become national leaders. The power of organising a large number of men into a corporate group depends on a special kind of genius. Such genius in our country runs to waste, a waste, as pitiful, it seems to me, as that of pulling down a star from the firmament for use as a lucifer match.

I remember still better his younger brother, my cousin Gunendra.[33] He likewise kept the house filled with his personality. His large, gracious heart embraced alike relatives, friends, guests and dependants. Whether in his broad south verandah, or on the lawn by the fountain, or at the tank-edge on the fishing platform, he presided over self-invited gatherings, like hospitality incarnate. His wide appreciation of art and talent kept him constantly radiant with enthusiasm. New ideas of festivity or frolic, theatricals or other entertainments, found in him a ready patron, and with his help would flourish and find fruition.

We were too young then to take any part in these doings, but the waves of merriment and life to which they gave rise came and beat at the doors of our curiosity. I remember how a burlesque composed by my eldest brother was once being rehearsed in my cousin's big drawing room. From our place against the verandah railings of our house we could hear, through the open windows opposite, roars of laughter mixed with the strains of a comic song, and would also occasionally catch glimpses of Akshay Mazumdar's extraordinary antics. We could not gather exactly what the song was about, but lived in hopes of being able to find that out sometime.

I recall how a trifling circumstance earned for me the special regard of cousin Gunendra. Never had I got a prize at school except once for good conduct. Of the three of us my nephew Satya was the best at his lessons. He once did well at some examination and was awarded a prize. As we came home I jumped off the carriage to give the great news to my cousin who was in the garden. "Satya has got a prize" I shouted as I ran to him. He drew me to his knees with a smile. "And have *you* not got a prize?" he asked. "No," said I, "not I, it's Satya." My genuine pleasure at Satya's success seemed to touch my cousin particularly. He turned to his friends and remarked on it as a very creditable trait. I well remember how mystified I felt at this, for I had not thought of my feeling in that light. This prize that I got for not getting a prize did not do me good. There is no harm in making gifts to children, but they should not be rewards. It is not healthy for youngsters to be made self-conscious.

After the mid-day meal cousin Gunendra would attend the estate offices in our part of the house. The office room of our elders was a sort of club where laughter and conversation were freely mixed with matters of business. My cousin would recline on a couch, and I would seize some opportunity of edging up to him.

He usually told me stories from Indian History. I still remember the surprise with which I heard how Clive, after establishing British rule in India, went back home and cut his own throat. On the one hand new history being made, on the other a tragic chapter hidden away in the mysterious darkness of a human heart. How could there be such dismal failure within and such brilliant success outside? This weighed heavily on my mind the whole day.

Some days cousin Gunendra would not be allowed to remain in any doubt as to the contents of my pocket. At the least encouragement out would come my manuscript book, unabashed. I need hardly state that my cousin was not a severe critic; in point of fact the opinions he expressed would have done splendidly as advertisements. None the less, when in any of my poetry my childishness became too obtrusive, he could not restrain his hearty "Ha! Ha!"

One day it was a poem on "Mother India" and as at the end of one line the only rhyme I could think of meant a cart, I had to drag in that cart in spite of there not being the vestige of a road by which it could reasonably arrive, —the insistent claims of rhyme would not hear of any excuses mere reason had to offer. The storm of laughter with which cousin Gunendra greeted it blew away the cart back over the same impossible path it had come by, and it has not been heard of since.

My eldest brother was then busy with his masterpiece "The Dream Journey," his cushion seat placed in the south verandah, a low desk before him. Cousin Gunendra would come and sit there for a time every morning. His immense capacity for enjoyment, like the breezes of spring, helped poetry to sprout. My eldest brother would go on alternately writing and reading out what he had written, his boisterous mirth at his own conceits making the verandah tremble. My brother wrote a great deal more than he finally used in his finished work, so fertile was his poetic inspiration. Like the superabounding mango flowerets which carpet the shade of the mango topes in spring time, the rejected pages of his "Dream Journey" were to be found scattered all over the house. Had anyone preserved them they would have been to-day a basketful of flowers adorning our Bengali literature.

Eavesdropping at doors and peeping round corners, we used to get our full share of this feast of poetry, so plentiful was it, with so much to spare. My eldest brother was then at the height of his wonderful powers; and from his pen surged, in untiring wave after wave, a tidal flood of poetic fancy, rhyme and expression, filling and overflowing its banks with an exuberantly joyful pæan of triumph. Did we quite understand "The Dream Journey"? But then did we need absolutely to understand in order to enjoy it? We might not have got at the wealth in the ocean depths-what could we have done with it if we had? —but we revelled in the delights of the waves on the shore; and how gaily, at their buffettings, did our life-blood course through every vein and artery!

The more I think of that period the more I realise that we have no longer the thing called a *mujlis*.[34] In our boyhood we beheld the dying rays of that intimate sociability which was characteristic of the last generation. Neighbourly feelings were then so strong that the *mujlis* was a necessity, and those who could contribute to its amenities were in great request. People now-a-days call on each other on business, or as a matter of social duty, but not to foregather by way of *mujlis*. They have not the time, nor are there the same intimate relations! What goings and comings we used to see, how merry the rooms and verandahs with the hum of conversation and the snatches of laughter! The faculty our predecessors had of becoming the centre of groups and gatherings, of starting and keeping up animated and amusing gossip, has vanished. Men still come and go, but those same verandahs and rooms seem empty and deserted.

In those days everything from furniture to festivity was designed to be enjoyed by the many, so that whatever of pomp or magnificence there might have been did not savour of hauteur. These appendages have since increased in quantity, but they have become unfeeling, and know not the art of making high and low alike feel at home. The bare-bodied, the indigently clad, no longer have the right to use and occupy them, without a permit, on the strength of their smiling faces alone. Those whom we now-a-days seek to imitate in our house-building and furnishing, they have their own society, with its wide hospitality. The mischief with us is that we have lost what we had, but have not the means of building up afresh on the European standard, with the result that our home-life has become joyless. We still meet for business or political purposes, but never for the pleasure of simply meeting one another. We have ceased to contrive opportunities to bring men together simply because we love our fellow-men. I can imagine nothing more ugly than this social miserliness; and, when I look back on those whose ringing laughter, coming straight from their hearts, used to lighten for us the burden of household cares, they seem to have been visitors from some other world.

# 19. LITERARY COMPANIONS

There came to me in my boyhood a friend whose help in my literary progress was invaluable. Akshay Chowdhury was a school-fellow of my fourth brother. He was an M. A. in English Literature for which his love was as great as his proficiency therein. On the other hand he had an equal fondness for our older Bengali authors and Vaishnava Poets. He knew hundreds of Bengali songs of unknown authorship, and on these he would launch, with voice uplifted, regardless of tune, or consequence, or of the express disapproval of his hearers. Nor could anything, within him or without, prevent his loudly beating time to his own music, for which the nearest table or book served his nimble fingers to rap a vigorous tattoo on, to help to enliven the audience.

He was also one of those with an inordinate capacity for extracting enjoyment from all and sundry. He was as ready to absorb every bit of goodness in a thing as he was lavish in singing its praises. He had an extraordinary gift as a lightning composer of lyrics and songs of no mean merit, but in which he himself had no pride of authorship. He took no further notice of the heaps of scattered scraps of paper on which his pencil writings had been indited. He was as indifferent to his powers as they were prolific.

One of his longer poetic pieces was much appreciated when it appeared in the *Bangadarsan*, and I have heard his songs sung by many who knew nothing at all about their composer.

A genuine delight in literature is much rarer than erudition, and it was this enthusiastic enjoyment in Akshay Babu which used to awaken my own literary appreciation. He was as liberal in his friendships as in his literary criticisms. Among strangers he was as a fish out of water, but among friends discrepancies in wisdom or age made no difference to him. With us boys he was a boy. When he took his leave, late in the evening, from the *mujlis* of our elders, I would buttonhole and drag him to our school room. There, with undiminished geniality he would make himself the life and soul of our little gathering, seated on the top of our study table. On many such occasions I have listened to him going into a rapturous dissertation on some English poem; engaged him in some appreciative discussion, critical inquiry, or hot dispute; or read to him some of my own writings and been rewarded in return with praise unsparing.

My fourth brother Jyotirindra was one of the chief helpers in my literary and emotional training. He was an enthusiast himself and loved to evoke enthusiasm in others. He did not allow the difference between our ages to be any bar to my free intellectual and sentimental intercourse with him. This great boon of freedom which he allowed me, none else would have dared to do; many even blamed him for it. His companionship made it possible for me to shake off my shrinking sensitiveness. It was as necessary for my soul after its rigorous repression during my infancy as are the monsoon clouds after a fiery summer.

But for such snapping of my shackles I might have become crippled for life. Those in authority are never tired of holding forth the possibility of the abuse of freedom as a reason for withholding it, but without that possibility freedom would not be really free. And the only way of learning how to use properly a thing is through its misuse. For myself, at least, I can truly say that what little mischief resulted from my freedom always led the way to the means of curing mischief. I have never been able to make my own anything which they tried to compel me to swallow by getting hold of me, physically or mentally, by the ears. Nothing but sorrow have I ever gained except when left freely to myself.

My brother Jyotirindra unreservedly let me go my own way to self-knowledge, and only since then could my nature prepare to put forth its thorns, it may be, but likewise its flowers. This experience of mine has led me to dread, not so much evil itself, as tyrannical attempts to create goodness. Of punitive police, political or moral, I have a wholesome horror. The state of slavery which is thus brought on is the worst form of cancer to which humanity is subject.

My brother at one time would spend days at his piano engrossed in the creation of new tunes. Showers of melody would stream from under his dancing fingers, while Akshay Babu and I, seated on either side, would be busy fitting words to the tunes as they grew into shape to help to hold them in our memories.[35] This is how I served my apprenticeship in the composition of songs.

While we were growing to boyhood music was largely cultivated in our family. This had the advantage of making it possible for me to imbibe it, without an effort, into my whole being. It had also the disadvantage of not giving me that technical mastery which the effort of learning step by step alone can give. Of what may be called proficiency in music, therefore, I acquired none.

Ever since my return from the Himalayas it was a case of my getting more freedom, more and more. The rule of the servants came to an end; I saw to it with many a device that the bonds of my school life were also loosened; nor to my home tutors did I give much scope. Gyan Babu, after taking me through "The Birth of the War-god" and one or two other books in a desultory fashion, went off to take up a legal career. Then came Braja Babu. The first day he put me on to translate "The Vicar of Wakefield." I found that I did not dislike the book; but when this encouraged him to make more elaborate arrangements for the advancement of my learning I made myself altogether scarce.

As I have said, my elders gave me up. Neither I nor they were troubled with any more hopes of my future. So I felt free to devote myself to filling up my manuscript book. And the writings which thus filled it were no better than could have been expected. My mind had nothing in it but hot vapour, and vapour-filled bubbles frothed and eddied round a vortex of lazy fancy, aimless and unmeaning. No forms were evolved, there was only the distraction of movement, a bubbling up, a bursting back into froth. What little of matter there was in it was not mine, but borrowed from other poets. What was my own was the restlessness, the seething tension within me. When motion has been born, while yet the balance of forces has not matured, then is there blind chaos indeed.

My sister-in-law[36] was a great lover of literature. She did not read simply to kill time, but the Bengali books which she read filled her whole mind. I was a partner in her literary enterprises. She was a devoted admirer of "The Dream Journey." So was I; the more particularly as, having been brought up in the atmosphere of its creation, its beauties had become intertwined with every fibre of my heart. Fortunately it was entirely beyond my power of imitation, so it never occurred to me to attempt anything like it.

"The Dream Journey" may be likened to a superb palace of Allegory, with innumerable halls, chambers, passages, corners and niches full of statuary and pictures, of wonderful design and workmanship; and in the grounds around gardens, bowers, fountains and shady nooks in profusion. Not only do poetic thought and fancy abound, but the richness and variety of language and expression is also marvellous. It is not a small thing, this creative power which can bring into being so magnificent a structure complete in all its artistic detail, and that is perhaps why the idea of attempting an imitation never occurred to me.

At this time Viharilal Chakravarti's series of songs called *Sarada Mangal* were coming out in the *Arya Darsan*. My sister-in-law was greatly taken with the sweetness of these lyrics. Most of them she knew by heart. She used often to invite the poet to our house and had embroidered for him a cushion-seat with her own hands. This gave me the opportunity of making friends with him. He came to have a great affection for me, and I took to dropping in at his house at all times of the day, morning, noon or evening. His heart was as large as his body, and a halo of fancy used to surround him like a poetic astral body which seemed to be his truer image. He was always full of true artistic joy, and whenever I have been to him I have breathed in my share of it. Often have I come upon him in his little room on the third storey, in the heat of noonday, sprawling on the cool polished cement floor, writing his poems. Mere boy though I was, his welcome was always so genuine and hearty that I never felt the least awkwardness in approaching him. Then, wrapt in his inspiration and forgetful of all surroundings, he would read out his poems or sing his songs to me. Not that he had much of the gift of song in his voice; but then he was not altogether tuneless, and one could get a fair idea of the intended melody.[37] When with eyes closed he raised his rich deep voice, its expressiveness made up for what it lacked in execution. I still seem to hear some of his songs as he sang them. I would also sometimes set his words to music and sing them to him.

He was a great admirer of Valmiki and Kalidas. I remember how once after reciting a description of the Himalayas from Kalidas with the full strength of his voice, he said: "The succession of long ā sounds here is not an accident. The poet has deliberately repeated this sound all the way from *Devatatma* down to *Nagadhiraja* as an assistance in realising the glorious expanse of the Himalayas."

At the time the height of my ambition was to become a poet like Vihari Babu. I might have even succeeded in working myself up to the belief that I was actually writing like him, but for my sister-in-law, his zealous devotee, who stood in the way. She would keep reminding me of a Sanskrit saying that the unworthy aspirant after poetic fame departs in jeers! Very possibly she knew that if my vanity was once allowed to get the upper hand it would be difficult afterwards to bring it under control. So neither my poetic abilities nor my powers of song readily received any praise from her; rather would she never let slip an opportunity of praising somebody else's singing at my expense; with the result that I gradually became quite convinced of the defects of my voice. Misgivings about my poetic powers also assailed me; but, as this was the only field of activity left in which I had any chance of retaining my self-respect, I could not allow the judgment of another to deprive me of all hope; moreover, so insistent was the spur within me that to stop my poetic adventure was a matter of sheer impossibility.

## 20. PUBLISHING

My writings so far had been confined to the family circle. Then was started the monthly called the *Gyanankur*, Sprouting Knowledge, and, as befitted its name it secured an embryo poet as one of its contributors. It began to publish all my poetic ravings indiscriminately, and to this day I have, in a corner of my mind, the fear that, when the day of judgment comes for me, some enthusiastic literary police-agent will institute a search in the inmost zenana of forgotten literature, regardless of the claims of privacy, and bring these out before the pitiless public gaze.

My first prose writing also saw the light in the pages of the *Gyanankur*. It was a critical essay and had a bit of a history.

A book of poems had been published entitled *Bhubanmohini Pratibha*.[38] Akshay Babu in the *Sadharani* and Bhudeb Babu in the *Education Gazette* hailed this new poet with effusive acclamation. A friend of mine, older than myself, whose friendship dates from then, would come and show me letters he had received signed *Bhubanmohini*. He was one of those whom the book had captivated and used frequently to send reverential offerings of books or cloth[39] to the address of the reputed authoress.

Some of these poems were so wanting in restraint both of thought and language that I could not bear the idea of their being written by a woman. The letters that were shown to me made it still less possible for me to believe in the womanliness of the writer. But my doubts did not shake my friend's devotion and he went on with the worship of his idol.

Then I launched into a criticism of the work of this writer. I let myself go, and eruditely held forth on the distinctive features of lyrics and other short poems, my great advantage being that printed matter is so unblushing, so impassively unbetraying of the writer's real attainments. My friend turned up in a great passion and hurled at me the threat that a b.a. was writing a reply. A b.a.! I was struck speechless. I felt the same as in my younger days when my nephew Satya had shouted for a policeman. I could see the triumphal pillar of argument, erected upon my nice distinctions, crumbling before my eyes at the merciless assaults of authoritative quotations; and the door effectually barred against my ever showing my face to the reading public again. Alas, my critique, under what evil star wert thou born! I spent day after day in the direst suspense. But, like Satya's policeman, the b.a. failed to appear.

## 21. BHANU SINGHA

As I have said I was a keen student of the series of old Vaishnava poems which were being collected and published by Babus Akshay Sarkar and Saroda Mitter. Their language, largely mixed with Maithili, I found difficult to understand; but for that very reason I took all the more pains to get at their meaning. My feeling towards them was that same eager curiosity with which I regarded the ungerminated sprout within the seed, or the undiscovered mystery under the dust covering of the earth. My enthusiasm was kept up with the hope of bringing to light some unknown poetical gems as I went deeper and deeper into the unexplored darkness of this treasure-house.

While I was so engaged, the idea got hold of me of enfolding my own writings in just such a wrapping of mystery. I had heard from Akshay Chowdhury the story of the English boy-poet Chatterton. What his poetry was like I had no idea, nor perhaps had Akshay Babu himself. Had we known, the story might have lost its charm. As it happened the melodramatic element in it fired my imagination; for had not so many been deceived by his successful imitation of the classics? And at last the unfortunate youth had died by his own hand. Leaving aside the suicide part I girded up my loins to emulate young Chatterton's exploits.

One noon the clouds had gathered thickly. Rejoicing in the grateful shade of the cloudy midday rest-hour, I lay prone on the bed in my inner room and wrote on a slate the imitation *Maithili* poem *Gahana kusuma kunja majhe*. I was greatly pleased with it and lost no time in reading it out to the first one I came across; of whose understanding a word of it there happened to be not the slightest danger, and who consequently could not but gravely nod and say, "Good, very good indeed!"

To my friend mentioned a while ago I said one day: "A tattered old manuscript has been discovered while rummaging in the *Adi Brahma Samaj* library and from this I have copied some poems by an old Vaishnava Poet named Bhanu Singha;"[40] with which I read some of my imitation poems to him. He was profoundly stirred. "These could not have been written even by *Vidyapati* or *Chandidas*!" he rapturously exclaimed. "I really must have that MS. to make over to Akshay Babu for publication."

Then I showed him my manuscript book and conclusively proved that the poems could not have been written by either *Vidyapati* or *Chandidas* because the author happened to be myself. My friend's face fell as he muttered, "Yes, yes, they're not half bad."

When these Bhanu Singha poems were coming out in the *Bharati*, Dr. Nishikanta Chatterjee was in Germany. He wrote a thesis on the lyric poetry of our country comparing it with that of Europe. Bhanu Singha was given a place of honour as one of the old poets such as no modern writer could have aspired to. This was the thesis on which Nishikanta Chatterjee got his Ph. D.!

Whoever Bhanu Singha might have been, had his writings fallen into the hands of latter-day me, I swear I would not have been deceived. The language might have passed muster; for that which the old poets wrote in was not their mother tongue, but an artificial language varying in the hands of different poets. But there was nothing artificial about their sentiments. Any attempt to test Bhanu Singha's poetry by its ring would have shown up the base metal. It had none of the ravishing melody of our ancient pipes, but only the tinkle of a modern, foreign barrel organ.

## 22. PATRIOTISM

From an outside point of view many a foreign custom would appear to have gained entry into our family, but at its heart flames a national pride which has never flickered. The genuine regard which my father had for his country never forsook him through all the revolutionary vicissitudes of his life, and this in his descendants has taken shape as a strong patriotic feeling. Love of country was, however, by no means a characteristic of the times of which I am writing. Our educated men then kept at arms' length both the language and thought of their native land. Nevertheless my elder brothers had always cultivated Bengali literature. When on one occasion some new connection by marriage wrote my father an English letter it was promptly returned to the writer.

The *Hindu Mela* was an annual fair which had been instituted with the assistance of our house. Babu Nabagopal Mitter was appointed its manager. This was perhaps the first attempt at a reverential realisation of India as our motherland. My second brother's popular national anthem *"Bharater Jaya,"* was composed, then. The singing of songs glorifying the motherland, the recitation of poems of the love of country, the exhibition of indigenous arts and crafts and the encouragement of national talent and skill were the features of this *Mela*.

On the occasion of Lord Curzon's Delhi durbar I wrote a prose-paper —at the time of Lord Lytton's it was a poem. The British Government of those days feared the Russians it is true, but not the pen of a 14-year old poet. So, though my poem lacked none of the fiery sentiments appropriate to my age, there were no signs of any consternation in the ranks of the authorities from Commander-in-chief down to Commissioner of Police. Nor did any lachrymose letter in the *Times* predict a speedy downfall of the Empire for this apathy of its local guardians. I recited my poem under a tree at the Hindu Mela and one of my hearers was Nabin Sen, the poet. He reminded me of this after I had grown up.

My fourth brother, Jyotirindra, was responsible for a political association of which old Rajnarain Bose was the president. It held its sittings in a tumbledown building in an obscure Calcutta lane. Its proceedings were enshrouded in mystery. This mystery was its only claim to be awe-inspiring, for as a matter of fact there was nothing in our deliberations or doings of which government or people need have been afraid. The rest of our family had no idea where we were spending our afternoons. Our front door would be locked, the meeting room in darkness, the watchword a Vedic *mantra*, our talk in whispers. These alone provided us with enough of a thrill, and we wanted nothing more. Mere child as I was, I also was a member. We surrounded ourselves with such an atmosphere of pure frenzy that we always seemed to be soaring aloft on the wings of our enthusiasm. Of bashfulness, diffidence or fear we had none, our main object being to bask in the heat of our own fervour.

Bravery may sometimes have its drawbacks; but it has always maintained a deep hold on the reverence of mankind. In the literature of all countries we find an unflagging endeavour to keep alive this reverence. So in whatever state a particular set of men in a particular locality may be, they cannot escape the constant impact of these stimulating shocks. We had to be content with responding to such shocks, as best we could, by letting loose our imagination, coming together, talking tall and singing fervently.

There can be no doubt that closing up all outlets and barring all openings to a faculty so deep-seated in the nature of man, and moreover so prized by him, creates an unnatural condition favourable to degenerate activity. It is not enough to keep open only the avenues to clerical employment in any comprehensive scheme of Imperial Government-if no road be left for adventurous daring the soul of man will pine for deliverance, and secret passages still be sought, of which the pathways are tortuous and the end unthinkable. I firmly believe that if in those days Government had paraded a frightfulness born of suspicion, then the comedy which the youthful members of this association had been at might have turned into grim tragedy. The play, however, is over, not a brick of Fort-William is any the worse, and we are now smiling at its memory.

My brother Jyotirindra began to busy himself with a national costume for all India, and submitted various designs to the association. The *Dhoti* was not deemed business-like; trousers were too foreign; so he hit upon a compromise which considerably detracted from the dhoti while failing to improve the trousers. That is to say, the trousers were decorated with the addition of a false dhoti-fold in front and behind. The fearsome thing that resulted from combining a turban with a *Sola-topee* our most enthusiastic member would not have had the temerity to call ornamental. No person of ordinary courage could have dared it, but my brother unflinchingly wore the complete suit in broad day-light, passing through the house of an afternoon to the carriage waiting outside, indifferent alike to the stare of relation or friend, door-keeper or coachman. There may be many a brave Indian ready to die for his country, but there are but few, I am sure, who even for the good of the nation would face the public streets in such pan-Indian garb.

Every Sunday my brother would get up a *Shikar* party. Many of those who joined in it, uninvited, we did not even know. There was a carpenter, a smith and others from all ranks of society. Bloodshed was the only thing lacking in this *shikar*, at least I cannot recall any. Its other appendages were so abundant and satisfying that we felt the absence of dead or wounded game to be a trifling circumstance of no account. As we were out from early morning, my sister-in-law furnished us with a plentiful supply of *luchis* with appropriate accompaniments; and as these did not depend upon the fortunes of our chase we never had to return empty.

The neighbourhood of Maniktola is not wanting in Villa-gardens. We would turn into any one of these at the end, and high-and low-born alike, seated on the bathing platform of a tank, would fling ourselves on the *luchis* in right good earnest, all that was left of them being the vessels they were brought in.

Braja Babu was one of the most enthusiastic of these blood-thirstless *shikaris*. He was the Superintendent of the Metropolitan Institution and had also been our private tutor for a time. One day he had the happy idea of accosting the *mali* (gardener) of a villa-garden into which we had thus trespassed with: "Hallo, has uncle been here lately!" The *mali* lost no time in saluting him respectfully before he replied: "No, Sir, the master hasn't been lately." "All right, get us some green cocoanuts off the trees." We had a fine drink after our *luchis* that day.

A Zamindar in a small way was among our party. He owned a villa on the river side. One day we had a picnic there together, in defiance of caste rules. In the afternoon there was a tremendous storm. We stood on the river-side stairs leading into the water and shouted out songs to its accompaniment. I cannot truthfully assert that all the seven notes of the scale could properly be distinguished in Rajnarain Babu's singing, nevertheless he sent forth his voice and, as in the old Sanskrit works the text is drowned by the notes, so in Rajnarain Babu's musical efforts the vigorous play of his limbs and features overwhelmed his feebler vocal performance; his head swung from side to side marking time, while the storm played havoc with his flowing beard. It was late in the night when we turned homewards in a hackney carriage. By that time the storm clouds had dispersed and the stars twinkled forth. The darkness had become intense, the atmosphere silent, the village roads deserted, and the thickets on either side filled with fireflies like a carnival of sparks scattered in some noiseless revelry.

One of the objects of our association was to encourage the manufacture of lucifer matches, and similar small industries. For this purpose each member had to contribute a tenth of his income. Matches had to be made, but matchwood was difficult to get; for though we all know with what fiery energy a bundle of *khangras*[41] can be wielded in capable hands, the thing that burns at its touch is not a lamp wick. After many experiments we succeeded in making a boxful of matches. The patriotic enthusiasm which was thus evidenced did not constitute their only value, for the money that was spent in their making might have served to light the family hearth for the space of a year. Another little defect was that these matches could not be got to burn unless there was a light handy to touch them up with. If they could only have inherited some of the patriotic flame of which they were born they might have been marketable even to-day.

News came to us that some young student was trying to make a power loom. Off we went to see it. None of us had the knowledge with which to test its practical usefulness, but in our capacity for believing and hoping we were inferior to none. The poor fellow had got into a bit of debt over the cost of his machine which we repaid for him. Then one day we found Braja Babu coming over to our house with a flimsy country towel tied round his head. "Made in our loom!" he shouted as with hands uplifted he executed a war-dance. The outside of Braja Babu's head had then already begun to ripen into grey!

At last some worldly-wise people came and joined our society, made us taste of the fruit of knowledge, and broke up our little paradise.

When I first knew Rajnarain Babu, I was not old enough to appreciate his many-sidedness. In him were combined many opposites. In spite of his hoary hair and beard he was as young as the youngest of us, his venerable exterior serving only as a white mantle for keeping his youth perpetually fresh. Even his extensive learning had not been able to do him any damage, for it left him absolutely simple. To the end of his life the incessant flow of his hearty laughter suffered no check, neither from the gravity of age, nor ill-health, nor domestic affliction, nor profundity of thought, nor variety of knowledge, all of which had been his in ample measure. He had been a favourite pupil of Richardson and brought up in an atmosphere of English learning, nevertheless he flung aside all obstacles due to his early habit and gave himself up lovingly and devotedly to Bengali literature. Though the meekest of men, he was full of fire which flamed its fiercest in his patriotism, as though to burn to ashes the shortcomings and destitution of his country. The memory of this smile-sweetened fervour-illumined lifelong-youthful saint is one that is worth cherishing by our countrymen.

## 23. THE BHARATI

On the whole the period of which I am writing was for me one of ecstatic excitement. Many a night have I spent without sleep, not for any particular reason but from a mere desire to do the reverse of the obvious. I would keep up reading in the dim light of our school room all alone; the distant church clock would chime every quarter as if each passing hour was being put up to auction; and the loud *Haribols* of the bearers of the dead, passing along Chitpore Road on their way to the Nimtollah cremation ground, would now and then resound. Through some summer moonlight nights I would be wandering about like an unquiet spirit among the lights and shadows of the tubs and pots on the garden of the roof-terrace.

Those who would dismiss this as sheer poetising would be wrong. The very earth in spite of its having aged considerably surprises us occasionally by its departure from sober stability; in the days of its youth, when it had not become hardened and crusty, it was effusively volcanic and indulged in many a wild escapade. In the days of man's first youth the same sort of thing happens. So long as the materials which go to form his life have not taken on their final shape they are apt to be turbulent in the process of their formation.

This was the time when my brother Jyotirindra decided to start the *Bharati* with our eldest brother as editor, giving us fresh food for enthusiasm. I was then just sixteen, but I was not left out of the editorial staff. A short time before, in all the insolence of my youthful vanity, I had written a criticism of the *Meghanadabadha*. As acidity is characteristic of the unripe mango so is abuse of the immature critic. When other powers are lacking, the power of pricking seems to be at its sharpest. I had thus sought immortality by leaving my scratches on that immortal epic. This impudent criticism was my first contribution to the Bharati.

In the first volume I also published a long poem called *Kavikahini*, The Poet's Story. It was the product of an age when the writer had seen practically nothing of the world except an exaggerated image of his own nebulous self. So the hero of the story was naturally a poet, not the writer as he was, but as he imagined or desired himself to seem. It would hardly be correct to say that he desired to *be* what he portrayed; that represented more what he thought was expected of him, what would make the world admiringly nod and say: "Yes, a poet indeed, quite the correct thing." In it was a great parade of universal love, that pet subject of the budding poet, which sounds as big as it is easy to talk about. While yet any truth has not dawned upon one's own mind, and others' words are one's only stock-in-trade, simplicity and restraint in expression are not possible. Then, in the endeavour to display magnified that which is really big in itself, it becomes impossible to avoid a grotesque and ridiculous exhibition.

When I blush to read these effusions of my boyhood I am also struck with the fear that very possibly in my later writings the same distortion, wrought by straining after effect, lurks in a less obvious form. The loudness of my voice, I doubt not, often drowns the thing I would say; and some day or other Time will find me out.

The *Kavikahini* was the first work of mine to appear in book form. When I went with my second brother to Ahmedabad, some enthusiastic friend of mine took me by surprise by printing and publishing it and sending me a copy. I cannot say that he did well, but the feeling that was roused in me at the time did not resemble that of an indignant judge. He got his punishment, however, not from the author, but from the public who hold the purse strings. I have heard that the dead load of the books lay, for many a long day, heavy on the shelves of the booksellers and the mind of the luckless publisher.

Writings of the age at which I began to contribute to the *Bharati* cannot possibly be fit for publication. There is no better way of ensuring repentance at maturity than to rush into print too early. But it has one redeeming feature: the irresistible impulse to see one's writings in print exhausts itself during early life. Who are the readers, what do they say, what printers' errors have remained uncorrected, these and the like worries run their course as infantile maladies and leave one leisure in later life to attend to one's literary work in a healthier frame of mind.

Bengali literature is not old enough to have elaborated those internal checks which can serve to control its votaries. As experience in writing is gained the Bengali writer has to evolve the restraining force from within himself. This makes it impossible for him to avoid the creation of a great deal of rubbish during a considerable length of time. The ambition to work wonders with the modest gifts at one's disposal is bound to be an obsession in the beginning, so that the effort to transcend at every step one's natural powers, and therewith the bounds of truth and beauty, is always visible in early writings. To recover one's normal self, to learn to respect one's powers as they are, is a matter of time.

However that may be, I have left much of youthful folly to be ashamed of, besmirching the pages of the *Bharati*; and this shames me not for its literary defects alone but for its atrocious impudence, its extravagant excesses and its high-sounding artificiality. At the same time I am free to recognise that the writings of that period were pervaded with an enthusiasm the value of which cannot be small. It was a period to which, if error was natural, so was the boyish faculty of hoping, believing and rejoicing. And if the fuel of error was necessary for feeding the flame of enthusiasm then while that which was fit to be reduced to ashes will have become ash, the good work done by the flame will not have been in vain in my life.

**PART V**

## 24. AHMEDABAD

When the *Bharati* entered upon its second year, my second brother proposed to take me to England; and when my father gave his consent, this further unasked favour of providence came on me as a surprise.

As a first step I accompanied my brother to Ahmedabad where he was posted as judge. My sister-in-law with her children was then in England, so the house was practically empty.

The Judge's house is known as *Shahibagh* and was a palace of the Badshahs of old. At the foot of the wall supporting a broad terrace flowed the thin summer stream of the Savarmati river along one edge of its ample bed of sand. My brother used to go off to his court, and I would be left all alone in the vast expanse of the palace, with only the cooing of the pigeons to break the midday stillness; and an unaccountable curiosity kept me wandering about the empty rooms.

Into the niches in the wall of a large chamber my brother had put his books. One of these was a gorgeous edition of Tennyson's works, with big print and numerous pictures. The book, for me, was as silent as the palace, and, much in the same way I wandered among its picture plates. Not that I could not make anything of the text, but it spoke to me more like inarticulate cooings than words. In my brother's library I also found a book of collected Sanskrit poems edited by Dr. Haberlin and printed at the old Serampore press. This was also beyond my understanding but the sonorous Sanskrit words, and the march of the metre, kept me tramping among the *Amaru Shataka* poems to the mellow roll of their drum call.

In the upper room of the palace tower was my lonely hermit cell, my only companions being a nest of wasps. In the unrelieved darkness of the night I slept there alone. Sometimes a wasp or two would drop off the nest on to my bed, and if perchance I happened to roll on one, the meeting was unpleasing to the wasp and keenly discomforting to me.

On moonlight nights pacing round and round the extensive terrace overlooking the river was one of my caprices. It was while so doing that I first composed my own tunes for my songs. The song addressed to the Rose-maiden was one of these, and it still finds a place in my published works.

Finding how imperfect was my knowledge of English I set to work reading through some English books with the help of a dictionary. From my earliest years it was my habit not to let any want of complete comprehension interfere with my reading on, quite satisfied with the structure which my imagination reared on the bits which I understood here and there. I am reaping even to-day both the good and bad effects of this habit.

## 25. ENGLAND

After six months thus spent in Ahmedabad we started for England. In an unlucky moment I began to write letters about my journey to my relatives and to the *Bharati*. Now it is beyond my power to call them back. These were nothing but the outcome of youthful bravado. At that age the mind refuses to admit that its greatest pride is in its power to understand, to accept, to respect; and that modesty is the best means of enlarging its domain. Admiration and praise are looked upon as a sign of weakness or surrender, and the desire to cry down and hurt and demolish with argument gives rise to this kind of intellectual fireworks. These attempts of mine to establish my superiority by revilement might have occasioned me amusement to-day, had not their want of straightness and common courtesy been too painful.

From my earliest years I had had practically no commerce with the outside world. To be plunged in this state, at the age of 17, into the midst of the social sea of England would have justified considerable misgiving as to my being able to keep afloat. But as my sister-in-law happened to be in Brighton with her children I weathered the first shock of it under her shelter.

Winter was then approaching. One evening as we were chatting round the fireside, the children came running to us with the exciting news that it had been snowing. We at once went out. It was bitingly cold, the sky filled with white moonlight, the earth covered with white snow. It was not the face of Nature familiar to me, but something quite different-like a dream. Everything near seemed to have receded far away, leaving the still white figure of an ascetic steeped in deep meditation. The sudden revelation, on the mere stepping outside a door, of such wonderful, such immense beauty had never before come upon me.

My days passed merrily under the affectionate care of my sister-in-law and in boisterous rompings with the children. They were greatly tickled at my curious English pronunciation, and though in the rest of their games I could whole-heartedly join, this I failed to see the fun of. How could I explain to them that there was no logical means of distinguishing between the sound of *a* in warm and *o* in worm. Unlucky that I was, I had to bear the brunt of the ridicule which was more properly the due of the vagaries of English spelling.

I became quite an adept in inventing new ways of keeping the children occupied and amused. This art has stood me in good stead many a time thereafter, and its usefulness for me is not yet over. But I no longer feel in myself the same unbounded profusion of ready contrivance. That was the first opportunity I had for giving my heart to children, and it had all the freshness and overflowing exuberance of such a first gift.

But I had not set out on this journey to exchange a home beyond the seas for the one on this side. The idea was that I should study Law and come back a barrister. So one day I was put into a public school in Brighton. The first thing the Headmaster said after scanning my features was: "What a splendid head you have!" This detail lingers in my memory because she, who at home was an enthusiast in her self-imposed duty of keeping my vanity in check, had impressed on me that my cranium[42] and features generally, compared with that of many another were barely of a medium order. I hope the reader will not fail to count it to my credit that I implicitly believed her, and inwardly deplored the parsimony of the Creator in the matter of my making. On many another occasion, finding myself estimated by my English acquaintances differently from what I had been accustomed to be by her, I was led to seriously worry my mind over the divergence in the standard of taste between the two countries!

One thing in the Brighton school seemed very wonderful: the other boys were not at all rude to me. On the contrary they would often thrust oranges and apples into my pockets and run away. I can only ascribe this uncommon behaviour of theirs to my being a foreigner.

I was not long in this school either-but that was no fault of the school. Mr. Tarak Palit[43] was then in England. He could see that this was not the way for me to get on, and prevailed upon my brother to allow him to take me to London, and leave me there to myself in a lodging house. The lodgings selected faced the Regent Gardens. It was then the depth of winter. There was not a leaf on the row of trees in front which stood staring at the sky with their scraggy snow-covered branches — a sight which chilled my very bones.

For the newly arrived stranger there can hardly be a more cruel place than London in winter. I knew no one near by, nor could I find my way about. The days of sitting alone at a window, gazing at the outside world, came back into my life. But the scene in this case was not attractive. There was a frown on its countenance; the sky turbid; the light lacking lustre like a dead man's eye; the horizon shrunk upon itself; with never an inviting smile from a broad hospitable world. The room was but scantily furnished, but there happened to be a harmonium which, after the daylight came to its untimely end, I used to play upon according to my fancy. Sometimes Indians would come to see me; and, though my acquaintance with them was but slight, when they rose to leave I felt inclined to hold them back by their coat-tails.

While living in these rooms there was one who came to teach me Latin. His gaunt figure with its worn-out clothing seemed no more able than the naked trees to withstand the winter's grip. I do not know what his age was but he clearly looked older than his years. Some days in the course of our lessons he would suddenly be at a loss for some word and look vacant and ashamed. His people at home counted him a crank. He had become possessed of a theory. He believed that in each age some one dominant idea is manifested in every human society in all parts of the world; and though it may take different shapes under different degrees of civilisation, it is at bottom one and the same; nor is such idea taken from one by another by any process of adoption, for this truth holds good even where there is no intercourse. His great preoccupation was the gathering and recording of facts to prove this theory. And while so engaged his home lacked food, his body clothes. His daughters had but scant respect for his theory and were perhaps constantly upbraiding him for his infatuation. Some days one could see from his face that he had lighted upon some new proof, and that his thesis had correspondingly advanced. On these occasions I would broach the subject, and wax enthusiastic at his enthusiasm. On other days he would be steeped in gloom, as if his burden was too heavy to bear. Then would our lessons halt at every step; his eyes wander away into empty space; and his mind refuse to be dragged into the pages of the first Latin Grammar. I felt keenly for the poor body-starved theory-burdened soul, and though I was under no delusion as to the assistance I got in my Latin, I could not make up my mind to get rid of him. This pretence of learning Latin lasted as long as I was at these lodgings. When on the eve of leaving them I offered to settle his dues he said piteously: "I have done nothing, and only wasted your time, I cannot accept any payment from you." It was with great difficulty that I got him at last to take his fees.

Though my Latin tutor had never ventured to trouble me with the proofs of his theory, yet up to this day I do not disbelieve it. I am convinced that the minds of men are connected through some deep-lying continuous medium, and that a disturbance in one part is by it secretly communicated to others.

Mr. Palit next placed me in the house of a coach named Barker. He used to lodge and prepare students for their examinations. Except his mild little wife there was not a thing with any pretensions to attractiveness about this household. One can understand how such a tutor can get pupils, for these poor creatures do not often get the chance of making a choice. But it is painful to think of the conditions under which such men get wives. Mrs. Barker had attempted to console herself with a pet dog, but when Barker wanted to punish his wife he tortured the dog. So that her affection for the unfortunate animal only made for an enlargement of her field of sensibility.

From these surroundings, when my sister-in-law sent for me to Torquay in Devonshire, I was only too glad to run off to her. I cannot tell how happy I was with the hills there, the sea, the flower-covered meadows, the shade of the pine woods, and my two little restlessly playful companions. I was nevertheless sometimes tormented with questionings as to why, when my eyes were so surfeited with beauty, my mind saturated with joy, and my leisure-filled days crossing over the limitless blue of space freighted with unalloyed happiness, there should be no call of poetry to me. So one day off I went along the rocky shore, armed with MS. book and umbrella, to fulfil my poet's destiny. The spot I selected was of undoubted beauty, for that did not depend on my rhyme or fancy. There was a flat bit of overhanging rock reaching out as with a perpetual eagerness over the waters; rocked on the foam-flecked waves of the liquid blue in front, the sunny sky slept smilingly to its lullaby; behind, the shade of the fringe of pines lay spread like the slipped off garment of some languorous wood nymph. Enthroned on that seat of stone I wrote a poem *Magnatari* (the sunken boat). I might have believed to-day that it was good, had I taken the precaution of sinking it then in the sea. But such consolation is not open to me, for it happens to be existing in the body; and though banished from my published works, a writ might yet cause it to be produced.

The messenger of duty however was not idle. Again came its call and I returned to London. This time I found a refuge in the household of Dr. Scott. One fine evening with bag and baggage I invaded his home. Only the white haired Doctor, his wife and their eldest daughter were there. The two younger girls, alarmed at this incursion of an Indian stranger had gone off to stay with a relative. I think they came back home only after they got the news of my not being dangerous.

In a very short time I became like one of the family. Mrs. Scott treated me as a son, and the heartfelt kindness I got from her daughters is rare even from one's own relations.

One thing struck me when living in this family-that human nature is everywhere the same. We are fond of saying, and I also believed, that the devotion of an Indian wife to her husband is something unique, and not to be found in Europe. But I at least was unable to discern any difference between Mrs. Scott and an ideal Indian wife. She was entirely wrapped up in her husband. With their modest means there was no fussing about of too many servants, and Mrs. Scott attended to every detail of her husband's wants herself. Before he came back home from his work of an evening, she would arrange his arm-chair and woollen slippers before the fire with her own hands. She would never allow herself to forget for a moment the things he liked, or the behaviour which pleased him. She would go over the house every morning, with their only maid, from attic to kitchen, and the brass rods on the stairs and the door knobs and fittings would be scrubbed and polished till they shone again. Over and above this domestic routine there were the many calls of social duty. After getting through all her daily duties she would join with zest in our evening readings and music, for it is not the least of the duties of a good housewife to make real the gaiety of the leisure hour.

Some evenings I would join the girls in a table-turning seance. We would place our fingers on a small tea table and it would go capering about the room. It got to be so that whatever we touched began to quake and quiver. Mrs. Scott did not quite like all this. She would sometimes gravely shake her head and say she had her doubts about its being right. She bore it bravely, however, not liking to put a damper on our youthful spirits. But one day when we put our hands on Dr. Scott's chimneypot to make it turn, that was too much for her. She rushed up in a great state of mind and forbade us to touch it. She could not bear the idea of Satan having anything to do, even for a moment, with her husband's head-gear.

In all her actions her reverence for her husband was the one thing that stood out. The memory of her sweet self-abnegation makes it clear to me that the ultimate perfection of all womanly love is to be found in reverence; that where no extraneous cause has hampered its true development woman's love naturally grows into worship. Where the appointments of luxury are in profusion, and frivolity tarnishes both day and night, this love is degraded, and woman's nature finds not the joy of its perfection.

I spent some months here. Then it was time for my brother to return home, and my father wrote to me to accompany him. I was delighted at the prospect. The light of my country, the sky of my country, had been silently calling me. When I said good bye Mrs. Scott took me by the hand and wept. "Why did you come to us," she said, "if you must go so soon?" That household no longer exists in London. Some of the members of the Doctor's family have departed to the other world, others are scattered in places unknown to me. But it will always live in my memory.

One winter's day, as I was passing through a street in Tunbridge Wells, I saw a man standing on the road side. His bare toes were showing through his gaping boots, his breast was partly uncovered. He said nothing to me, perhaps because begging was forbidden, but he looked up at my face just for a moment. The coin I gave him was perhaps more valuable than he expected, for, after I had gone on a bit, he came after me and said: "Sir, you have given me a gold piece by mistake," with which he offered to return it to me. I might not have particularly remembered this, but for a similar thing which happened on another occasion. When I first reached the Torquay railway station a porter took my luggage to the cab outside. After searching my purse for small change in vain, I gave him half-a-crown as the cab started. After a while he came running after us, shouting to the cabman to stop. I thought to myself that finding me to be such an innocent he had hit upon some excuse for demanding more. As the cab stopped he said: "You must have mistaken a half-crown piece for a penny, Sir!"

I cannot say that I have never been cheated while in England, but not in any way which it would be fair to hold in remembrance. What grew chiefly upon me, rather, was the conviction that only those who are trustworthy know how to trust. I was an unknown foreigner, and could have easily evaded payment with impunity, yet no London shopkeeper ever mistrusted me.

During the whole period of my stay in England I was mixed up in a farcical comedy which I had to play out from start to finish. I happened to get acquainted with the widow of some departed high Anglo-Indian official. She was good enough to call me by the pet-name Ruby. Some Indian friend of hers had composed a doleful poem in English in memory of her husband. It is needless to expatiate on its poetic merit or felicity of diction. As my ill-luck would have it, the composer had indicated that the dirge was to be chanted to the mode *Behaga*. So the widow one day entreated me to sing it to her thus. Like the silly innocent that I was, I weakly acceded. There was unfortunately no one there but I who could realise the atrociously ludicrous way in which the *Behaga* mode combined with those absurd verses. The widow seemed intensely touched to hear the Indian's lament for her husband sung to its native melody. I thought that there the matter ended, but that was not to be.

I frequently met the widowed lady at different social gatherings, and when after dinner we joined the ladies in the drawing room, she would ask me to sing that *Behaga*. Everyone else would anticipate some extraordinary specimen of Indian music and would add their entreaties to hers. Then from her pocket would come forth printed copies of that fateful composition, and my ears begin to redden and tingle. And at last, with bowed head and quavering voice I would have to make a beginning–but too keenly conscious that to none else in the room but me was this performance sufficiently heartrending. At the end, amidst much suppressed tittering, there would come a chorus of "Thank you very much!" "How interesting!" And in spite of its being winter I would perspire all over. Who would have predicted at my birth or at his death what a severe blow to me would be the demise of this estimable Anglo-Indian!

Then, for a time, while I was living with Dr. Scott and attending lectures at the University College, I lost touch with the widow. She was in a suburban locality some distance away from London, and I frequently got letters from her inviting me there. But my dread of that dirge kept me from accepting these invitations. At length I got a pressing telegram from her. I was on my way to college when this telegram reached me and my stay in England was then about to come to its close. I thought to myself I ought to see the widow once more before my departure, and so yielded to her importunity.

Instead of coming home from college I went straight to the railway station. It was a horrible day, bitterly cold, snowing and foggy. The station I was bound for was the terminus of the line. So I felt quite easy in mind and did not think it worth while to inquire about the time of arrival.

All the station platforms were coming on the right hand side, and in the right hand corner seat I had ensconced myself reading a book. It had already become so dark that nothing was visible outside. One by one the other passengers got down at their destinations. We reached and left the station just before the last one. Then the train stopped again, but there was nobody to be seen, nor any lights or platform. The mere passenger has no means of divining why trains should sometimes stop at the wrong times and places, so, giving up the attempt, I went on with my reading. Then the train began to move backwards. There seems to be no accounting for railway eccentricity, thought I as I once more returned to my book. But when we came right back to the previous station, I could remain indifferent no longer. "When are we getting to ——" I inquired at the station. "You are just coming from there," was the reply. "Where are we going now, then?" I asked, thoroughly flurried. "To London." I thereupon understood that this was a shuttle train. On inquiring about the next train to —— I was informed that there were no more trains that night. And in reply to my next question I gathered that there was no inn within five miles.

I had left home after breakfast at ten in the morning, and had had nothing since. When abstinence is the only choice, an ascetic frame of mind comes easy. I buttoned up my thick overcoat to the neck and seating myself under a platform lamp went on with my reading. The book I had with me was Spencer's *Data of Ethics*, then recently published. I consoled myself with the thought that I might never get another such opportunity of concentrating my whole attention on such a subject.

After a short time a porter came and informed me that a special was running and would be in in half an hour. I felt so cheered up by the news that I could not go on any longer with the *Data of Ethics*. Where I was due at seven I arrived at length at nine. "What is this, Ruby?" asked my hostess. "Whatever have you been doing with yourself?" I was unable to take much pride in the account of my wonderful adventures which I gave her. Dinner was over; nevertheless, as my misfortune was hardly my fault, I did not expect condign punishment, especially as the dispenser was a woman. But all that the widow of the high Anglo-Indian official said to me was: "Come along, Ruby, have a cup of tea."

I never was a tea-drinker, but in the hope that it might be of some assistance in allaying my consuming hunger I managed to swallow a cup of strong decoction with a couple of dry biscuits. When I at length reached the drawing room I found a gathering of elderly ladies and among them one pretty young American who was engaged to a nephew of my hostess and seemed busy going through the usual premarital love passages.

"Let's have some dancing," said my hostess. I was neither in the mood nor bodily condition for that exercise. But it is the docile who achieve the most impossible things in this world; so, though the dance was primarily got up for the benefit of the engaged couple, I had to dance with the ladies of considerably advanced age, with only the tea and biscuits between myself and starvation.

But my sorrows did not end here. "Where are you putting up for the night?" asked my hostess. This was a question for which I was not prepared. While I stared at her, speechless, she explained that as the local inn would close at midnight I had better betake myself thither without further delay. Hospitality, however, was not entirely wanting for I had not to find the inn unaided, a servant showing me the way there with a lantern. At first I thought this might prove a blessing in disguise, and at once proceeded to make inquiries for food: flesh, fish or vegetable, hot or cold, anything! I was told that drinks I could have in any variety but nothing to eat. Then I looked to slumber for forgetfulness, but there seemed to be no room even in her world-embracing lap. The sand-stone floor of the bed-room was icy cold, an old bedstead and worn-out wash-stand being its only furniture.

In the morning the Anglo-Indian widow sent for me to breakfast. I found a cold repast spread out, evidently the remnants of last night's dinner. A small portion of this, lukewarm or cold, offered to me last night could not have hurt anyone, while my dancing might then have been less like the agonised wrigglings of a landed carp.

After breakfast my hostess informed me that the lady for whose delectation I had been invited to sing was ill in bed, and that I would have to serenade her from her bed-room door. I was made to stand up on the staircase landing. Pointing to a closed door the widow said: "That's where she is." And I gave voice to that *Behaga* dirge facing the mysterious unknown on the other side. Of what happened to the invalid as the result I have yet received no news.

273

After my return to London I had to expiate in bed the consequences of my fatuous complaisance. Dr. Scott's girls implored me, on my conscience, not to take this as a sample of English hospitality. It was the effect of India's salt, they protested.

## 26. LOKEN PALIT

While I was attending lectures on English literature at the University College, Loken Palit was my class fellow. He was about 4 years younger than I. At the age I am writing these reminiscences a difference of 4 years is not perceptible. But it is difficult for friendship to bridge the gulf between 17 and 13. Lacking the weight of years the boy is always anxious to keep up the dignity of seniority. But this did not raise any barrier in my mind in the case of the boy Loken, for I could not feel that he was in any way my junior.

Boy and girl students sat together in the College library for study. This was the place for our tete-a-tete. Had we been fairly quiet about it none need have complained, but my young friend was so surcharged with high spirits that at the least provocation they would burst forth as laughter. In all countries girls have a perverse degree of application to their studies, and I feel repentant as I recall the multitude of reproachful blue eyes which vainly showered disapprobation on our unrestrained merriment. But in those days I felt not the slightest sympathy with the distress of disturbed studiousness. By the grace of Providence I have never had a headache in my life, nor a moment of compunction for interrupted school studies.

With our laughter as an almost unbroken accompaniment we managed also to do a bit of literary discussion, and, though Loken's reading of Bengali literature was less extensive than mine, he made up for that by the keenness of his intellect. Among the subjects we discussed was Bengali orthography.

The way it arose was this. One of the Scott girls wanted me to teach her Bengali. When taking her through the alphabet I expressed my pride that Bengali spelling has a conscience, and does not delight in overstepping rules at every step. I made clear to her how laughable would have been the waywardness of English spelling but for the tragic compulsion we were under to cram it for our examinations. But my pride had a fall. It transpired that Bengali spelling was quite as impatient of bondage, but that habit had blinded me to its transgressions.

Then I began to search for the laws regulating its lawlessness. I was quite surprised at the wonderful assistance which Loken proved to be in this matter.

After Loken had got into the Indian Civil Service, and returned home, the work, which had in the University College library had its source in rippling merriment, flowed on in a widening stream. Loken's boisterous delight in literature was as the wind in the sails of my literary adventure. And when at the height of my youth I was driving the tandem of prose and poetry at a furious rate, Loken's unstinted appreciation kept my energies from flagging for a moment. Many an extraordinary prose or poetical flight have I taken in his bungalow in the moffussil. On many an occasion did our literary and musical gatherings assemble under the auspices of the evening star to disperse, as did the lamplights at the breezes of dawn, under the morning star.

Of the many lotus flowers at *Saraswati's*[44] feet the blossom of friendship must be her favorite. I have not come across much of golden pollen in her lotus bank, but have nothing to complain of as regards the profusion of the sweet savour of good-fellowship.

## 27. THE BROKEN HEART

While in England I began another poem, which I went on with during my journey home, and finished after my return. This was published under the name of *Bhagna Hriday*, The Broken Heart. At the time I thought it very good. There was nothing strange in the writer's thinking so; but it did not fail to gain the appreciation of the readers of the time as well. I remember how, after it came out, the chief minister of the late Raja of Tipperah called on me solely to deliver the message that the Raja admired the poem and entertained high hopes of the writer's future literary career.

About this poem of my eighteenth year let me set down here what I wrote in a letter when I was thirty:

When I began to write the *Bhagna Hriday* I was eighteen-neither in my childhood nor my youth. This borderland age is not illumined with the direct rays of Truth; —its reflection is seen here and there, and the rest is shadow. And like twilight shades its imaginings are long-drawn and vague, making the real world seem like a world of phantasy. The curious part of it is that not only was I eighteen, but everyone around me seemed to be eighteen likewise; and we all flitted about in the same baseless, substanceless world of imagination, where even the most intense joys and sorrows seemed like the joys and sorrows of dreamland. There being nothing real to weigh them against, the trivial did duty for the great.

This period of my life, from the age of fifteen or sixteen to twenty-two or twenty-three, was one of utter disorderliness.

When, in the early ages of the Earth, land and water had not yet distinctly separated, huge misshapen amphibious creatures walked the trunk-less forests growing on the oozing silt. Thus do the passions of the dim ages of the immature mind, as disproportionate and curiously shaped, haunt the unending shades of its trackless, nameless wildernesses. They know not themselves, nor the aim of their wanderings; and, because they do not, they are ever apt to imitate something else. So, at this age of unmeaning activity, when my undeveloped powers, unaware of and unequal to their object, were jostling each other for an outlet, each sought to assert superiority through exaggeration.

When milk-teeth are trying to push their way through, they work the infant into a fever. All this agitation finds no justification till the teeth are out and have begun assisting in the absorption of food. In the same way do our early passions torment the mind, like a malady, till they realise their true relationship with the outer world.

The lessons I learnt from my experiences at that stage are to be found in every moral text-book, but are not therefore to be despised. That which keeps our appetites confined within us, and checks their free access to the outside, poisons our life. Such is selfishness which refuses to give free play to our desires, and prevents them from reaching their real goal, and that is why it is always accompanied by festering untruths and extravagances. When our desires find unlimited freedom in good work they shake off their diseased condition and come back to their own nature; —that is their true end, there also is the joy of their being.

The condition of my immature mind which I have described was fostered both by the example and precept of the time, and I am not sure that the effects of these are not lingering on to the present day. Glancing back at the period of which I tell, it strikes me that we had gained more of stimulation than of nourishment out of English Literature. Our literary gods then were Shakespeare, Milton and Byron; and the quality in their work which stirred us most was strength of passion. In the social life of Englishmen passionate outbursts are kept severely in check, for which very reason, perhaps, they so dominate their literature, making its characteristic to be the working out of extravagantly vehement feelings to an inevitable conflagration. At least this uncontrolled excitement was what we learnt to look on as the quintessence of English literature.

In the impetuous declamation of English poetry by Akshay Chowdhury, our initiator into English literature, there was the wildness of intoxication. The frenzy of Romeo's and Juliet's love, the fury of King Lear's impotent lamentation, the all-consuming fire of Othello's jealousy, these were the things that roused us to enthusiastic admiration. Our restricted social life, our narrower field of activity, was hedged in with such monotonous uniformity that tempestuous feelings found no entrance; —all was as calm and quiet as could be. So our hearts naturally craved the life-bringing shock of the passionate emotion in English literature. Ours was not the æsthetic enjoyment of literary art, but the jubilant welcome by stagnation of a turbulent wave, even though it should stir up to the surface the slime of the bottom.

Shakespeare's contemporary literature represents the war-dance of the day when the Renascence came to Europe in all the violence of its reaction against the severe curbing and cramping of the hearts of men. The examination of good and evil, beauty and ugliness, was not the main object, —man then seemed consumed with the anxiety to break through all barriers to the inmost sanctuary of his being, there to discover the ultimate image of his own violent desire. That is why in this literature we find such poignant, such exuberant, such unbridled expression.

The spirit of this bacchanalian revelry of Europe found entrance into our demurely well-behaved social world, woke us up, and made us lively. We were dazzled by the glow of unfettered life which fell upon our custom-smothered heart, pining for an opportunity to disclose itself.

There was another such day in English literature when the slow-measure of Pope's common time gave place to the dance-rhythm of the French revolution. This had Byron for its poet. And the impetuosity of his passion also moved our veiled heart-bride in the seclusion of her corner.

In this wise did the excitement of the pursuit of English literature come to sway the heart of the youth of our time, and at mine the waves of this excitement kept beating from every side. The first awakening is the time for the play of energy, not its repression.

And yet our case was so different from that of Europe. There the excitability and impatience of bondage was a reflection from its history into its literature. Its expression was consistent with its feeling. The roaring of the storm was heard because a storm was really raging. The breeze therefrom that ruffled our little world sounded in reality but little above a murmur. Therein it failed to satisfy our minds, so that our attempts to imitate the blast of a hurricane led us easily into exaggeration, —a tendency which still persists and may not prove easy of cure.

And for this, the fact that in English literature the reticence of true art has not yet appeared, is responsible. Human emotion is only one of the ingredients of literature and not its end, —which is the beauty of perfect fulness consisting in simplicity and restraint. This is a proposition which English literature does not yet fully admit.

Our minds from infancy to old age are being moulded by this English literature alone. But other literatures of Europe, both classical and modern, of which the art-form shows the well-nourished development due to a systematic cultivation of self-control, are not subjects of our study; and so, as it seems to me, we are yet unable to arrive at a correct perception of the true aim and method of literary work.

Akshay Babu, who had made the passion in English literature living to us, was himself a votary of the emotional life. The importance of realising truth in the fulness of its perfection seemed less apparent to him than that of feeling it in the heart. He had no intellectual respect for religion, but songs of *Shyāmā*, the dark Mother, would bring tears to his eyes. He felt no call to search for ultimate reality; whatever moved his heart served him for the time as the truth, even obvious coarseness not proving a deterrent.

Atheism was the dominant note of the English prose writings then in vogue, —Bentham, Mill and Comte being favourite authors. Theirs was the reasoning in terms of which our youths argued. The age of Mill constitutes a natural epoch in English History. It represents a healthy reaction of the body politic; these destructive forces having been brought in, temporarily, to rid it of accumulated thought-rubbish. In our country we received these in the letter, but never sought to make practical use of them, employing them only as a stimulant to incite ourselves to moral revolt. Atheism was thus for us a mere intoxication.

For these reasons educated men then fell mainly into two classes. One class would be always thrusting themselves forward with unprovoked argumentation to cut to pieces all belief in God. Like the hunter whose hands itch, no sooner he spies a living creature on the top or at the foot of a tree, to kill it, whenever these came to learn of a harmless belief lurking anywhere in fancied security, they felt stirred up to sally forth and demolish it. We had for a short time a tutor of whom this was a pet diversion. Though I was a mere boy, even I could not escape his onslaughts. Not that his attainments were of any account, or that his opinions were the result of any enthusiastic search for the truth, being mostly gathered from others' lips. But though I fought him with all my strength, unequally matched in age as we were, I suffered many a bitter defeat. Sometimes I felt so mortified I almost wanted to cry.

The other class consisted not of believers, but religious epicureans, who found comfort and solace in gathering together, and steeping themselves in pleasing sights, sounds and scents galore, under the garb of religious ceremonial; they luxuriated in the paraphernalia of worship. In neither of these classes was doubt or denial the outcome of the travail of their quest.

Though these religious aberrations pained me, I cannot say I was not at all influenced by them. With the intellectual impudence of budding youth this revolt also found a place. The religious services which were held in our family I would have nothing to do with, I had not accepted them for my own. I was busy blowing up a raging flame with the bellows of my emotions. It was only the worship of fire, the giving of oblations to increase its flame-with no other aim. And because my endeavour had no end in view it was measureless, always reaching beyond any assigned limit.

As with religion, so with my emotions, I felt no need for any underlying truth, my excitement being an end in itself. I call to mind some lines of a poet of that time:

> My heart is mine
> I have sold it to none,
> Be it tattered and torn and worn away,
> My heart is mine!

From the standpoint of truth the heart need not worry itself so; for nothing compels it to wear itself to tatters. In truth sorrow is not desirable, but taken apart its pungency may appear savoury. This savour our poets often made much of; leaving out the god in whose worship they were indulging. This childishness our country has not yet succeeded in getting rid of. So even to-day, when we fail to see the truth of religion, we seek in its observance an artistic gratification. So, also, much of our patriotism is not service of the mother-land, but the luxury of bringing ourselves into a desirable attitude of mind toward the country.

**PART VI**

## 28. EUROPEAN MUSIC

When I was in Brighton I once went to hear some Prima Donna. I forget her name. It may have been Madame Neilson or Madame Albani. Never before had I come across such an extraordinary command over the voice. Even our best singers cannot hide their sense of effort; nor are they ashamed to bring out, as best they can, top notes or bass notes beyond their proper register. In our country the understanding portion of the audience think no harm in keeping the performance up to standard by dint of their own imagination. For the same reason they do not mind any harshness of voice or uncouthness of gesture in the exponent of a perfectly formed melody; on the contrary, they seem sometimes to be of opinion that such minor external defects serve better to set off the internal perfection of the composition, —as with the outward poverty of the Great Ascetic, Mahadeva, whose divinity shines forth naked.

This feeling seems entirely wanting in Europe. There, outward embellishment must be perfect in every detail, and the least defect stands shamed and unable to face the public gaze. In our musical gatherings nothing is thought of spending half-an-hour in tuning up the *Tanpuras*, or hammering into tone the drums, little and big. In Europe such duties are performed beforehand, behind the scenes, for all that comes in front must be faultless. There is thus no room for any weak spot in the singer's voice. In our country a correct and artistic exposition[45] of the melody is the main object, thereon is concentrated all the effort. In Europe the voice is the object of culture, and with it they perform impossibilities. In our country the virtuoso is satisfied if he has heard the song; in Europe, they go to hear the singer.

That is what I saw that day in Brighton. To me it was as good as a circus. But, admire the performance as I did, I could not appreciate the song. I could hardly keep from laughing when some of the *cadenzas* imitated the warbling of birds. I felt all the time that it was a misapplication of the human voice. When it came to the turn of a male singer I was considerably relieved. I specially liked the tenor voices which had more of human flesh and blood in them, and seemed less like the disembodied lament of a forlorn spirit.

After this, as I went on hearing and learning more and more of European music, I began to get into the spirit of it; but up to now I am convinced that our music and theirs abide in altogether different apartments, and do not gain entry to the heart by the self-same door.

European music seems to be intertwined with its material life, so that the text of its songs may be as various as that life itself. If we attempt to put our tunes to the same variety of use they tend to lose their significance, and become ludicrous; for our melodies transcend the barriers of everyday life, and only thus can they carry us so deep into Pity, so high into Aloofness; their function being to reveal a picture of the inmost inexpressible depths of our being, mysterious and impenetrable, where the devotee may find his hermitage ready, or even the epicurean his bower, but where there is no room for the busy man of the world.

I cannot claim that I gained admittance to the soul of European music. But what little of it I came to understand from the outside attracted me greatly in one way. It seemed to me so romantic. It is somewhat difficult to analyse what I mean by that word. What I would refer to is the aspect of variety, of abundance, of the waves on the sea of life, of the ever-changing light and shade on their ceaseless undulations. There is the opposite aspect-of pure extension, of the unwinking blue of the sky, of the silent hint of immeasureability in the distant circle of the horizon. However that may be, let me repeat, at the risk of not being perfectly clear, that whenever I have been moved by European music I have said to myself: it is romantic, it is translating into melody the evanescence of life.

Not that we wholly lack the same attempt in some forms of our music; but it is less pronounced, less successful. Our melodies give voice to the star-spangled night, to the first reddening of dawn. They speak of the sky-pervading sorrow which lowers in the darkness of clouds; the speechless deep intoxication of the forest-roaming spring.

## 29. VALMIKI PRATIBHA

We had a profusely decorated volume of Moore's Irish Melodies: and often have I listened to the enraptured recitation of these by Akshay Babu. The poems combined with the pictorial designs to conjure up for me a dream picture of the Ireland of old. I had not then actually heard the original tunes, but had sung these Irish Melodies to myself to the accompaniment of the harps in the pictures. I longed to hear the real tunes, to learn them, and sing them to Akshay Babu. Some longings unfortunately do get fulfilled in this life, and die in the process. When I went to England I did hear some of the Irish Melodies sung, and learnt them too, but that put an end to my keenness to learn more. They were simple, mournful and sweet, but they somehow did not fit in with the silent melody of the harp which filled the halls of the Old Ireland of my dreams.

When I came back home I sung the Irish melodies I had learnt to my people. "What is the matter with Rabi's voice?" they exclaimed. "How funny and foreign it sounds!" They even felt my speaking voice had changed its tone.

From this mixed cultivation of foreign and native melody was born the *Valmiki Pratibha*.[46] The tunes in this musical drama are mostly Indian, but they have been dragged out of their classic dignity; that which soared in the sky was taught to run on the earth. Those who have seen and heard it performed will, I trust, bear witness that the harnessing of Indian melodic modes to the service of the drama has proved neither derogatory nor futile. This conjunction is the only special feature of *Valmiki Pratibha*. The pleasing task of loosening the chains of melodic forms and making them adaptable to a variety of treatment completely engrossed me.

Several of the songs of *Valmiki Pratibha* were set to tunes originally severely classic in mode; some of the tunes were composed by my brother Jyotirindra; a few were adapted from European sources. The *Telena*[47] style of Indian modes specially lends itself to dramatic purposes and has been frequently utilized in this work. Two English tunes served for the drinking songs of the robber band, and an Irish melody for the lament of the wood nymphs.

*Valmiki Pratibha* is not a composition which will bear being read. Its significance is lost if it is not heard sung and seen acted. It is not what Europeans call an Opera, but a little drama set to music. That is to say, it is not primarily a musical composition. Very few of the songs are important or attractive by themselves; they all serve merely as the musical text of the play.

Before I went to England we occasionally used to have gatherings of literary men in our house, at which music, recitations and light refreshments were served up. After my return one more such gathering was held, which happened to be the last. It was for an entertainment in this connection that the *Valmiki Pratibha* was composed. I played *Valmiki* and my niece, Pratibha, took the part of *Saraswati* —which bit of history remains recorded in the name.

I had read in some work of Herbert Spencer's that speech takes on tuneful inflexions whenever emotion comes into play. It is a fact that the tone or tune is as important to us as the spoken word for the expression of anger, sorrow, joy and wonder. Spencer's idea that, through a development of these emotional modulations of voice, man found music, appealed to me. Why should it not do, I thought to myself, to act a drama in a kind of recitative based on this idea. The *Kathakas*[48] of our country attempt this to some extent, for they frequently break into a chant which, however, stops short of full melodic form. As blank verse is more elastic than rhymed, so such chanting, though not devoid of rhythm, can more freely adapt itself to the emotional interpretation of the text, because it does not attempt to conform to the more rigorous canons of tune and time required by a regular melodic composition. The expression of feeling being the object, these deficiencies in regard to form do not jar on the hearer.

Encouraged by the success of this new line taken in the *Valmiki Pratibha*, I composed another musical play of the same class. It was called the *Kal Mrigaya*, The Fateful Hunt. The plot was based on the story of the accidental killing of the blind hermit's only son by King Dasaratha. It was played on a stage erected on our roof-terrace, and the audience seemed profoundly moved by its pathos. Afterwards, much of it was, with slight changes, incorporated in the *Valmiki Pratibha*, and this play ceased to be separately published in my works.

Long afterwards, I composed a third musical play, *Mayar Khela*, the Play of *Maya*, an operetta of a different type. In this the songs were important, not the drama. In the others a series of dramatic situations were strung on a thread of melody; this was a garland of songs with just a thread of dramatic plot running through. The play of feeling, and not action, was its special feature. In point of fact I was, while composing it, saturated with the mood of song.

The enthusiasm which went to the making of *Valmiki Pratibha* and *Kal Mrigaya* I have never felt for any other work of mine. In these two the creative musical impulse of the time found expression.

My brother, Jyotirindra, was engaged the live-long day at his piano, refashioning the classic melodic forms at his pleasure. And, at every turn of his instrument, the old modes took on unthought-of shapes and expressed new shades of feeling. The melodic forms which had become habituated to their pristine stately gait, when thus compelled to march to more lively unconventional measures, displayed an unexpected agility and power; and moved us correspondingly. We could plainly hear the tunes speak to us while Akshay Babu and I sat on either side fitting words to them as they grew out of my brother's nimble fingers. I do not claim that our *libretto* was good poetry but it served as a vehicle for the tunes.

In the riotous joy of this revolutionary activity were these two musical plays composed, and so they danced merrily to every measure, whether or not technically correct, indifferent as to the tunes being homelike or foreign.

On many an occasion has the Bengali reading public been grievously exercised over some opinion or literary form of mine, but it is curious to find that the daring with which I had played havoc with accepted musical notions did not rouse any resentment; on the contrary those who came to hear departed pleased. A few of Akshay Babu's compositions find place in the *Valmiki Pratibha* and also adaptations from Vihari Chakravarti's *Sarada Mangal* series of songs.

I used to take the leading part in the performance of these musical dramas. From my early years I had a taste for acting, and firmly believed that I had a special aptitude for it. I think I proved that my belief was not ill-founded. I had only once before done the part of Aleek Babu in a farce written by my brother Jyotirindra. So these were really my first attempts at acting. I was then very young and nothing seemed to fatigue or trouble my voice.

In our house, at the time, a cascade of musical emotion was gushing forth day after day, hour after hour, its scattered spray reflecting into our being a whole gamut of rainbow colours. Then, with the freshness of youth, our new-born energy, impelled by its virgin curiosity, struck out new paths in every direction. We felt we would try and test everything, and no achievement seemed impossible. We wrote, we sang, we acted, we poured ourselves out on every side. This was how I stepped into my twentieth year.

Of these forces which so triumphantly raced our lives along, my brother Jyotirindra was the charioteer. He was absolutely fearless. Once, when I was a mere lad, and had never ridden a horse before, he made me mount one and gallop by his side, with no qualms about his unskilled companion. When at the same age, while we were at Shelidah, (the head-quarters of our estate,) news was brought of a tiger, he took me with him on a hunting expedition. I had no gun, —it would have been more dangerous to me than to the tiger if I had. We left our shoes at the outskirts of the jungle and crept in with bare feet. At last we scrambled up into a bamboo thicket, partly stripped of its thorn-like twigs, where I somehow managed to crouch behind my brother till the deed was done; with no means of even administering a shoe-beating to the unmannerly brute had he dared lay his offensive paws on me!

Thus did my brother give me full freedom both internal and external in the face of all dangers. No usage or custom was a bondage for him, and so was he able to rid me of my shrinking diffidence.

## 30. EVENING SONGS

In the state of being confined within myself, of which I have been telling, I wrote a number of poems which have been grouped together, under the title of the *Heart-Wilderness*, in Mohita Babu's edition of my works. In one of the poems subsequently published in a volume called *Morning Songs*, the following lines occur:

> There is a vast wilderness whose name is *Heart*;
> Whose interlacing forest branches dandle and rock darkness like an infant.
> I lost my way in its depths.

from which came the idea of the name for this group of poems.

Much of what I wrote, when thus my life had no commerce with the outside, when I was engrossed in the contemplation of my own heart, when my imaginings wandered in many a disguise amidst causeless emotions and aimless longings, has been left out of that edition; only a few of the poems originally published in the volume entitled *Evening Songs* finding a place there, in the *Heart-Wilderness* group.

My brother Jyotirindra and his wife had left home travelling on a long journey, and their rooms on the third storey, facing the terraced-roof, were empty. I took possession of these and the terrace, and spent my days in solitude. While thus left in communion with my self alone, I know not how I slipped out of the poetical groove into which I had fallen. Perhaps being cut off from those whom I sought to please, and whose taste in poetry moulded the form I tried to put my thoughts into, I naturally gained freedom from the style they had imposed on me.

I began to use a slate for my writing. That also helped in my emancipation. The manuscript books in which I had indulged before seemed to demand a certain height of poetic flight, to work up to which I had to find my way by a comparison with others. But the slate was clearly fitted for my mood of the moment. "Fear not," it seemed to say. "Write just what you please, one rub will wipe all away!"

As I wrote a poem or two, thus unfettered, I felt a great joy well up within me. "At last," said my heart, "what I write is my own!" Let no one mistake this for an accession of pride. Rather did I feel a pride in my former productions, as being all the tribute I had to pay them. But I refuse to call the realisation of self, self-sufficiency. The joy of parents in their first-born is not due to any pride in its appearance, but because it is their very own. If it happens to be an extraordinary child they may also glory in that-but that is different.

In the first flood-tide of that joy I paid no heed to the bounds of metrical form, and as the stream does not flow straight on but winds about as it lists, so did my verse. Before, I would have held this to be a crime, but now I felt no compunction. Freedom first breaks the law and then makes laws which brings it under true Self-rule.

The only listener I had for these erratic poems of mine was Akshay Babu. When he heard them for the first time he was as surprised as he was pleased, and with his approbation my road to freedom was widened.

The poems of Vihari Chakravarti were in a 3-beat metre. This triple time produces a rounded-off globular effect, unlike the square-cut multiple of 2. It rolls on with ease, it glides as it dances to the tinkling of its anklets. I was once very fond of this metre. It felt more like riding a bicycle than walking. And to this stride I had got accustomed. In the *Evening Songs*, without thinking of it, I somehow broke off this habit. Nor did I come under any other particular bondage. I felt entirely free and unconcerned. I had no thought or fear of being taken to task.

The strength I gained by working, freed from the trammels of tradition, led me to discover that I had been searching in impossible places for that which I had within myself. Nothing but want of self-confidence had stood in the way of my coming into my own. I felt like rising from a dream of bondage to find myself unshackled. I cut extraordinary capers just to make sure I was free to move.

To me this is the most memorable period of my poetic career. As poems my *Evening Songs* may not have been worth much, in fact as such they are crude enough. Neither their metre, nor language, nor thought had taken definite shape. Their only merit is that for the first time I had come to write what I really meant, just according to my pleasure. What if those compositions have no value, that pleasure certainly had.

## 31. AN ESSAY ON MUSIC

I had been proposing to study for the bar when my father had recalled me home from England. Some friends concerned at this cutting short of my career pressed him to send me off once again. This led to my starting on a second voyage towards England, this time with a relative as my companion. My fate, however, had so strongly vetoed my being called to the bar that I was not even to reach England this time. For a certain reason we had to disembark at Madras and return home to Calcutta. The reason was by no means as grave as its outcome, but as the laugh was not against *me*, I refrain from setting it down here. From both my attempted pilgrimages to *Lakshmi's*[49] shrine I had thus to come back repulsed. I hope, however, that the Law-god, at least, will look on me with a favourable eye for that I have not added to the encumbrances on the Bar-library premises.

My father was then in the Mussoorie hills. I went to him in fear and trembling. But he showed no sign of irritation, he rather seemed pleased. He must have seen in this return of mine the blessing of Divine Providence.

The evening before I started on this voyage I read a paper at the Medical College Hall on the invitation of the Bethune Society. This was my first public reading. The Reverend K. M. Banerji was the president. The subject was Music. Leaving aside instrumental music, I tried to make out that to bring out better what the words sought to express was the chief end and aim of vocal music. The text of my paper was but meagre. I sang and acted songs throughout illustrating my theme. The only reason for the flattering eulogy which the President bestowed on me at the end must have been the moving effect of my young voice together with the earnestness and variety of its efforts. But I must make the confession to-day that the opinion I voiced with such enthusiasm that evening was wrong.

The art of vocal music has its own special functions and features. And when it happens to be set to words the latter must not presume too much on their opportunity and seek to supersede the melody of which they are but the vehicle. The song being great in its own wealth, why should it wait upon the words? Rather does it begin where mere words fail. Its power lies in the region of the inexpressible; it tells us what the words cannot.

So the less a song is burdened with words the better. In the classic style of Hindustan[50] the words are of no account and leave the melody to make its appeal in its own way. Vocal music reaches its perfection when the melodic form is allowed to develop freely, and carry our consciousness with it to its own wonderful plane. In Bengal, however, the words have always asserted themselves so, that our provincial song has failed to develop her full musical capabilities, and has remained content as the handmaiden of her sister art of poetry. From the old *Vaishnava* songs down to those of Nidhu Babu she has displayed her charms from the background. But as in our country the wife rules her husband through acknowledging her dependence, so our music, though professedly in attendance only, ends by dominating the song.

I have often felt this while composing my songs. As I hummed to myself and wrote the lines:

> Do not keep your secret to yourself, my love,
> But whisper it gently to me, only to me.

I found that the words had no means of reaching by themselves the region into which they were borne away by the tune. The melody told me that the secret, which I was so importunate to hear, had mingled with the green mystery of the forest glades, was steeped in the silent whiteness of moonlight nights, peeped out of the veil of the illimitable blue behind the horizon-and is the one intimate secret of Earth, Sky and Waters.

In my early boyhood I heard a snatch of a song:

> Who dressed you, love, as a foreigner?

This one line painted such wonderful pictures in my mind that it haunts me still. One day I sat down to set to words a composition of my own while full of this bit of song. Humming my tune I wrote to its accompaniment:

> I know you, O Woman from the strange land!
> Your dwelling is across the Sea.

Had the tune not been there I know not what shape the rest of the poem might have taken; but the magic of the melody revealed to me the stranger in all her loveliness. It is she, said my soul, who comes and goes, a messenger to this world from the other shore of the ocean of mystery. It is she, of whom we now and again catch glimpses in the dewy Autumn mornings, in the scented nights of Spring, in the inmost recesses of our hearts-and sometimes we strain skywards to hear her song. To the door of this world-charming stranger the melody, as I say, wafted me, and so to her were the rest of the words addressed.

Long after this, in a street in Bolpur, a mendicant *Baul* was singing as he walked along:

> How does the unknown bird flit in and out of the cage!
> Ah, could I but catch it, I'd ring its feet with my love!

I found this *Baul* to be saying the very same thing. The unknown bird sometimes surrenders itself within the bars of the cage to whisper tidings of the bondless unknown beyond. The heart would fain hold it near to itself for ever, but cannot. What but the melody of song can tell us of the goings and comings of the unknown bird?

That is why I am always reluctant to publish books of the words of songs, for therein the soul must needs be lacking.

## 32. THE RIVER-SIDE

When I returned home from the outset of my second voyage to England, my brother Jyotirindra and sister-in-law were living in a river-side villa at Chandernagore, and there I went to stay with them.

The Ganges again! Again those ineffable days and nights, languid with joy, sad with longing, attuned to the plaintive babbling of the river along the cool shade of its wooded banks. This Bengal sky-full of light, this south breeze, this flow of the river, this right royal laziness, this broad leisure stretching from horizon to horizon and from green earth to blue sky, all these were to me as food and drink to the hungry and thirsty. Here it felt indeed like home, and in these I recognised the ministrations of a Mother.

That was not so very long ago, and yet time has wrought many changes. Our little river-side nests, clustering under their surrounding greenery, have been replaced by mills which now, dragon-like, everywhere rear their hissing heads, belching forth black smoke. In the midday glare of modern life even our hours of mental siesta have been narrowed down to the lowest limit, and hydra-headed unrest has invaded every department of life. Maybe, this is for the better, but I, for one, cannot account it wholly to the good.

These lovely days of mine at the riverside passed by like so many dedicated lotus blossoms floating down the sacred stream. Some rainy afternoons I spent in a veritable frenzy, singing away old *Vaishnava* songs to my own tunes, accompanying myself on a harmonium. On other afternoons, we would drift along in a boat, my brother Jyotirindra accompanying my singing with his violin. And as, beginning with the *Puravi*,[51] we went on varying the mode of our music with the declining day, we saw, on reaching the *Behaga*, the western sky close the doors of its factory of golden toys, and the moon on the east rise over the fringe of trees.

Then we would row back to the landing steps of the villa and seat ourselves on a quilt spread on the terrace facing the river. By then a silvery peace rested on both land and water, hardly any boats were about, the fringe of trees on the bank was reduced to a deep shadow, and the moonlight glimmered over the smooth flowing stream.

The villa we were living in was known as 'Moran's Garden'. A flight of stone-flagged steps led up from the water to a long, broad verandah which formed part of the house. The rooms were not regularly arranged, nor all on the same level, and some had to be reached by short flights of stairs. The big sitting room overlooking the landing steps had stained glass windows with coloured pictures.

One of the pictures was of a swing hanging from a branch half-hidden in dense foliage, and in the checkered light and shade of this bower, two persons were swinging; and there was another of a broad flight of steps leading into some castle-like palace, up and down which men and women in festive garb were going and coming. When the light fell on the windows, these pictures shone wonderfully, seeming to fill the river-side atmosphere with holiday music. Some far-away long-forgotten revelry seemed to be expressing itself in silent words of light; the love thrills of the swinging couple making alive with their eternal story the woodlands of the river bank.

The topmost room of the house was in a round tower with windows opening to every side. This I used as my room for writing poetry. Nothing could be seen from thence save the tops of the surrounding trees, and the open sky. I was then busy with the *Evening Songs* and of this room I wrote:

> There, where in the breast of limitless space clouds are laid to sleep,
> I have built my house for thee, O Poesy!

## 33. MORE ABOUT THE EVENING SONGS

At this time my reputation amongst literary critics was that of being a poet of broken cadence and lisping utterance. Everything about my work was dubbed misty, shadowy. However little I might have relished this at the time, the charge was not wholly baseless. My poetry did in fact lack the backbone of worldly reality. How, amidst the ringed-in seclusion of my early years, was I to get the necessary material?

But one thing I refuse to admit. Behind this charge of vagueness was the sting of the insinuation of its being a deliberate affectation-for the sake of effect. The fortunate possessor of good eye-sight is apt to sneer at the youth with glasses, as if he wears them for ornament. While a reflection on the poor fellow's infirmity may be permissible, it is too bad to charge him with pretending not to see.

The nebula is not an outside creation-it merely represents a phase; and to leave out all poetry which has not attained definiteness would not bring us to the truth of literature. If any phase of man's nature has found true expression, it is worth preserving-it may be cast aside only if not expressed truly. There is a period in man's life when his feelings are the pathos of the inexpressible, the anguish of vagueness. The poetry which attempts its expression cannot be called baseless-at worst it may be worthless; but it is not necessarily even that. The sin is not in the thing expressed, but in the failure to express it.

There is a duality in man. Of the inner person, behind the outward current of thoughts, feelings and events, but little is known or recked; but for all that, he cannot be got rid of as a factor in life's progress. When the outward life fails to harmonise with the inner, the dweller within is hurt, and his pain manifests itself in the outer consciousness in a manner to which it is difficult to give a name, or even to describe, and of which the cry is more akin to an inarticulate wail than words with more precise meaning.

The sadness and pain which sought expression in the *Evening Songs* had their roots in the depths of my being. As one's sleep-smothered consciousness wrestles with a nightmare in its efforts to awake, so the submerged inner self struggles to free itself from its complexities and come out into the open. These *Songs* are the history of that struggle. As in all creation, so in poetry, there is the opposition of forces. If the divergence is too wide, or the unison too close, there is, it seems to me, no room for poetry. Where the pain of discord strives to attain and express its resolution into harmony, there does poetry break forth into music, as breath through a flute.

When the *Evening Songs* first saw the light they were not hailed with any flourish of trumpets, but none the less they did not lack admirers. I have elsewhere told the story of how at the wedding of Mr. Ramesh Chandra Dutt's eldest daughter, Bankim Babu was at the door, and the host was welcoming him with the customary garland of flowers. As I came up Bankim Babu eagerly took the garland and placing it round my neck said: "The wreath to him, Ramesh, have you not read his *Evening Songs*?" And when Mr. Dutt avowed he had not yet done so, the manner in which Bankim Babu expressed his opinion of some of them amply rewarded me.

The *Evening Songs* gained for me a friend whose approval, like the rays of the sun, stimulated and guided the shoots of my newly sprung efforts. This was Babu Priyanath Sen. Just before this the *Broken Heart* had led him to give up all hopes of me. I won him back with these *Evening Songs*. Those who are acquainted with him know him as an expert navigator of all the seven seas[52] of literature, whose highways and byways, in almost all languages, Indian and foreign, he is constantly traversing. To converse with him is to gain glimpses of even the most out of the way scenery in the world of ideas. This proved of the greatest value to me.

He was able to give his literary opinions with the fullest confidence, for he had not to rely on his unaided taste to guide his likes and dislikes. This authoritative criticism of his also assisted me more than I can tell. I used to read to him everything I wrote, and but for the timely showers of his discriminate appreciation it is hard to say whether these early ploughings of mine would have yielded as they have done.

## 34. MORNING SONGS

At the river-side I also did a bit of prose writing, not on any definite subject or plan, but in the spirit that boys catch butterflies. When spring comes within, many-coloured short-lived fancies are born and flit about in the mind, ordinarily unnoticed. In these days of my leisure, it was perhaps the mere whim to collect them which had come upon me. Or it may have been only another phase of my emancipated self which had thrown out its chest and decided to write just as it pleased; what I wrote not being the object, it being sufficient unto itself that it was I who wrote. These prose pieces were published later under the name of *Vividha Prabandha*, Various Topics, but they expired with the first edition and did not get a fresh lease of life in a second.

At this time, I think, I also began my first novel, *Bauthakuranir Hat*.

After we had stayed for a time by the river, my brother Jyotirindra took a house in Calcutta, on Sudder Street near the Museum. I remained with him. While I went on here with the novel and the *Evening Songs*, a momentous revolution of some kind came about within me.

One day, late in the afternoon, I was pacing the terrace of our Jorasanko house. The glow of the sunset combined with the wan twilight in a way which seemed to give the approaching evening a specially wonderful attractiveness for me. Even the walls of the adjoining house seemed to grow beautiful. Is this uplifting of the cover of triviality from the everyday world, I wondered, due to some magic in the evening light? Never!

I could see at once that it was the effect of the evening which had come within me; its shades had obliterated my *self*. While the self was rampant during the glare of day, everything I perceived was mingled with and hidden by it. Now, that the self was put into the background, I could see the world in its own true aspect. And that aspect has nothing of triviality in it, it is full of beauty and joy.

Since this experience I tried the effect of deliberately suppressing my *self* and viewing the world as a mere spectator, and was invariably rewarded with a sense of special pleasure. I remember I tried also to explain to a relative how to see the world in its true light, and the incidental lightening of one's own sense of burden which follows such vision; but, as I believe, with no success.

Then I gained a further insight which has lasted all my life.

The end of Sudder Street, and the trees on the Free School grounds opposite, were visible from our Sudder Street house. One morning I happened to be standing on the verandah looking that way. The sun was just rising through the leafy tops of those trees. As I continued to gaze, all of a sudden a covering seemed to fall away from my eyes, and I found the world bathed in a wonderful radiance, with waves of beauty and joy swelling on every side. This radiance pierced in a moment through the folds of sadness and despondency which had accumulated over my heart, and flooded it with this universal light.

That very day the poem, *The Awakening of the Waterfall*, gushed forth and coursed on like a veritable cascade. The poem came to an end, but the curtain did not fall upon the joy aspect of the Universe. And it came to be so that no person or thing in the world seemed to me trivial or unpleasing. A thing that happened the next day or the day following seemed specially astonishing.

There was a curious sort of person who came to me now and then, with a habit of asking all manner of silly questions. One day he had asked: "Have you, sir, seen God with your own eyes?" And on my having to admit that I had not, he averred that he had. "What was it you saw?" I asked. "He seethed and throbbed before my eyes!" was the reply.

It can well be imagined that one would not ordinarily relish being drawn into abstruse discussions with such a person. Moreover, I was at the time entirely absorbed in my own writing. Nevertheless as he was a harmless sort of fellow I did not like the idea of hurting his susceptibilities and so tolerated him as best I could.

This time, when he came one afternoon, I actually felt glad to see him, and welcomed him cordially. The mantle of his oddity and foolishness seemed to have slipped off, and the person I so joyfully hailed was the real man whom I felt to be in nowise inferior to myself, and moreover closely related. Finding no trace of annoyance within me at sight of him, nor any sense of my time being wasted with him, I was filled with an immense gladness, and felt rid of some enveloping tissue of untruth which had been causing me so much needless and uncalled for discomfort and pain.

As I would stand on the balcony, the gait, the figure, the features of each one of the passers-by, whoever they might be, seemed to me all so extraordinarily wonderful, as they flowed past, — waves on the sea of the universe. From infancy I had seen only with my eyes, I now began to see with the whole of my consciousness. I could not look upon the sight of two smiling youths, nonchalantly going their way, the arm of one on the other's shoulder, as a matter of small moment; for, through it I could see the fathomless depths of the eternal spring of Joy from which numberless sprays of laughter leap up throughout the world.

I had never before marked the play of limbs and lineaments which always accompanies even the least of man's actions; now I was spell-bound by their variety, which I came across on all sides, at every moment. Yet I saw them not as being apart by themselves, but as parts of that amazingly beautiful greater dance which goes on at this very moment throughout the world of men, in each of their homes, in their multifarious wants and activities.

Friend laughs with friend, the mother fondles her child, one cow sidles up to another and licks its body, and the immeasurability behind these comes direct to my mind with a shock which almost savours of pain.

When of this period I wrote:

I know not how of a sudden my heart flung open its doors,
And let the crowd of worlds rush in, greeting each other, —

it was no poetic exaggeration. Rather I had not the power to express all I felt.

For some time together I remained in this self-forgetful state of bliss. Then my brother thought of going to the Darjeeling hills. So much the better, thought I. On the vast Himalayan tops I shall be able to see more deeply into what has been revealed to me in Sudder Street; at any rate I shall see how the Himalayas display themselves to my new gift of vision.

But the victory was with that little house in Sudder Street. When, after ascending the mountains, I looked around, I was at once aware I had lost my new vision. My sin must have been in imagining that I could get still more of truth from the outside. However sky-piercing the king of mountains may be, he can have nothing in his gift for me; while He who is the Giver can vouchsafe a vision of the eternal universe in the dingiest of lanes, and in a moment of time.

I wandered about amongst the firs, I sat near the falls and bathed in their waters, I gazed at the grandeur of Kinchinjunga through a cloudless sky, but in what had seemed to me these likeliest of places, I found *it* not. I had come to know it, but could see it no longer. While I was admiring the gem the lid had suddenly closed, leaving me staring at the enclosing casket. But, for all the attractiveness of its workmanship, there was no longer any danger of my mistaking it for merely an empty box.

My *Morning Songs* came to an end, their last echo dying out with *The Echo* which I wrote at Darjeeling. This apparently proved such an abstruse affair that two friends laid a wager as to its real meaning. My only consolation was that, as I was equally unable to explain the enigma to them when they came to me for a solution, neither of them had to lose any money over it. Alas! The days when I wrote excessively plain poems about *The Lotus* and *A Lake* had gone forever.

But does one write poetry to explain any matter? What is felt within the heart tries to find outside shape as a poem. So when after listening to a poem anyone says he has not understood, I feel nonplussed. If someone smells a flower and says he does not understand, the reply to him is: there is nothing to understand, it is only a scent. If he persists, saying: *that* I know, but what does it all *mean*? Then one has either to change the subject, or make it more abstruse by saying that the scent is the shape which the universal joy takes in the flower.

That words have meanings is just the difficulty. That is why the poet has to turn and twist them in metre and verse, so that the meaning may be held somewhat in check, and the feeling allowed a chance to express itself.

This utterance of feeling is not the statement of a fundamental truth, or a scientific fact, or a useful moral precept. Like a tear or a smile it is but a picture of what is taking place within. If Science or Philosophy may gain anything from it they are welcome, but that is not the reason of its being. If while crossing a ferry you can catch a fish you are a lucky man, but that does not make the ferry boat a fishing boat, nor should you abuse the ferryman if he does not make fishing his business.

*The Echo* was written so long ago that it has escaped attention and I am now no longer called upon to render an account of its meaning. Nevertheless, whatever its other merits or defects may be, I can assure my readers that it was not my intention to propound a riddle, or insidiously convey any erudite teaching. The fact of the matter was that a longing had been born within my heart, and, unable to find any other name, I had called the thing I desired an Echo.

When from the original fount in the depths of the Universe streams of melody are sent forth abroad, their echo is reflected into our heart from the faces of our beloved and the other beauteous things around us. It must be, as I suggested, this Echo which we love, and not the things themselves from which it happens to be reflected; for that which one day we scarce deign to glance at, may be, on another, the very thing which claims our whole devotion.

I had so long viewed the world with external vision only, and so had been unable to see its universal aspect of joy. When of a sudden, from some innermost depth of my being, a ray of light found its way out, it spread over and illuminated for me the whole universe, which then no longer appeared like heaps of things and happenings, but was disclosed to my sight as one whole. This experience seemed to tell me of the stream of melody issuing from the very heart of the universe and spreading over space and time, re-echoing thence as waves of joy which flow right back to the source.

When the artist sends his song forth from the depths of a full heart that is joy indeed. And the joy is redoubled when this same song is wafted back to him as hearer. If, when the creation of the Arch-Poet is thus returning back to him in a flood of joy, we allow it to flow over our consciousness, we at once, immediately, become aware, in an inexpressible manner, of the end to which this flood is streaming. And as we become aware our love goes forth; and our *selves* are moved from their moorings and would fain float down the stream of joy to its infinite goal. This is the meaning of the longing which stirs within us at the sight of Beauty.

The stream which comes from the Infinite and flows toward the finite-that is the True, the Good; it is subject to laws, definite in form. Its echo which returns towards the Infinite is Beauty and Joy; which are difficult to touch or grasp, and so make us beside ourselves. This is what I tried to say by way of a parable or a song in *The Echo*. That the result was not clear is not to be wondered at, for neither was the attempt then clear unto itself.

Let me set down here part of what I wrote in a letter, at a more advanced age, about the *Morning Songs*.

"There is none in the World, all are in my heart" —is a state of mind belonging to a particular age. When the heart is first awakened it puts forth its arms and would grasp the whole world, like the teething infant which thinks everything meant for its mouth. Gradually it comes to understand what it really wants and what it does not. Then do its nebulous emanations shrink upon themselves, get heated, and heat in their turn.

To begin by wanting the whole world is to get nothing. When desire is concentrated, with the whole strength of one's being upon any one object whatsoever it might be, then does the gateway to the Infinite become visible. The morning songs were the first throwing forth of my inner self outwards, and consequently they lack any signs of such concentration.

This all-pervading joy of a first outflow, however, has the effect of leading us to an acquaintance with the particular. The lake in its fulness seeks an outlet as a river. In this sense the permanent later love is narrower than first love. It is more definite in the direction of its activities, desires to realise the whole in each of its parts, and is thus impelled on towards the infinite. What it finally reaches is no longer the former indefinite extension of the heart's own inner joy, but a merging in the infinite reality which was outside itself, and thereby the attainment of the complete truth of its own longings.

In Mohita Babu's edition these *Morning Songs* have been placed in the group of poems entitled *Nishkraman*, The Emergence. For in these was to be found the first news of my coming out of the *Heart Wilderness* into the open world. Thereafter did this pilgrim heart make its acquaintance with that world, bit by bit, part by part, in many a mood and manner. And at the end, after gliding past all the numerous landing steps of ever-changing impermanence, it will reach the infinite, —not the vagueness of indeterminate possibility, but the consummation of perfect fulness of Truth.

From my earliest years I enjoyed a simple and intimate communion with Nature. Each one of the cocoanut trees in our garden had for me a distinct personality. When, on coming home from the Normal School, I saw behind the skyline of our roof-terrace blue-grey water-laden clouds thickly banked up, the immense depth of gladness which filled me, all in a moment, I can recall clearly even now. On opening my eyes every morning, the blithely awakening world used to call me to join it like a playmate; the perfervid noonday sky, during the long silent watches of the siesta hours, would spirit me away from the work-a-day world into the recesses of its hermit cell; and the darkness of night would open the door to its phantom paths, and take me over all the seven seas and thirteen rivers, past all possibilities and impossibilities, right into its wonder-land.

Then one day, when, with the dawn of youth, my hungry heart began to cry out for its sustenance, a barrier was set up between this play of inside and outside. And my whole being eddied round and round my troubled heart, creating a vortex within itself, in the whirls of which its consciousness was confined.

This loss of the harmony between inside and outside, due to the over-riding claims of the heart in its hunger, and consequent restriction of the privilege of communion which had been mine, was mourned by me in the *Evening Songs*. In the *Morning Songs* I celebrated the sudden opening of a gate in the barrier, by what shock I know not, through which I regained the lost one, not only as I knew it before, but more deeply, more fully, by force of the intervening separation.

Thus did the First Book of my life come to an end with these chapters of union, separation and reunion. Or, rather, it is not true to say it has come to an end. The same subject has still to be continued through more elaborate solutions of worse complexities, to a greater conclusion. Each one comes here to finish but one book of life, which, during the progress of its various parts, grows spiral-wise on an ever-increasing radius. So, while each segment may appear different from the others at a cursory glance, they all really lead back to the self-same starting centre.

The prose writings of the *Evening Songs* period were published, as I have said, under the name of *Vividha Prabandha*. Those others which correspond to the time of my writing the *Morning Songs* came out under the title of *Alochana*, Discussions. The difference between the characteristics of these two would be a good index of the nature of the change that had in the meantime taken place within me.

**PART VII**

# 35. RAJENDRAHAL MITRA

It was about this time that my brother Jyotirindra had the idea of founding a Literary Academy by bringing together all the men of letters of repute. To compile authoritative technical terms for the Bengali language and in other ways to assist in its growth was to be its object-therein differing but little from the lines on which the modern *Sahitya Parishat*, Academy of Literature, has taken shape.

Dr. Rajendrahal Mitra took up the idea of this Academy with enthusiasm, and he was eventually its president for the short time it lasted. When I went to invite Pandit Vidyasagar to join it, he gave a hearing to my explanation of its objects and the names of the proposed members, then said: "My advice to you is to leave us out-you will never accomplish anything with big wigs; they can never be got to agree with one another." With which he refused to come in. Bankim Babu became a member, but I cannot say that he took much interest in the work.

To be plain, so long as this academy lived Rajendrahal Mitra did everything single-handed. He began with Geographical terms. The draft list was made out by Dr. Rajendrahal himself and was printed and circulated for the suggestions of the members. We had also an idea of transliterating in Bengali the name of each foreign country as pronounced by itself.

Pandit Vidyasagar's prophecy was fulfilled. It did not prove possible to get the big wigs to do anything. And the academy withered away shortly after sprouting. But Rajendrahal Mitra was an all-round expert and was an academy in himself. My labours in this cause were more than repaid by the privilege of his acquaintance. I have met many Bengali men of letters in my time but none who left the impression of such brilliance.

I used to go and see him in the office of the Court of Wards in Maniktala. I would go in the mornings and always find him busy with his studies, and with the inconsiderateness of youth, I felt no hesitation in disturbing him. But I have never seen him the least bit put out on that account. As soon as he saw me he would put aside his work and begin to talk to me. It is a matter of common knowledge that he was somewhat hard of hearing, so he hardly ever gave me occasion to put him any question. He would take up some broad subject and talk away upon it, and it was the attraction of these discourses which drew me there. Converse with no other person ever gave me such a wealth of suggestive ideas on so many different subjects. I would listen enraptured.

I think he was a member of the text-book committee and every book he received for approval, he read through and annotated in pencil. On some occasions he would select one of these books for the text of discourses on the construction of the Bengali language in particular or Philology in general, which were of the greatest benefit to me. There were few subjects which he had not studied and anything he had studied he could clearly expound.

If we had not relied on the other members of the Academy we had tried to found, but left everything to Dr. Rajendrahal, the present *Sahitya Parishat* would have doubtless found the matters it is now occupied with left in a much more advanced state by that one man alone.

Dr. Rajendrahal Mitra was not only a profound scholar, but he had likewise a striking personality which shone through his features. Full of fire as he was in his public life, he could also unbend graciously so as to talk on the most difficult subjects to a stripling like myself without any trace of a patronising tone. I even took advantage of his condescension to the extent of getting a contribution, *Yama's Dog*, from him for the Bharabi. There were other great contemporaries of his with whom I would not have ventured to take such liberties, nor would I have met with the like response if I had.

And yet when he was on the war path his opponents on the Municipal Corporation or the Senate of the University were mortally afraid of him. In those days Kristo Das Pal was the tactful politician, and Rajendrahal Mitra the valiant fighter.

For the purposes of the Asiatic Society's publications and researches, he had to employ a number of Sanscrit Pandits to do the mechanical work for him. I remember how this gave certain envious and mean-minded detractors the opportunity of saying that everything was really done by these Pandits while Rajendrahal fraudulently appropriated all the credit. Even to-day we very often find the tools arrogating to themselves the lion's share of the achievement, imagining the wielder to be a mere ornamental figurehead. If the poor pen had a mind it would as certainly have bemoaned the unfairness of its getting all the stain and the writer all the glory!

It is curious that this extraordinary man should have got no recognition from his countrymen even after his death. One of the reasons may be that the national mourning for Vidyasagar, whose death followed shortly after, left no room for a recognition of the other bereavement. Another reason may be that his main contributions being outside the pale of Bengali literature, he had been unable to reach the heart of the people.

## 36. KARWAR

Our Sudder Street party next transferred itself to Karwar on the West Sea coast. Karwar is the headquarters of the Kanara district in the Southern portion of the Bombay Presidency. It is the tract of the Malaya Hills of Sanskrit literature where grow the cardamum creeper and the Sandal Tree. My second brother was then Judge there.

The little harbour, ringed round with hills, is so secluded that it has nothing of the aspect of a port about it. Its crescent shaped beach throws out its arms to the shoreless open sea like the very image of an eager striving to embrace the infinite. The edge of the broad sandy beach is fringed with a forest of casuarinas, broken at one end by the *Kalanadi* river which here flows into the sea after passing through a gorge flanked by rows of hills on either side.

I remember how one moonlit evening we went up this river in a little boat. We stopped at one of Shivaji's old hill forts, and stepping ashore found our way into the clean-swept little yard of a peasant's home. We sat on a spot where the moonbeams fell glancing off the top of the outer enclosure, and there dined off the eatables we had brought with us. On our way back we let the boat glide down the river. The night brooded over the motionless hills and forests, and on the silent flowing stream of this little *Kalanadi*, throwing over all its moonlight spell. It took us a good long time to reach the mouth of the river, so, instead of returning by sea, we got off the boat there and walked back home over the sands of the beach. It was then far into the night, the sea was without a ripple, even the ever-troubled murmur of the casuarinas was at rest. The shadow of the fringe of trees along the vast expanse of sand hung motionless along its border, and the ring of blue-grey hills around the horizon slept calmly beneath the sky.

Through the deep silence of this illimitable whiteness we few human creatures walked along with our shadows, without a word. When we reached home my sleep had lost itself in something still deeper. The poem which I then wrote is inextricably mingled with that night on the distant seashore. I do not know how it will appeal to the reader apart from the memories with which it is entwined. This doubt led to its being left out of Mohita Babu's edition of my works. I trust that a place given to it among my reminiscences may not be deemed unfitting.

> Let me sink down, losing myself in the depths of midnight.
> Let the Earth leave her hold of me, let her free me from her obstacle of dust.
> Keep your watch from afar, O stars, drunk though you be with moonlight,
> And let the horizon hold its wings still around me.
> Let there be no song, no word, no sound, no touch; nor sleep, nor awakening, —
> But only the moonlight like a swoon of ecstasy over the sky and my being.
> The world seems to me like a ship with its countless pilgrims,
> Vanishing in the far-away blue of the sky,
> Its sailors' song becoming fainter and fainter in the air,
> While I sink in the bosom of the endless night, fading away from myself, dwindling
> into a point.

It is necessary to remark here that merely because something has been written when feelings are brimming over, it is not therefore necessarily good. Such is rather a time when the utterance is thick with emotion. Just as it does not do to have the writer entirely removed from the feeling to which he is giving expression, so also it does not conduce to the truest poetry to have him too close to it. Memory is the brush which can best lay on the true poetic colour. Nearness has too much of the compelling about it and the imagination is not sufficiently free unless it can get away from its influence. Not only in poetry, but in all art, the mind of the artist must attain a certain degree of aloofness-the *creator* within man must be allowed the sole control. If the subject matter gets the better of the creation, the result is a mere replica of the event, not a reflection of it through the Artist's mind.

## 37. NATURE'S REVENGE

Here in Karwar I wrote the *Prakritir Pratishodha*, Nature's Revenge, a dramatic poem. The hero was a Sanyasi (hermit) who had been striving to gain a victory over Nature by cutting away the bonds of all desires and affections and thus to arrive at a true and profound knowledge of self. A little girl, however, brought him back from his communion with the infinite to the world and into the bondage of human affection. On so coming back the *Sanyasi* realised that the great is to be found in the small, the infinite within the bounds of form, and the eternal freedom of the soul in love. It is only in the light of love that all limits are merged in the limitless.

The sea beach of Karwar is certainly a fit place in which to realise that the beauty of Nature is not a mirage of the imagination, but reflects the joy of the Infinite and thus draws us to lose ourselves in it. Where the universe is expressing itself in the magic of its laws it may not be strange if we miss its infinitude; but where the heart gets into immediate touch with immensity in the beauty of the meanest of things, is any room left for argument?

Nature took the *Sanyasi* to the presence of the Infinite, enthroned on the finite, by the pathway of the heart. In the *Nature's Revenge* there were shown on the one side the wayfarers and the villagers, content with their home-made triviality and unconscious of anything beyond; and on the other the *Sanyasi* busy casting away his all, and himself, into the self-evolved infinite of his imagination. When love bridged the gulf between the two, and the hermit and the householder met, the seeming triviality of the finite and the seeming emptiness of the infinite alike disappeared.

This was to put in a slightly different form the story of my own experience, of the entrancing ray of light which found its way into the depths of the cave into which I had retired away from all touch with the outer world, and made me more fully one with Nature again. This *Nature's Revenge* may be looked upon as an introduction to the whole of my future literary work; or, rather this has been the subject on which all my writings have dwelt-the joy of attaining the Infinite within the finite.

On our way back from Karwar I wrote some songs for the *Nature's Revenge* on board ship. The first one filled me with a great gladness as I sang, and wrote it sitting on the deck:

> Mother, leave your darling boy to us,
> And let us take him to the field where we graze our cattle.[53]

The sun has risen, the buds have opened, the cowherd boys are going to the pasture; and they would not have the sunlight, the flowers, and their play in the grazing grounds empty. They want their *Shyam* (Krishna) to be with them there, in the midst of all these. They want to see the Infinite in all its carefully adorned loveliness; they have turned out so early because they want to join in its gladsome play, in the midst of these woods and fields and hills and dales-not to admire from a distance, nor in the majesty of power. Their equipment is of the slightest. A simple yellow garment and a garland of wild-flowers are all the ornaments they require. For where joy reigns on every side, to hunt for it arduously, or amidst pomp and circumstances, is to lose it.

Shortly after my return from Karwar, I was married. I was then 22 years of age.

## 38. PICTURES AND SONGS

*Chhabi o Gan*, Picture and Songs, was the title of a book of poems most of which were written at this time.

We were then living in a house with a garden in Lower Circular Road. Adjoining it on the south was a large *Busti*.[54] I would often sit near a window and watch the sights of this populous little settlement. I loved to see them at their work and play and rest, and in their multifarious goings and comings. To me it was all like a living story.

A faculty of many-sightedness possessed me at this time. Each little separate picture I ringed round with the light of my imagination and the joy of my heart; every one of them, moreover, being variously coloured by a pathos of its own. The pleasure of thus separately marking off each picture was much the same as that of painting it, both being the outcome of the desire to see with the mind what the eye sees, and with the eye what the mind imagines.

Had I been a painter with the brush I would doubtless have tried to keep a permanent record of the visions and creations of that period when my mind was so alertly responsive. But that instrument was not available to me. What I had was only words and rhythms, and even with these I had not yet learnt to draw firm strokes, and the colours went beyond their margins. Still, like young folk with their first paint box, I spent the livelong day painting away with the many coloured fancies of my new-born youth. If these pictures are now viewed in the light of that twenty-second year of my life, some features may be discerned even through their crude drawing and blurred colouring.

I have said that the first book of my literary life came to an end with the *Morning Songs*. The same subject was then continued under a different rendering. Many a page at the outset of this Book, I am sure, is of no value. In the process of making a new beginning much in the way of superfluous preliminary has to be gone through. Had these been leaves of trees they would have duly dropped off. Unfortunately, leaves of books continue to stick fast even when they are no longer wanted. The feature of these poems was the closeness of attention devoted even to trifling things. *Pictures and Songs* seized every opportunity of giving value to these by colouring them with feelings straight from the heart.

Or, rather, that was not it. When the string of the mind is properly attuned to the universe then at each point the universal song can awaken its sympathetic vibrations. It was because of this music roused within that nothing then felt trivial to the writer. Whatever my eyes fell upon found a response within me. Like children who can play with sand or stones or shells or whatever they can get (for the spirit of play is within them), so also we, when filled with the song of youth, become aware that the harp of the universe has its variously tuned strings everywhere stretched, and the nearest may serve as well as any other for our accompaniment, there is no need to seek afar.

## 39. AN INTERVENING PERIOD

Between the *Pictures and Songs* and the *Sharps and Flats*, a child's magazine called the *Balaka* sprang up and ended its brief days like an annual plant. My second sister-in-law felt the want of an illustrated magazine for children. Her idea was that the young people of the family would contribute to it, but as she felt that that alone would not be enough, she took up the editorship herself and asked me to help with contributions. After one or two numbers of the *Balaka* had come out I happened to go on a visit to Rajnarayan Babu at Deoghur. On the return journey the train was crowded and as there was an unshaded light just over the only berth I could get, I could not sleep. I thought I might as well take this opportunity of thinking out a story for the *Balaka*. In spite of my efforts to get hold of the story it eluded me, but sleep came to the rescue instead. I saw in a dream the stone steps of a temple stained with the blood of victims of the sacrifice; —a little girl standing there with her father asking him in piteous accents: "Father, what is this, why all this blood?" and the father, inwardly moved, trying with a show of gruffness to quiet her questioning. As I awoke I felt I had got my story. I have many more such dream-given stories and other writings as well. This dream episode I worked into the annals of King Gobinda Manikya of Tipperah and made out of it a little serial story, *Rajarshi*, for the *Balaka*.

Those were days of utter freedom from care. Nothing in particular seemed to be anxious to express itself through my life or writings. I had not yet joined the throng of travellers on the path of Life, but was a mere spectator from my roadside window. Many a person hied by on many an errand as I gazed on, and every now and then Spring or Autumn, or the Rains would enter unasked and stay with me for a while.

But I had not only to do with the seasons. There were men of all kinds of curious types who, floating about like boats adrift from their anchorage, occasionally invaded my little room. Some of them sought to further their own ends, at the cost of my inexperience, with many an extraordinary device. But they need not have taken any extraordinary pains to get the better of me. I was then entirely unsophisticated, my own wants were few, and I was not at all clever in distinguishing between good and bad faith. I have often gone on imagining that I was assisting with their school fees students to whom fees were as superfluous as their unread books.

Once a long-haired youth brought me a letter from an imaginary sister in which she asked me to take under my protection this brother of hers who was suffering from the tyranny of a stepmother as imaginary as herself. The brother was not imaginary, that was evident enough. But his sister's letter was as unnecessary for me as expert marksmanship to bring down a bird which cannot fly.

Another young fellow came and informed me that he was studying for the B.A., but could not go up for his examination as he was afflicted with some brain trouble. I felt concerned, but being far from proficient in medical science, or in any other science, I was at a loss what advice to give him. But he went on to explain that he had seen in a dream that my wife had been his mother in a former birth, and that if he could but drink some water which had touched her feet he would get cured. "Perhaps you don't believe in such things," he concluded with a smile. My belief, I said, did not matter, but if he thought he could get cured, he was welcome, with which I procured him a phial of water which was supposed to have touched my wife's feet. He felt immensely better, he said. In the natural course of evolution from water he came to solid food. Then he took up his quarters in a corner of my room and began to hold smoking parties with his friends, till I had to take refuge in flight from the smoke laden air. He gradually proved beyond doubt that his brain might have been diseased, but it certainly was not weak.

After this experience it took no end of proof before I could bring myself to put my trust in children of previous births. My reputation must have spread for I next received a letter from a daughter. Here, however, I gently but firmly drew the line.

All this time my friendship with Babu Srish Chandra Magundar ripened apace. Every evening he and Prija Babu would come to this little room of mine and we would discuss literature and music far into the night. Sometimes a whole day would be spent in the same way. The fact is my *self* had not yet been moulded and nourished into a strong and definite personality and so my life drifted along as light and easy as an autumn cloud.

## 40. BANKIM CHANDRA

This was the time when my acquaintance with Bankim Babu began. My first sight of him was a matter of long before. The old students of Calcutta University had then started an annual reunion, of which Babu Chandranath Basu was the leading spirit. Perhaps he entertained a hope that at some future time I might acquire the right to be one of them; anyhow I was asked to read a poem on the occasion. Chandranath Babu was then quite a young man. I remember he had translated some martial German poem into English which he proposed to recite himself on the day, and came to rehearse it to us full of enthusiasm. That a warrior poet's ode to his beloved sword should at one time have been his favourite poem will convince the reader that even Chandranath Babu was once young; and moreover that those times were indeed peculiar.

While wandering about in the crush at the Students' reunion, I suddenly came across a figure which at once struck me as distinguished beyond that of all the others and who could not have possibly been lost in any crowd. The features of that tall fair personage shone with such a striking radiance that I could not contain my curiosity about him-he was the only one there whose name I felt concerned to know that day. When I learnt he was Bankim Babu I marvelled all the more, it seemed to me such a wonderful coincidence that his appearance should be as distinguished as his writings. His sharp aquiline nose, his compressed lips, and his keen glance all betokened immense power. With his arms folded across his breast he seemed to walk as one apart, towering above the ordinary throng-this is what struck me most about him. Not only that he looked an intellectual giant, but he had on his forehead the mark of a true prince among men.

One little incident which occurred at this gathering remains indelibly impressed on my mind. In one of the rooms a Pandit was reciting some Sanskrit verses of his own composition and explaining them in Bengali to the audience. One of the allusions was not exactly coarse, but somewhat vulgar. As the Pandit was proceeding to expound this Bankim Babu, covering his face with his hands, hurried out of the room. I was near the door and can still see before me that shrinking, retreating figure.

After that I often longed to see him, but could not get an opportunity. At last one day, when he was Deputy Magistrate of Hawrah, I made bold to call on him. We met, and I tried my best to make conversation. But I somehow felt greatly abashed while returning home, as if I had acted like a raw and bumptious youth in thus thrusting myself upon him unasked and unintroduced.

Shortly after, as I added to my years, I attained a place as the youngest of the literary men of the time; but what was to be my position in order of merit was not even then settled. The little reputation I had acquired was mixed with plenty of doubt and not a little of condescension. It was then the fashion in Bengal to assign each man of letters a place in comparison with a supposed compeer in the West. Thus one was the Byron of Bengal, another the Emerson and so forth. I began to be styled by some the Bengal Shelley. This was insulting to Shelley and only likely to get me laughed at.

My recognised cognomen was the Lisping Poet. My attainments were few, my knowledge of life meagre, and both in my poetry and my prose the sentiment exceeded the substance. So that there was nothing there on which anyone could have based his praise with any degree of confidence. My dress and behaviour were of the same anomalous description. I wore my hair long and indulged probably in an ultra-poetical refinement of manner. In a word I was eccentric and could not fit myself into everyday life like the ordinary man.

At this time Babu Akshay Sarkar had started his monthly review, the *Nabajiban*, New Life, to which I used occasionally to contribute. Bankim Babu had just closed the chapter of his editorship of the *Banga Darsan*, the Mirror of Bengal, and was busy with religious discussions for which purpose he had started the monthly, *Prachar*, the Preacher. To this also I contributed a song or two and an effusive appreciation of *Vaishnava* lyrics.

From now I began constantly to meet Bankim Babu. He was then living in Bhabani Dutt's street. I used to visit him frequently, it is true, but there was not much of conversation. I was then of the age to listen, not to talk. I fervently wished we could warm up into some discussion, but my diffidence got the better of my conversational powers. Some days Sanjib Babu[55] would be there reclining on his bolster. The sight would gladden me, for he was a genial soul. He delighted in talking and it was a delight to listen to his talk. Those who have read his prose writing must have noticed how gaily and airily it flows on like the sprightliest of conversation. Very few have this gift of conversation, and fewer still the art of translating it into writing.

This was the time when Pandit Sashadhar rose into prominence. Of him I first heard from Bankim Babu. If I remember right Bankim Babu was also responsible for introducing him to the public. The curious attempt made by Hindu orthodoxy to revive its prestige with the help of western science soon spread all over the country. Theosophy for some time previously had been preparing the ground for such a movement. Not that Bankim Babu even thoroughly identified himself with this cult. No shadow of Sashadhar was cast on his exposition of Hinduism as it found expression in the *Prachar* —that was impossible.

I was then coming out of the seclusion of my corner as my contributions to these controversies will show. Some of these were satirical verses, some farcical plays, others letters to newspapers. I thus came down into the arena from the regions of sentiment and began to spar in right earnest.

In the heat of the fight I happened to fall foul of Bankim Babu. The history of this remains recorded in the *Prachar* and *Bharati* of those days and need not be repeated here. At the close of this period of antagonism Bankim Babu wrote me a letter which I have unfortunately lost. Had it been here the reader could have seen with what consummate generosity Bankim Babu had taken the sting out of that unfortunate episode.

**PART VIII**

## 41. THE STEAMER HULK

Lured by an advertisement in some paper my brother Jyotirindra went off one afternoon to an auction sale, and on his return informed us that he had bought a steel hulk for seven thousand rupees; all that now remained being to put in an engine and some cabins for it to become a full-fledged steamer.

My brother must have thought it a great shame that our countrymen should have their tongues and pens going, but not a single line of steamers. As I have narrated before, he had tried to light matches for his country, but no amount of rubbing availed to make them strike. He had also wanted power-looms to work, but after all his travail only one little country towel was born, and then the loom stopped. And now that he wanted Indian steamers to ply, he bought an empty old hulk, which in due course, was filled, not only with engines and cabins, but with loss and ruin as well. And yet we should remember that all the loss and hardship due to his endeavours fell on him alone, while the gain of experience remained in reserve for the whole country. It is these uncalculating, unbusinesslike spirits who keep the business-fields of the country flooded with their activities. And, though the flood subsides as rapidly as it comes, it leaves behind fertilising silt to enrich the soil. When the time for reaping arrives no one thinks of these pioneers; but those who have cheerfully staked and lost their all, during life, are not likely, after death, to mind this further loss of being forgotten.

On one side was the European Flotilla Company, on the other my brother Jyotirindra alone; and how tremendous waxed that battle of the mercantile fleets, the people of Khulna and Barisal may still remember. Under the stress of competition steamer was added to steamer, loss piled on loss, while the income dwindled till it ceased to be worth while to print tickets. The golden age dawned on the steamer service between Khulna and Barisal. Not only were the passengers carried free of charge, but they were offered light refreshments *gratis* as well! Then was formed a band of volunteers who, with flags and patriotic songs, marched the passengers in procession to the Indian line of steamers. So while there was no want of passengers to carry, every other kind of want began to multiply apace.

Arithmetic remained uninfluenced by patriotic fervour; and while enthusiasm flamed higher and higher to the tune of patriotic songs, three times three went on steadily making nine on the wrong side of the balance sheet.

One of the misfortunes which always pursues the unbusinesslike is that, while they are as easy to read as an open book, they never learn to read the character of others. And since it takes them the whole of their lifetime and all their resources to find out this weakness of theirs, they never get the chance of profiting by experience. While the passengers were having free refreshments, the staff showed no signs of being starved either, but nevertheless the greatest gain remained with my brother in the ruin he so valiantly faced.

The daily bulletins of victory or disaster which used to arrive from the theatre of action kept us in a fever of excitement. Then one day came the news that the steamer *Swadeshi* had fouled the Howrah bridge and sunk. With this last loss my brother completely overstepped the limits of his resources, and there was nothing for it but to wind up the business.

## 42. BEREAVEMENTS

In the meantime death made its appearance in our family. Before this, I had never met Death face to face. When my mother died I was quite a child. She had been ailing for quite a long time, and we did not even know when her malady had taken a fatal turn. She used all along to sleep on a separate bed in the same room with us. Then in the course of her illness she was taken for a boat trip on the river, and on her return a room on the third storey of the inner apartments was set apart for her.

On the night she died we were fast asleep in our room downstairs. At what hour I cannot tell, our old nurse came running in weeping and crying: "O my little ones, you have lost your all!" My sister-in-law rebuked her and led her away, to save us the sudden shock at dead of night. Half awakened by her words, I felt my heart sink within me, but could not make out what had happened. When in the morning we were told of her death, I could not realize all that it meant for me.

As we came out into the verandah we saw my mother laid on a bedstead in the courtyard. There was nothing in her appearance which showed death to be terrible. The aspect which death wore in that morning light was as lovely as a calm and peaceful sleep, and the gulf between life and its absence was not brought home to us.

Only when her body was taken out by the main gateway, and we followed the procession to the cremation ground, did a storm of grief pass through me at the thought that mother would never return by this door and take again her accustomed place in the affairs of her household. The day wore on, we returned from the cremation, and as we turned into our lane I looked up at the house towards my father's rooms on the third storey. He was still in the front verandah sitting motionless in prayer.

She who was the youngest daughter-in-law of the house took charge of the motherless little ones. She herself saw to our food and clothing and all other wants, and kept us constantly near, so that we might not feel our loss too keenly. One of the characteristics of the living is the power to heal the irreparable, to forget the irreplaceable. And in early life this power is strongest, so that no blow penetrates too deeply, no scar is left permanently. Thus the first shadow of death which fell on us left no darkness behind; it departed as softly as it came, only a shadow.

When, in later life, I wandered about like a madcap, at the first coming of spring, with a handful of half-blown jessamines tied in a corner of my muslin scarf, and as I stroked my forehead with the soft, rounded, tapering buds, the touch of my mother's fingers would come back to me; and I clearly realised that the tenderness which dwelt in the tips of those lovely fingers was the very same as that which blossoms every day in the purity of these jessamine buds; and that whether we know it or not, this tenderness is on the earth in boundless measure.

The acquaintance which I made with Death at the age of twenty-four was a permanent one, and its blow has continued to add itself to each succeeding bereavement in an ever lengthening chain of tears. The lightness of infant life can skip aside from the greatest of calamities, but with age evasion is not so easy, and the shock of that day I had to take full on my breast.

That there could be any gap in the unbroken procession of the joys and sorrows of life was a thing I had no idea of. I could therefore see nothing beyond, and this life I had accepted as all in all. When of a sudden death came and in a moment made a gaping rent in its smooth-seeming fabric, I was utterly bewildered. All around, the trees, the soil, the water, the sun, the moon, the stars, remained as immovably true as before; and yet the person who was as truly there, who, through a thousand points of contact with life, mind, and heart, was ever so much more true for me, had vanished in a moment like a dream. What perplexing self-contradiction it all seemed to me as I looked around! How was I ever to reconcile that which remained with that which had gone?

The terrible darkness which was disclosed to me through this rent, continued to attract me night and day as time went on. I would ever and anon return to take my stand there and gaze upon it, wondering what there was left in place of what had gone. Emptiness is a thing man cannot bring himself to believe in; that which is *not*, is untrue; that which is untrue, is not. So our efforts to find something, where we see nothing, are unceasing.

Just as a young plant, surrounded by darkness, stretches itself, as it were on tiptoe, to find its way out into the light, so when death suddenly throws the darkness of negation round the soul it tries and tries to rise into the light of affirmation. And what other sorrow is comparable to the state wherein darkness prevents the finding of a way out of the darkness?

And yet in the midst of this unbearable grief, flashes of joy seemed to sparkle in my mind, now and again, in a way which quite surprised me. That life was not a stable permanent fixture was itself the sorrowful tidings which helped to lighten my mind. That we were not prisoners for ever within a solid stone wall of life was the thought which unconsciously kept coming uppermost in rushes of gladness. That which I had held I was made to let go-this was the sense of loss which distressed me, —but when at the same moment I viewed it from the standpoint of freedom gained, a great peace fell upon me.

The all-pervading pressure of worldly existence compensates itself by balancing life against death, and thus it does not crush us. The terrible weight of an unopposed life force has not to be endured by man, —this truth came upon me that day as a sudden, wonderful revelation.

With the loosening of the attraction of the world, the beauty of nature took on for me a deeper meaning. Death had given me the correct perspective from which to perceive the world in the fulness of its beauty, and as I saw the picture of the Universe against the background of Death I found it entrancing.

At this time I was attacked with a recrudescence of eccentricity in thought and behaviour. To be called upon to submit to the customs and fashions of the day, as if they were something soberly and genuinely real, made me want to laugh. I *could* not take them seriously. The burden of stopping to consider what other people might think of me was completely lifted off my mind. I have been about in fashionable book shops with a coarse sheet draped round me as my only upper garment, and a pair of slippers on my bare feet. Through hot and cold and wet I used to sleep out on the verandah of the third storey. There the stars and I could gaze at each other, and no time was lost in greeting the dawn.

This phase had nothing to do with any ascetic feeling. It was more like a holiday spree as the result of discovering the schoolmaster Life with his cane to be a myth, and thereby being able to shake myself free from the petty rules of his school. If, on waking one fine morning we were to find gravitation reduced to only a fraction of itself, would we still demurely walk along the high road? Would we not rather skip over many-storied houses for a change, or on encountering the monument take a flying jump, rather than trouble to walk round it? That was why, with the weight of worldly life no longer clogging my feet, I could not stick to the usual course of convention.

Alone on the terrace in the darkness of night I groped all over like a blind man trying to find upon the black stone gate of death some device or sign. Then when I woke with the morning light falling on that unscreened bed of mine, I felt, as I opened my eyes, that my enveloping haze was becoming transparent; and, as on the clearing of the mist the hills and rivers and forests of the scene shine forth, so the dew-washed picture of the world-life, spread out before me, seemed to become renewed and ever so beautiful.

## 43. THE RAINS AND AUTUMN

According to the Hindu calendar, each year is ruled by a particular planet. So have I found that in each period of life a particular season assumes a special importance. When I look back to my childhood I can best recall the rainy days. The wind-driven rain has flooded the verandah floor. The row of doors leading into the rooms are all closed. Peari, the old scullery maid, is coming from the market, her basket laden with vegetables, wading through the slush and drenched with the rain. And for no rhyme or reason I am careering about the verandah in an ecstasy of joy.

This also comes back to me: —I am at school, our class is held in a colonnade with mats as outer screens; cloud upon cloud has come up during the afternoon, and they are now heaped up, covering the sky; and as we look on, the rain comes down in close thick showers, the thunder at intervals rumbling long and loud; some mad woman with nails of lightning seems to be rending the sky from end to end; the mat walls tremble under the blasts of wind as if they would be blown in; we can hardly see to read, for the darkness. The Pandit gives us leave to close our books. Then leaving the storm to do the romping and roaring for us, we keep swinging our dangling legs; and my mind goes right away across the far-off unending moor through which the Prince of the fairy tale passes.

I remember, moreover, the depth of the *Sravan*[56] nights. The pattering of the rain finding its way through the gaps of my slumber, creates within a gladsome restfulness deeper than the deepest sleep. And in the wakeful intervals I pray that the morning may see the rain continue, our lane under water, and the bathing platform of the tank submerged to the last step.

But at the age of which I have just been telling, Autumn is on the throne beyond all doubt. Its life is to be seen spread under the clear transparent leisure of *Aswin*.[57] And in the molten gold of this autumn sunshine, softly reflected from the fresh dewy green outside, I am pacing the verandah and composing, in the mode *Jogiya*, the song:

> In this morning light I do not know what it is that my heart desires.

The autumn day wears on, the house gong sounds 12 noon, the mode changes; though my mind is still filled with music, leaving no room for call of work or duty; and I sing:

> What idle play is this with yourself, my heart,
> through the listless hours?

Then in the afternoon I am lying on the white floorcloth of my little room, with a drawing book trying to draw pictures, —by no means an arduous pursuit of the pictorial muse, but just a toying with the desire to make pictures. The most important part is that which remains in the mind, and of which not a line gets drawn on the paper. And in the meantime the serene autumn afternoon is filtering through the walls of this little Calcutta room filling it, as a cup, with golden intoxication.

I know not why, but all my days of that period I see as if through this autumn sky, this autumn light-the autumn which ripened for me my songs as it ripens the corn for the tillers; the autumn which filled my granary of leisure with radiance; the autumn which flooded my unburdened mind with an unreasoning joy in fashioning song and story.

The great difference which I see between the Rainy-season of my childhood and the Autumn of my youth is that in the former it is outer Nature which closely hemmed me in keeping me entertained with its numerous troupe, its variegated make-up, its medley of music; while the festivity which goes on in the shining light of autumn is in man himself. The play of cloud and sunshine is left in the background, while the murmurs of joy and sorrow occupy the mind. It is our gaze which gives to the blue of the autumn sky its wistful tinge and human yearning which gives poignancy to the breath of its breezes.

My poems have now come to the doors of men. Here informal goings and comings are not allowed. There is door after door, chamber within chamber. How many times have we to return with only a glimpse of the light in the window, only the sound of the pipes from within the palace gates lingering in our ears. Mind has to treat with mind, will to come to terms with will, through many tortuous obstructions, before giving and taking can come about. The foundation of life, as it dashes into these obstacles, splashes and foams over in laughter and tears, and dances and whirls through eddies from which one cannot get a definite idea of its course.

## 44. SHARPS AND FLATS

*Sharps and Flats* is a serenade from the streets in front of the dwelling of man, a plea to be allowed an entry and a place within that house of mystery.

> This world is sweet, —I do not want to die.
> I wish to dwell in the ever-living life of Man.

This is the prayer of the individual to the universal life.

When I started for my second voyage to England, I made the acquaintance on board ship of Asutosh Chaudhuri. He had just taken the M. A. degree of the Calcutta University and was on his way to England to join the Bar. We were together only during the few days the steamer took from Calcutta to Madras, but it became quite evident that depth of friendship does not depend upon length of acquaintance. Within this short time he so drew me to him by his simple natural qualities of heart, that the previous life-long gap in our acquaintance seemed always to have been filled with our friendship.

When Ashu came back from England he became one of us.[58] He had not as yet had time or opportunity to pierce through all the barriers with which his profession is hedged in, and so become completely immersed in it. The money-bags of his clients had not yet sufficiently loosened the strings which held their gold, and Ashu was still an enthusiast in gathering honey from various gardens of literature. The spirit of literature which then saturated his being had nothing of the mustiness of library morocco about it, but was fragrant with the scent of unknown exotics from over the seas. At his invitation I enjoyed many a picnic amidst the spring time of those distant woodlands.

He had a special taste for the flavour of French literature. I was then writing the poems which came to be published in the volume entitled *Kadi o Komal*, Sharps and Flats. Ashu could discern resemblances between many of my poems and old French poems he knew. According to him the common element in all these poems was the attraction which the play of world-life had for the poet, and this had found varied expression in each and every one of them. The unfulfilled desire to enter into this larger life was the fundamental motive throughout.

"I will arrange and publish these poems for you," said Ashu, and accordingly that task was entrusted to him. The poem beginning *This world is sweet* was the one he considered to be the keynote of the whole series and so he placed it at the beginning of the volume.

Ashu was very possibly right. When in childhood I was confined to the house, I offered my heart in my wistful gaze to outside nature in all its variety through the openings in the parapet of our inner roof-terrace. In my youth the world of men in the same way exerted a powerful attraction on me. To that also I was then an outsider and looked out upon it from the roadside. My mind standing on the brink called out, as it were, with an eager waving of hands to the ferryman sailing away across the waves to the other side. For Life longed to start on life's journey.

It is not true that my peculiarly isolated social condition was the bar to my plunging into the midst of the world-life. I see no sign that those of my countrymen who have been all their lives in the thick of society feel, any more than I did, the touch of its living intimacy. The life of our country has its high banks, and its flight of steps, and, on its dark waters falls the cool shade of the ancient trees, while from within the leafy branches over-head the *koel* cooes forth its ravishing old-time song. But for all that it is stagnant water. Where is its current, where are the waves, when does the high tide rush in from the sea?

Did I then get from the neighbourhood on the other side of our lane an echo of the victorious pæan with which the river, falling and rising, wave after wave, cuts its way through walls of stone to the sea? No! My life in its solitude was simply fretting for want of an invitation to the place where the festival of world-life was being held.

Man is overcome by a profound depression while nodding through his voluptuously lazy hours of seclusion, because in this way he is deprived of full commerce with life. Such is the despondency from which I have always painfully struggled to get free. My mind refused to respond to the cheap intoxication of the political movements of those days, devoid, as they seemed, of all strength of national consciousness, with their complete ignorance of the country, their supreme indifference to real service of the motherland. I was tormented by a furious impatience, an intolerable dissatisfaction with myself and all around me. Much rather, I said to myself, would I be an Arab Bedouin!

While in other parts of the world there is no end to the movement and clamour of the revelry of free life, we, like the beggar maid, stand outside and longingly look on. When have we had the wherewithal to deck ourselves for the occasion and go and join in it? Only in a country where the spirit of separation reigns supreme, and innumerable petty barriers divide one from another, need this longing to realise the larger life of the world in one's own remain unsatisfied.

I strained with the same yearning towards the world of men in my youth, as I did in my childhood towards outside nature from within the chalk-ring drawn round me by the servants. How rare, how unattainable, how far away it seemed! And yet if we cannot get into touch with it, if from it no breeze can blow, no current come, if no road be there for the free goings and comings of travellers, then the dead things that accumulate around us never get removed, but continue to be heaped up till they smother all life.

During the Rains there are only dark clouds and showers. And in the Autumn there is the play of light and shade in the sky, but that is not all-absorbing; for there is also the promise of corn in the fields. So in my poetical career, when the rainy season was in the ascendant there were only my vaporous fancies which stormed and showered; my utterance was misty, my verses were wild. And with the *Sharps and Flats* of my Autumn, not only was there the play of cloud-effects in the sky, but out of the ground crops were to be seen rising. Then, in the commerce with the world of reality, both language and metre attempted definiteness and variety of form.

Thus ends another Book. The days of coming together of inside and outside, kin and stranger, are closing in upon my life. My life's journey has now to be completed through the dwelling places of men. And the good and evil, joy and sorrow, which it thus encountered, are not to be lightly viewed as pictures. What makings and breakings, victories and defeats, clashings and minglings, are here going on!

I have not the power to disclose and display the supreme art with which the Guide of my life is joyfully leading me through all its obstacles, antagonisms and crookednesses towards the fulfilment of its innermost meaning. And if I cannot make clear all the mystery of this design, whatever else I may try to show is sure to prove misleading at every step. To analyse the image is only to get at its dust, not at the joy of the artist.

So having escorted them to the door of the inner sanctuary I take leave of my readers.

# Footnotes

1.  Neither the secondary curtain nor the drop is again used during the play. The action is continuous, either on the front stage, or on the rear stage, the latter being darkened when not actually in use.

2.  A jingling sentence in the Bengali Child's Primer.

3.  Exercises in two-syllables.

4.  Roofed colonnade or balcony. The writer's family house is an irregular three-storied mass of buildings, which had grown with the joint family it sheltered, built round several courtyards or quadrangles, with long colonnades along the outer faces, and narrower galleries running round each quadrangle, giving access to the single rows of rooms.

5.  The men's portion of the house is the outer; and the women's the inner.

6.  These Bustees or settlements consisting of tumbledown hovels, existing side by side with palatial buildings, are still one of the anomalies of Calcutta.

7.  Corresponding to "Wonderland."

8.  There are innumerable renderings of the Ramayana in the Indian languages.

9.  A kind of crisp unsweetened pancake taken like bread along with the other courses.

10. Food while being eaten, and utensils or anything else touched by the hand engaged in conveying food to the mouth, are considered ceremonially unclean.

11. The writer is the youngest of seven brothers. The sixth brother is here meant.

12. Obsolete word meaning bee.

13. The lane, a blind one, leads, at right angles to the front verandah, from the public main road to the grounds round the house.

14. God of Death.

15. Goddess of Learning.

16. The Jupiter Pluvius of Hindu Mythology.

17. The King of the Yakshas is the Pluto of Hindu Mythology.

18. Corresponding to Lethe.

19. Krishna's playground.

20. Correspondence clerk.

21. Spices wrapped in betel leaf.

22. It is considered sinful for non-brahmins to cast glances on neophytes during the process of their sacred-thread investiture, before the ceremony is complete.

23. Two novices in the hermitage of the sage Kanva, mentioned in the Sanskrit drama, Sakuntala.

24. The text for self-realisation.

25. Bards or reciters.

26.	The Cow and the Brahmin are watchwords of modern Hindu Orthodoxy.

27.	An instrument on which the keynote is strummed to accompany singing.

28.	A large proportion of words in the literary Bengali are derived unchanged from the Sanskrit.

29.	Servants call the master and mistress father, and mother, and the children brothers and sisters.

30.	Name of Vishnu in his aspect of slayer of the proud demon, Madhu.

31.	Nirada is a Sanscrit word meaning *cloud*, being a compound of *nira* = water and *da* = giver. In Bengali it is pronounced *nirode*.

32.	Betel-leaf and spices.

33.	Father of the well-known artists Gaganendra and Abanindra.

34.	In Bengali this word has come to mean an informal uninvited gathering.

35.	Systems of notation were not then in use. One of the most popular of the present-day systems was subsequently devised by the writer's brother here mentioned.

36.	The new bride of the house, wife of the writer's fourth brother, above-mentioned.

37.	It may be helpful to the foreign reader to explain that the expert singer of Indian music improvises more or less on the tune outline made over to him by the original composer, so that the latter need not necessarily do more than give a correct idea of such outline.

38.	This would mean "the genius of Bhubanmohini" if that be taken as the author's name.

39.	Gifts of cloth for use as wearing apparel are customary by way of ceremonial offerings of affection, respect or seasonable greeting.

40.	The old Vaishnava poets used to bring their name into the last stanza of the poem, this serving as their signature. Bhanu and Rabi both mean the Sun.

41.	The dried and stripped centre-vein of a cocoanut leaf gives a long tapering stick of the average thickness of a match stick, and a bundle of these goes to make the common Bengal household broom which in the hands of the housewife is popularly supposed to be useful in keeping the whole household in order from husband downwards. Its effect on a bare back is here alluded to.

42.	There was a craze for phrenology at the time.

43.	Latterly Sir Tarak Palit, a life-long friend of the writer's second brother.

44.	Saraswati, the goddess of learning, is depicted in Bengal as clad in white and seated among a mass of lotus flowers.

45.	With Indian music it is not a mere question of correctly rendering a melody exactly as composed, but the theme of the original composition is the subject of an improvised interpretative elaboration by the expounding Artist.

46.	Valmiki Pratibha means the genius of Valmiki. The plot is based on the story of Valmiki, the robber chief, being moved to pity and breaking out into a metrical lament on witnessing the grief of one of a pair of cranes whose mate was killed by a hunter. In the metre which so came to him he afterwards composed his *Ramayana*.

47.	Some Indian classic melodic compositions are designed on a scheme of accentuation, for which purpose the music is set, not to words, but to unmeaning notation-sounds representing drum-beats or plectrum-impacts which in Indian music are of a considerable variety of tone, each having its own sound-symbol. The *Telena* is one such style of composition.

48. Reciters of Puranic legendary lore.

49. The Goddess of Wealth.

50. As distinguished generally from different provincial styles, but chiefly from the Dravidian style prevalent in the South.

51. Many of the Hindustani classic modes are supposed to be best in keeping with particular seasons of the year, or times of the day.

52. The world, as the Indian boy knows it from fairy tale and folklore, has seven seas and thirteen rivers.

53. This is addressed to Yashoda, mother of Krishna, by his playmates. Yashoda would dress up her darling every morning in his yellow garment with a peacock plume in his hair. But when it came to the point, she was nervous about allowing him, young as he was, to join the other cowherd boys at the pasturage. So it often required a great deal of persuasion before they would be allowed to take charge of him. This is part of the *Vaishnava* parable of the child aspect of Krishna's play with the world.

54. A Busti is an area thickly packed with shabby tiled huts, with narrow pathways running through, and connecting it with the main street. These are inhabited by domestic servants, the poorer class of artisans and the like. Such settlements were formerly scattered throughout the town even in the best localities, but are now gradually disappearing from the latter.

55. One of Bankim Babu's brothers.

56. The month corresponding to July-August, the height of the rainy season.

57. The month of Aswin corresponds to September-October, the long vacation time for Bengal.

58. Referring to his marriage with the writer's niece, Pratibha.

Made in the USA
Middletown, DE
01 June 2022

66480322R00176